SOCIOLOGY OF CRIME

SOCIOLOGY OF CRIME

Dr. Bindeshwari Pd. Mandal

CENTRUM PRESS
NEW DELHI-110002 (INDIA)

CENTRUM PRESS
H.O.: 4360/4, Ansari Road, Daryaganj,
New Delhi-110002 (India)
Tel: 23278000, 23261597, 23255577, 23286875
B.O.: No. 1015, Ist Main Road, BSK IIIrd Stage,
IIIrd Phase, IIIrd Block, Bangalore-560085 (INDIA)
Tel: 080-41723429
Email: centrumpress@gmail.com
Visit us at: www.centrumpress.com

Sociology of Crime

First Edition, 2011

ISBN 978-93-80921-53-2

PRINTED IN INDIA

Printed at Tarun Offset Printers, Delhi-110053

Contents

Preface

In Sociology, crime is identified as a deviant behaviour. It is deviant in that it goes against accepted or written rules and laws that guide a society. All deviant behaviour isn't a crime. Whether a behaviour is a crime is determined from one society to the next. Understanding sociology will give you a better understanding of how crime affects society as a whole. To understand crime and sociology, one must first understand the "Conflict Theory" founded by Karl Marx. Conflict theory sees society as two struggling groups engaged in conflict over resources. Under this theory, it is believed that the capitalist class (or the society elites) commit acts of deviance just as the working class does. The main difference is that society elites determine the rules regarding what is deviant. This difference among the people will always lead to conflict. This idea explains why there is crime in societies and why it will never cease to be. Sociologists classify crimes by three types: crimes against a person, crimes against property and victimless crimes. Crimes against a person include any offences where violence is used or threatened. Mugging and assault are examples of crimes against a person. Crimes against property include theft of property or damage done to someone else's property. Burglary and arson are crimes against property. Finally, victimless crimes are crimes that are against the law, but no victim exists. Prostitution and marijuana are common examples of victimless crimes. In sociology, all crimes fall into one of these three categories.

In order to identify who commits crimes and why they do it, the study of sociology utilizes age, gender, race, social class, and ethnicity. These features are helpful when breaking down what demographics commit which types of crime. By using this information, sociologists have been able to determine that younger individuals in society are more likely to commit crimes than older ones. They found out that men are more likely to commit a crime than women. A more appropriate example to the study of sociology and crime is that violent crimes are most often perpetrated by poor individuals. White-collar crime is more prevalent among the wealthy, and the laws involved in that sort of crime are less frequently enforced.

Studying crime together with sociology is important due to the effects that crime has on society. In addition to the victims of the crime, the rest of society is charged with the responsibility of paying for the incarceration of hundreds of thousands of criminals each year. Crimes against property often have devastating financial impacts on areas of high crime, particularly urban areas filled with low-income individuals unlikely to report crimes committed against them. Studying crime and sociology together seeks to identify why these individuals turn to crime, and it shows how we, as a society, can prevent it. With nearly 300 individuals under the age of 19 incarcerated in federal prisons, learning how to prevent children from turning into lifetime criminals is a current goal of sociologists. Finding alternative rehabilitation facilities is a first step in making sure underage offenders don't perfect their criminal skills while in the presence of career criminals.

Understanding crime and sociology together has great significance for the future of any society. By identifying the "who" and the "why" of crime, we are better equipped to find solutions that don't lead to a life of crime. For example, removing a child from an abusive home is the first step in making certain that child does not learn to express himself in only a physical manner. Without understanding the make up of the criminal, it is not possible to understand his or her motives. Sociology seeks to understand these individuals and their situations. By doing so, the goal is to determine a way to treat these individuals that will reduce their recidivism rate. A lower crime rate has a positive effect on society as a whole, including more money available for more necessary projects, greater property value in urban areas and less children incarcerated.

This book fulfills the long felt necessity of a text dealing with concepts of this subject. It can also prove to be a worthy companion and guide for the students, users and researchers.

1

Introduction

Crime is the breach of rules or laws for which some governing authority (via mechanisms such as legal systems) can ultimately prescribe a conviction. Individual human societies may each define crime and crimes differently. While every crime violates the law, not every violation of the law counts as a crime; for example: breaches of contract and of other civil law may rank as "offences" or as "infractions". Modern societies generally regard crimes as offences against the public or the state, distinguished from *torts* (offences against private parties that can give rise to a civil cause of action).

When informal relationships and sanctions prove insufficient to establish and maintain a desired social order, a government or a state may impose more formalized or stricter systems of social control. With institutional and legal machinery at their disposal, agents of the State can compel populations to conform to codes, and can opt to punish or attempt to reform those who do not conform.

Authorities employ various mechanisms to regulate (encouraging or discouraging) certain behaviours in general. Governing or administering agencies may for example codify rules into laws, police citizens and visitors to ensure that they comply with those laws, and implement other policies and practices which legislators or administrators have prescribed with the aim of discouraging or preventing crime. In addition, authorities provide remedies and sanctions, and collectively these constitute a criminal justice system. Legal sanctions vary widely in their severity, they may include (for example) incarceration of temporary character aimed at reforming the convict. Some jurisdictions have penal codes written to inflict permanent harsh punishments: legal mutilation, capital punishment or life without parole.

The sociologist Richard Quinney has written about the relationship between society and crime. When Quinney states "crime is a social phenomenon" he envisages both how individuals conceive crime and how populations perceive it, based on societal norms.

The label of "crime" and the accompanying social stigma normally confine their scope to those activities seen as injurious to the general population or to the State, including some that cause serious loss or damage to individuals. Those who apply the labels of "crime" or "criminal" intend to assert the hegemony of a dominant population, or to reflect a consensus of condemnation for the identified behaviour and to justify any punishments prescribed by the State (in the event that standard processing tries and convicts an accused person of a crime).

Usually a natural person perpetrates a crime, but legal persons may also commit crimes.

Definition

A normative definition views crime as deviant behaviour that violates prevailing norms – cultural standards prescribing how humans ought to behave normally. This approach considers the complex realities surrounding the concept of crime and seeks to understand how changing social, political, psychological, and economic conditions may affect changing definitions of crime and the form of the legal, law-enforcement, and penal responses made by society.

These structural realities remain fluid and often contentious. For example: as cultures change and the political environment shifts, societies may criminalise or decriminalise certain behaviours, which will directly affect the statistical crime rates, influence the allocation of resources for the enforcement of laws, and (re-)influence the general public opinion.

Similarly, changes in the collection and/or calculation of data on crime may affect the public perceptions of the extent of any given "crime problem". All such adjustments to crime statistics, allied with the experience of people in their everyday lives, shape attitudes on the extent to which the State should use law or social engineering to enforce or encourage any particular social norm. Behaviour can be controlled and influenced in many ways without having to resort to the criminal justice system.

Indeed, in those cases where no clear consensus exists on a given norm, the drafting of criminal law by the group in power to prohibit the behaviour of another group may seem to some observers an improper limitation of the second group's freedom, and the ordinary members of society have less respect for the law or laws in general — whether the authorities actually enforce the disputed law or not.

Legislatures can pass laws (called *mala prohibita*) that define crimes which violate social norms. These laws vary from time to time and from place to place: note variations in gambling laws, for example, and the prohibition or encouragement of duelling in history. Other crimes, called *mala in se*, count as outlawed in almost all societies, (murder, theft and rape, for example).

English criminal law and the related criminal law of Commonwealth countries can define offences which the courts alone have developed over the years, without any actual legislation: common law offences. The courts used the concept of *malum in se* to develop various common law offences.

Criminalization

One can view criminalization as a procedure deployed by society as a pre-emptive, harm-reduction device, using the threat of punishment as a deterrent to anyone proposing to engage in the behaviour causing harm. The State becomes involved because governing entities can become convinced that the costs of not criminalizing (through allowing the harms to continue unabated) outweigh the costs of criminalizing it (restricting individual liberty, for example, in order to minimize harm to others).

Criminalization may provide future harm-reduction at least to the outside population, assuming those shamed or incarcerated or otherwise restrained for committing crimes start out more prone to criminal behaviour. Likewise, one might assume that criminalizing acts which in themselves do not harm other people ("victimless crimes") may prevent subsequent harmful acts (assuming that people "prone" to commit these acts may tend to commit harmful actions in general). Some see the criminalization of "victimless crimes" as a pretext for imposing personal, religious or moral convictions on otherwise productive citizens or taxpayers.

Some commentators may see criminalization as a way to make potential criminals pay or suffer for their prospective crimes. In this case, criminalization becomes a way to set the price that one must pay to society for certain actions considered detrimental to society as a whole. An extreme view might see criminalization as State-sanctioned revenge.

States control the process of criminalization because:

- Even if victims recognize their own role as victims, they may not have the resources to investigate and seek legal redress for the injuries suffered: the enforcers formally appointed by the State often have better access to expertise and resources.
- The victims may only want compensation for the injuries suffered, while remaining indifferent to a possible desire for deterrence.
- Fear of retaliation may deter victims or witnesses of crimes from taking any action. Even in policed societies, fear may inhibit from reporting incidents or from co-operating in a trial.
- Victims, on their own, may lack the economies of scale which might allow them to administer a penal system, let alone to collect any fines levied by a court. Garoupa & Klerman (2002) warn that a rent-seeking government has as its primary motivation to maximize revenue and so, if offenders have sufficient wealth, a rent-seeking government will act more aggressively than a social-welfare-maximizing government in enforcing laws against minor crimes (usually with a fixed penalty such as parking and routine traffic violations), but more laxly in enforcing laws against major crimes.

- As a result of the crime, victims may die or become incapacitated.

History

The idea of crime has a long history. Some religious communities regard sin as a crime; some may even highlight the crime of sin very early in legendary or mythological accounts of origins — note the tale of Adam and Eve and the theory of original sin. What one group considers a crime may cause or ignite war or conflict. However, the earliest known civilizations had codes of law, containing both civil and penal rules mixed together, though not always in recorded form.

The Sumerians produced the earliest surviving written codes. Urukagina had an early code that has not survived; a later king, Ur-Nammu, left the earliest extant written law-system, the Code of Ur-Nammu, which prescribed a formal system of penalties for specific cases in 57 articles. The Sumerians later issued other codes, including the "code of Lipit-Ishtar". This code, from the 20th century BCE, contains some fifty articles, and scholars have reconstructed it by comparing several sources.

The Sumerian was deeply conscious of his personal rights and resented any encroachment on them, whether by his King, his superior, or his equal. No wonder that the Sumerians were the first to compile laws and law codes. — Kramer

Successive legal codes in Babylon, including the code of Hammurabi (ca. 1790 BC), reflected Mesopotamian society's belief that law derived from the will of the gods. Many states at this time functioned as theocracies, with codes of conduct largely religious in origin or reference.

Sir Henry Maine (1861) studied the ancient codes available in his day, and failed to find any criminal law in the "modern" sense of the word. While modern systems distinguish between offences against the "State" or "Community", and offences against the "Individual", the so-called penal law of ancient communities did not deal with "crimes" (Latin: *crimina*), but with "wrongs" (Latin: *delicta*). Thus the Hellenic laws treated all forms of theft, assault, rape, and murder as private wrongs, and left action for enforcement up to the victims or their survivors. The earliest systems seem to have lacked formal courts.

The Romans systematized law and applied their system across the Roman Empire. Again, the initial rules of Roman Law regarded assaults as a matter of private compensation. The most significant Roman Law concept involved *dominion*. The *pater familias* owned all the family and its property (including slaves); the *pater* enforced matters involving interference with any property. The *Commentaries* of Gaius (written between 130 and 180 AD) on the Twelve Tables treated *furtum* (in modern parlance: "theft") as a tort.

Similarly, assault and violent robbery involved trespass as to the *pater's* property (so, for example, the rape of a slave could become the subject of compensation to the *pater* as having trespassed on his "property"), and breach of such laws created a *vinculum juris* (an obligation of law) that only the payment of monetary compensation (modern "damages") could discharge. Similarly, the consolidated Teutonic laws of the Germanic tribes, included a complex system of monetary compensations for what courts would now consider the complete range of criminal offences against the person, from murder down.

Even though Rome abandoned its Britannic provinces around 400 AD, the Germanic mercenaries – who had largely become instrumental in enforcing Roman rule in Britannia – acquired ownership of land there and continued to use a mixture of Roman and Teutonic Law, with much written down under the early Anglo-Saxon Kings. But only when a more centralized English monarchy emerged following the Norman invasion, and when the kings of England attempted to assert power over the land and its peoples, did the modern concept emerge, namely of a crime not only as an offence against the "individual", but also as a wrong against the "State".

This idea came from common law, and the earliest conception of a criminal act involved events of such major significance that the "State" had to usurp the usual functions of the civil tribunals, and direct a special law or *privilegium* against the perpetrator. All the earliest English criminal trials involved wholly extraordinary and arbitrary courts without any settled law to apply, whereas the civil (delictual) law operated in a highly developed and consistent manner (except where a King wanted to raise money by selling a new form of writ). The development of the idea that the "State" dispenses justice in a court only emerges in parallel with or after the emergence of the concept of sovereignty.

In continental Europe, Roman law persisted, but with a stronger influence from the Christian Church. Coupled with the more diffuse political structure based on smaller feudal units, various different legal traditions emerged, remaining more strongly rooted in Roman jurisprudence, but modified to meet the prevailing political climate.

In Scandinavia the effect of Roman law did not become apparent until the 17th century, and the courts grew out of the *things* — the assemblies of the people. The people decided the cases (usually with largest freeholders dominating). This system later gradually developed into a system with a royal judge nominating a number of the most esteemed men of the parish as his board, fulfilling the function of "the people" of yore.

From the Hellenic system onwards, the policy rationale for requiring the payment of monetary compensation for wrongs committed has involved the avoidance of feuding between clans and families. If compensation could mollify families' feelings, this would help to keep the peace. On the other hand, the institution of oaths also played down the threat of feudal warfare. Both in archaic Greece and in medieval Scandinavia, an accused person walked free if he could get a sufficient number of male relatives to swear him unguilty. (Compare the United Nations Security Council, in which the veto power of the permanent members ensures that the organization does not become involved in crises where it could not enforce its decisions.)

These means of restraining private feuds did not always work, and sometimes prevented the fulfilment of justice. But in the earliest times the "state" did not always provide an independent policing force. Thus criminal law grew out what 21st-century lawyers would call torts; and, in real terms, many acts and omissions classified as crimes actually overlap with civil-law concepts.

The development of sociological thought from the 19th century onwards prompted some fresh views on crime and criminality, and fostered the beginnings of criminology as a study of crime in society. Nietzsche noted a link between crime and creativity – in *The Birth of Tragedy* he asserted: "The best and brightest that man can acquire he must obtain by crime". In the 20th century Michel Foucault in *Discipline and Punish* made a study of criminalization as a coercive method of state control.

Natural-law Theory

Justifying the State's use of force to coerce compliance with its laws has proven a consistent theoretical problem. One of the earliest justifications involved the theory of natural law. This posits that the nature of the world or of human beings underlies the standards of morality or constructs them. Thomas Aquinas wrote in the 13th century: "the rule and measure of human acts is the reason, which is the first principle of human acts". He regarded people as by nature rational beings, concluding that it becomes morally appropriate that they should behave in a way that conforms to their rational nature. Thus, to be valid, any law must conform to natural law and coercing people to conform to that law is morally acceptable. In the 1760s William Blackstone (1979: 41) described the thesis:

"This law of nature, being co-eval with mankind and dictated by God himself, is of course superior in obligation to any other. It is binding over all the globe, in all countries, and at all times: no human laws are of any validity, if contrary to this; and such of them as are valid derive all their force, and all their authority, mediately or immediately, from this original."

But John Austin (1790–1859), an early positivist, applied utilitarianism in accepting the calculating nature of human beings and the existence of an objective morality. He denied that the legal validity of a norm depends on whether its content conforms to morality. Thus in Austinian terms a moral code can objectively determine what people ought to do, the law can embody whatever norms the legislature decrees to achieve social utility, but every individual remains free to choose what he or she will do. Similarly, Hart (1961) saw the law as an aspect of sovereignty, with lawmakers able to adopt any law as a means to a moral end.

Thus the necessary and sufficient conditions for the truth of a proposition of law simply involved internal logic and consistency, and that the state's agents used state power with responsibility. Ronald Dworkin (2005) rejects Hart's theory and proposes that all individuals should expect the equal respect and concern of those who govern them as a fundamental political right. He offers a theory of compliance overlaid by a theory of deference (the citizen's duty to obey the law) and a theory of enforcement, which identifies the legitimate goals of enforcement and punishment. Legislation must conform to a theory of legitimacy, which describes the circumstances under which a particular person or group is entitled to make law, and a theory of legislative justice, which describes the law they are entitled or obliged to make.

Indeed, despite everything, the majority of natural-law theorists have accepted the idea of enforcing the prevailing morality as a primary function of the law. This view entails the problem that it makes any moral criticism of the law impossible: if conformity with natural law forms a necessary condition for legal validity, all valid law must, by definition, count as morally just. Thus, on this line of reasoning, the legal validity of a norm necessarily entails its moral justice.

One can solve this problem by granting some degree of moral relativism and accepting that norms may evolve over time and, therefore, one can criticize the continued enforcement of old laws in the light of the current norms. People may find such law acceptable, but the use of State power to coerce citizens to comply with that law lacks moral justification. More recent conceptions of the theory characterise crime as the violation of individual rights.

Since society considers so many rights as natural (hence the term "right") rather than man-made, what constitutes a crime also counts as natural, in contrast to laws (seen as man-made). Adam Smith illustrates this view, saying that a smuggler would be an excellent citizen, "...had not the laws of his country made that a crime which nature never meant to be so."

Natural-law theory therefore distinguishes between "criminality" (which derives from human nature) and "illegality" (which originates with the interests of those in power). Lawyers sometimes express the two concepts with the phrases *malum in se* and *malum prohibitum* respectively. They regard a "crime *malum in se*" as inherently criminal; whereas a "crime *malum prohibitum*" (the argument goes) counts as criminal only because the law has decreed it so.

This view leads to a seeming paradox: one can perform an illegal act without committing a crime, while a criminal act could be perfectly legal. Many Enlightenment thinkers (such as Adam Smith and the American Founding Fathers) subscribed to this view to some extent, and it remains influential among so-called classical liberals and libertarians.

Distinctions

Governments criminalise antisocial behaviour — and treat it within a system of offences against society — in order to justify the imposition of punishment. Authorities make a series of distinctions depending on the passive subject of the crime (the victim), or on the offended interest(s), in crimes against:

- honour
- the administration of justice
- law and order
- patrimony
- the person
- personality of the State
- personality rights
- public administration
- public economy, industry, and commerce
- public morality
- religious sentiment and faith
- rights of the citizen.

Or one can categorise crimes depending on the related punishment, with sentencing tariffs prescribed in line with the perceived seriousness of the offence. Thus fines and noncustodial sentences may address the crimes seen as least serious, with lengthy imprisonment or (in some jurisdictions) capital punishment reserved for the most serious.

Types

Researchers and commentators may classify crime into categories, including:

- property crime
- public order crime
- violent crime.

Analysts can also group crimes by severity, some common category-terms including:

- Federal crimes (US, Canada, and Australia)
- felonies (US and previously UK)
- indictable offences (UK)
- infractions (US)
- misdemeanors (US and previously UK)
- summary offences (UK).

U.S. Classification

In the United States since 1930, the FBI has tabulated Uniform Crime Reports (UCR) annually from crime data submitted by law enforcement agencies across the United States. Officials compile this data at the city, county, and state levels into the Uniform crime reports (UCR). They classify violations of laws which derive from common law as Part I crimes in UCR data, further categorised as violent or property crimes. Part I violent crimes include murder and criminal homicide (voluntary manslaughter), forcible rape, aggravated assault, and robbery; while Part I property crimes include burglary, arson, larceny/theft, and motor-vehicle theft. All other crimes count come under Part II.

For convenience, such lists usually include infractions although, in the U.S., they may come into the sphere not of the criminal law, but rather of the civil law. Compare tortfeasance.

Booking-arrests require detention for a time-frame ranging 1 to 24 hours.

Crimes in International Law

Crimes defined by treaty as crimes against international law include:

- crimes against peace
- crimes of apartheid
- genocide
- piracy
- the slave trade
- waging a war of aggression
- war crimes.

From the point of view of State-centric law, extraordinary procedures (usually international courts) may prosecute such crimes. Note the role of the International Criminal Court at The Hague in the Netherlands.

Popular opinion often associates international law with the concept of opposing terrorism — seen as a crime as distinct from warfare.

Religion and Crime

Different religious traditions may promote distinct norms of behaviour, and these in turn may clash or harmonise with the perceived interests of a state. Socially accepted or imposed religious morality has influenced secular jurisdictions on issues that may otherwise concern only an individual's conscience. Activities sometimes criminalized on religious grounds include (for example) alcohol-consumption (prohibition), abortion and stem-cell research. In various historical and present-day societies institutionalized religions have established systems of earthly justice which punish crimes against the divine will and against specific devotional, organizational and other rules under specific codes, such as Islamic *sharia* or Roman Catholic canon law.

Military Jurisdictions and States of Emergency

In the military sphere, authorities can prosecute both regular crimes and specific acts (such as mutiny or desertion) under martial-law codes that either supplant or extend civil codes in times of (for example) war.

Many constitutions contain provisions to curtail freedoms and criminalize otherwise tolerated behaviours under a state of emergency in the event of war, natural disaster or civil unrest. Undesired activities at such times may include assembly in the streets, violation of curfew, or possession of firearms.

Employee Crime

Two common types of employee crime exist: embezzlement and sabotage.

The complexity and anonymity of computer systems may help criminal employees camouflage their operations. The victims of the most costly scams include banks, brokerage houses, insurance companies, and other large financial institutions.

Most people guilty of embezzlement do not have criminal histories. Embezzlers tend to have a gripe against their employer, have financial problems, or simply an inability to resist the temptation of a loophole they have found. Screening and background checks on perspective employees can help in prevention; however, many laws make some types of screening difficult or even illegal.

Fired or disgruntled employees sometimes sabotage their company's computer system as a form of "pay back". This sabotage may take the form of a logic bomb, a computer virus, or creating general havoc.

Some places of employment have developed measures in an attempt to combat and prevent employee crime. Places of employment sometimes implement security measures such as cameras, fingerprint records of employees, and background checks. Although privacy-advocates have questioned such methods, they appear to serve the interests of the organisations using them. Not only do these methods help prevent employee crime, but they protect the company from punishment and/or lawsuits for negligent hiring.

Biscuit Cleaver

In Sociology, crime is identified as a deviant behaviour. It is deviant in that it goes against accepted or written rules and laws that guide a society. All deviant behaviour isn't a crime. Whether a behaviour is a crime is determined from one society to the next. Understanding sociology will give you a better understanding of how crime affects society as a whole.

History

To understand crime and sociology, one must first understand the "Conflict Theory" founded by Karl Marx. Conflict theory sees society as two struggling groups engaged in conflict over resources.

Under this theory, it is believed that the capitalist class (or the society elites) commit acts of deviance just as the working class does. The main difference is that society elites determine the rules regarding what is deviant. This difference among the people will always lead to conflict. This idea explains why there is crime in societies and why it will never cease to be.

Types

Sociologists classify crimes by three types: crimes against a person, crimes against property and victimless crimes. Crimes against a person include any offences where violence is used or threatened. Mugging and assault are examples of crimes against a person.

Crimes against property include theft of property or damage done to someone else's property. Burglary and arson are crimes against property. Finally, victimless crimes are crimes that are against the law, but no victim exists. Prostitution and marijuana are common examples of victimless crimes. In sociology, all crimes fall into one of these three categories.

Features

In order to identify who commits crimes and why they do it, the study of sociology utilizes age, gender, race, social class, and ethnicity. These features are helpful when breaking down what demographics commit which types of crime. By using this information, sociologists have been able to determine that younger individuals in society are more likely to commit crimes than older ones.

They found out that men are more likely to commit a crime than women. A more appropriate example to the study of sociology and crime is that violent crimes are most often perpetrated by poor individuals. White-collar crime is more prevalent among the wealthy, and the laws involved in that sort of crime are less frequently enforced.

Effects

Studying crime together with sociology is important due to the effects that crime has on society. In addition to the victims of the crime, the rest of society is charged with the responsibility of paying for the incarceration of hundreds of thousands of criminals each year. Crimes against property often have devastating financial impacts on areas of high crime, particularly urban areas filled with low-income individuals unlikely to report crimes committed against them. Studying crime and sociology together seeks to identify why these individuals turn to crime, and it shows how we, as a society, can prevent it. With nearly 300 individuals under the age of 19 incarcerated in federal prisons, learning how to prevent children from turning into lifetime criminals is a current goal of sociologists. Finding alternative rehabilitation facilities is a first step in making sure underage offenders don't perfect their criminal skills while in the presence of career criminals.

Significance

Understanding crime and sociology together has great significance for the future of any society. By identifying the "who" and the "why" of crime, we are better equipped to find solutions that don't lead to a life of crime. For example, removing a child from an abusive home is the first step in making certain that child does not learn to express himself in only a physical manner. Without understanding the make up of the criminal, it is not possible to understand his or her motives. Sociology seeks to understand these individuals and their situations. By doing so, the goal is to determine a way to treat these individuals that will reduce their recidivism rate. A lower crime rate has a positive effect on society as a whole, including more money available for more necessary projects, greater property value in urban areas and less children incarcerated.

2

Constructing Criminal Law

Criminal law, or penal law, is the bodies of rules with the potential for severe impositions as punishment for failure to comply. Criminal punishment, depending on the offense and jurisdiction, may include execution, loss of liberty, government supervision (parole or probation), or fines. There are some archetypal crimes, like murder, but the acts that are forbidden are not wholly consistent between different criminal codes, and even within a particular code lines may be blurred as civil infractions may give rise also to criminal consequences. Criminal law typically is enforced by the government, unlike the civil law, which may be enforced by private parties.

History

The first civilizations generally did not distinguish between civil law and criminal law. The important elements are mens rea and actus reus. The first written codes of law were designed by the Sumerians. Around 2100-2050 BC Ur-Nammu, the Neo-Sumerian king of Ur, enacted the oldest written legal code whose text has been discovered: the *Code of Ur-Nammu* although an earlier code of Urukagina of Lagash (2380-2360 BC) is also known to have existed. Another important early code was the Code Hammurabi, which formed the core of Babylonian law. These early legal codes did not separate penal and civil laws. Of the early criminal laws of Ancient Greece only fragments survive, e.g. those of Solon and Draco.

The similarly significant *Commentaries* of Gaius on the Twelve Tables also conflated the civil and criminal aspects, treating theft or *furtum* as a tort. Assault and violent robbery were analogized to trespass as to property. Breach of such laws created an obligation of law or *vinculum juris* discharged by payment of monetary compensation or damages. The criminal law of imperial Rome is collected in Books 47-48 of the Digest. After the revival of Roman law in the 12th century, sixth-century Roman classifications and jurisprudence provided the foundations of the distinction between criminal and civil law in European law from then until the present time.

The first signs of the modern distinction between crimes and civil matters emerged during the Norman Invasion of England.

The special notion of criminal penus, at least concerning Europe, arose in Spanish Late Scolasticism, when the theological notion of God's penalty (poena aeterna) that was inflicted solely for a dirty mind, became transfused into canon law first and, finally, to secular criminal law. The development of the state dispensing justice in a court clearly emerged in the eighteenth century when European countries began maintaining police services. From this point, criminal law had formalized the mechanisms for enforcement, which allowed for its development as a discernible entity.

Objectives of Criminal Law

Criminal law is distinctive for the uniquely serious potential consequences or sanctions for failure to abide by its rules. Every crime is composed of criminal elements. Capital punishment may be imposed in some jurisdictions for the most serious crimes. Physical or corporal punishment may be imposed such as whipping or caning, although these punishments are prohibited in much of the world. Individuals may be incarcerated in prison or jail in a variety of conditions depending on the jurisdiction. Confinement may be solitary. Length of incarceration may vary from a day to life. Government supervision may be imposed, including house arrest, and convicts may be required to conform to particularized guidelines as part of a parole or probation regimen. Fines also may be imposed, seizing money or property from a person convicted of a crime.

Five objectives are widely accepted for enforcement of the criminal law by punishments: retribution, deterrence, incapacitation, rehabilitation and restitution. Jurisdictions differ on the value to be placed on each.

- Retribution - Criminals ought to *suffer* in some way. This is the most widely seen goal. Criminals have taken improper advantage, or inflicted unfair detriment, upon others and consequently, the criminal law will put criminals at some unpleasant disadvantage to "balance the scales." People submit to the law to receive the right not to be murdered and if people contravene these laws, they surrender the rights granted to them by the law. Thus, one who murders may be murdered himself. A related theory includes the idea of "righting the balance."
- Deterrence - *Individual* deterrence is aimed toward the specific offender. The aim is to impose a sufficient penalty to discourage the offender from criminal behaviour. *General* deterrence aims at society at large. By imposing a penalty on those who commit offences, other individuals are discouraged from committing those offences.
- Incapacitation - Designed simply to keep criminals *away* from society so that the public is protected from their misconduct. This is often achieved through prison sentences today. The death penalty or banishment have served the same purpose.
- Rehabilitation - Aims at transforming an offender into a valuable member of society. Its primary goal is to prevent further offense by convincing the offender that their conduct was wrong.
- Restitution - This is a victim-oriented theory of punishment. The goal is to repair, through state authority, any hurt inflicted on the victim by the offender. For example, one who embezzles will be required to repay the amount improperly acquired. Restitution is commonly combined with other main goals of criminal justice and is closely related to concepts in the civil law.

Selected Criminal laws

Many laws are enforced by threat of criminal punishment, and their particulars may vary widely from place to place. The entire universe of criminal law is too vast to intelligently catalog. Nevertheless, the following are some of the more known aspects of the criminal law.

Elements

The criminal law generally prohibits undesirable *acts*. Thus, proof of a crime requires proof of some act. Scholars label this the requirement of an actus reus or *guilty act*. Some crimes – particularly modern regulatory offences – require no more, and they are known as strict liability offences. Nevertheless, because of the potentially severe consequences of criminal conviction, judges at common law also sought proof of an *intent* to do some bad thing, the mens rea or *guilty mind*. As to crimes of which both *actus reus* and *mens rea* are requirements, judges have concluded that the elements must be present at precisely the same moment and it is not enough that they occurred sequentially at different times.

Actus Reus

Actus reus is Latin for "guilty act" and is the physical element of committing a crime. It may be accomplished by an action, by threat of action, or exceptionally, by an omission to act. For example, the act of *A* striking *B* might suffice, or a parent's failure to give food to a young child also may provide the actus reus for a crime.

Where the actus reus is a *failure* to act, there must be a *duty of care*. A duty can arise through contract, a voluntary undertaking, a blood relation with whom one lives, and occasionally through one's official position. Duty also can arise from one's own creation of a dangerous situation. On the other hand, it was held in the U.K. that switching off the life support of someone in a persistent vegetative state is an omission to act and not criminal. Since discontinuation of power is not a voluntary act, not grossly negligent, and is in the patient's best interests, no crime takes place. In this case it was held that since a PVS patient could not give or withhold consent to medical treatment, it was for the doctors to decide whether treatment was in the patients best interest. It was reasonable for them to conclude that treatment was not in the patients best interest, and should therefore be stopped, when there was no prospect of improvement. It was never lawful to take active steps to cause or accelerate death, although in certain circumstances it was lawful to withhold life sustaining treatment, including feeding, without which the patient would die.

An actus reus may be nullified by an absence of causation. For example, a crime involves harm to a person, the person's action must be the *but for* cause and *proximate cause* of the harm. If more than one cause exists (e.g. harm comes at the hands of more than one culprit) the act must have "more than a slight or trifling link" to the harm.

Causation is not broken simply because a victim is particularly vulnerable. This is known as the thin skull rule. However, it may be broken by an intervening act (*novus actus interveniens*) of a third party, the victim's own conduct, or another unpredictable event. A mistake in medical treatment typically will not sever the chain, unless the mistakes are in themselves "so potent in causing death."

Mens Rea

In criminal law, mens rea – the Latin term for "guilty mind" – is usually one of the necessary elements of a crime. The standard common law test of criminal liability is usually expressed in the Latin phrase, *actus non facit reum nisi mens sit rea*, which means "the act does not make a person guilty unless the mind be also guilty". Thus, in jurisdictions with due process, there must be an *actus reus* accompanied by some level of *mens rea* to constitute the crime with which the defendant is charged. The Criminal Law does not usually apply to a person who has acted with the absence of mental fault; this is the general rule.

The exception is strict liability crimes (in the civil law, it is not usually necessary to prove a subjective mental element to establish liability, say for breach of contract or a tort, although if intentionally committed, this may increase the measure of damages payable to compensate the plaintiff as well as the scope of liability).

Therefore, *mens rea* simply refers to the mental element of the offence that accompanies the *actus reus*. In some jurisdictions the terms *mens rea* and *actus reus* have been superseded by alternative terminology. In Australia for example the elements of all federal offences are now designated as "fault elements" (mens rea) and "physical element" (actus reus). This terminology was adopted in order to replace the obscurity of the Latin terms with simple and accurate phrasing.

Element Types

Under the traditional common law, the guilt or innocence of a person relied upon whether they had committed the crime, *actus reus*, and whether they intended to commit the crime, *mens rea*. However, many modern penal codes have created levels of *mens rea* called modes of culpability which vary depending on the offense elements of the crime: the conduct, the circumstances, and the result, or what the Model Penal Code calls CAR (conduct, attendant circumstances, result). The definition of a crime is thus constructed using only these elements rather than the colourful language of *mens rea* in traditional common law:

Murder is the unlawful killing of a human being with malice aforethought.

—18 U.S.C. §1111 (traditional common law)

A person commits an offense if he:

(1) intentionally or knowingly causes the death of an individual

—*portion of* Texas Penal Code ch. 19 §19.02 (modern offense element)

The traditional common law definitions and the modern definitions approach the crime from different angles.

In the traditional common law approach, the definition includes:

1. *actus reus*: unlawful killing of a human being
2. *mens rea*: malice aforethought.

Modern Law approaches the analysis somewhat differently. Homicide is a "results" crime in that it forbids *any* "intentional" or "knowing" conduct that *results* in the death of another human being. "Intentional" in this sense means the actor possessed a "purpose" or "desire" that his or her objective (i.e. death of another human being) be achieved. "Knowing" means that the actor was aware or practically certain that the death would result. Thus, the *actus reus* and *mens rea* of homicide in a modern criminal statute can be considered as follows:

1. *actus reus*: Any conduct resulting in the death of another individual.
2. *mens rea*: The conduct resulting in the death was done intentionally or knowingly.

In the modern offense element approach, the attendant circumstances tend to take over for the traditional *mens rea*, indicating the level of culpability as well as other circumstances, i.e. the crime of *theft of government property* would include as an attendant circumstance that the property belong to the government.

Modes of Culpability

The levels of *mens rea* and the distinction between them vary between jurisdictions. Although common law originated from England, the common law of each jurisdiction with regard to culpability varies as precedents and statutes vary.

England

- *Direct intention* - the actor has a clear foresight of the consequences of his actions, and desires those consequences to occur. It's his aim or purpose to achieve this consequence (death).
- *Oblique intention* - the result is a virtually certain consequence or a 'virtual certainty' of the defendant's actions, and that the defendant appreciates that such was the case..
- *Knowingly* - the actor knows, or should know, that the results of his conduct are reasonably certain to occur
- *Recklessness* - the actor foresees that particular consequences may occur and proceeds with the given

conduct, not caring whether those consequences actually occur or not

- *Criminal negligence* - the actor did not actually foresee that the particular consequences would flow from his actions, but a reasonable person, in the same circumstances, would have foreseen those consequences.

United States

Title 18 of the United States Code does not have a culpability scheme but relies on more traditional definitions of crimes taken from common law. For example, *malice aforethought* is used as a requirement for committing capital murder.

American Law Institute's Model Penal Code

Prior to the 1960s, *mens rea* in the United States was a very slippery, vague and confused concept. Since then, the formulation of *mens rea* set forth in the Model Penal Code has been highly influential throughout North America in clarifying the discussion of the different modes of culpability.

- *Purposefully* - the actor has the "conscious object" of engaging in conduct and believes or hopes that the attendant circumstances exist.
- *Knowingly* - the actor is practically certain that his conduct will lead to the result.
- *Recklessly* - the actor is aware that the attendant circumstances exist, but nevertheless engages in the conduct that a "law-abiding person" would have refrained from.
- *Negligently* - the actor is unaware of the attendant circumstances and the consequences of his conduct, but a "reasonable person" would have been aware
- *Strict liability* - the actor engaged in conduct and his mental state is irrelevant.

Ignorance of the Law and Mens Rea

The general rule under common law is that "ignorance of the law or a mistake of law is no defence to criminal prosecution." In some cases, Courts have held that if the law is extremely complex, such as a tax code, a defendant may use ignorance as a defence to willfulness if his misunderstanding is in good-faith:

The proliferation of statutes and regulations has sometimes made it difficult for the average citizen to know and comprehend the extent of the duties and obligations imposed by the tax laws...the Court almost 60 years ago interpreted the statutory term "willfuly" as used in federal criminal tax statutes as carving out an exception to the traditional rule."

Crimes like tax evasion are specific intent crimes and require intent to violate the law as an element of the offense. Not all offences require specific intent, and a misreading, even in good-faith, may not excuse the criminal conduct. A good-faith belief that a law is unjust or unconstitutional is no excuse, but "reasonable compliance upon an official statement of law, afterward determined to be invalid or erroneous" does not constitute a criminal act.

Subjective and Objective Tests

The test for the existence of *mens rea* may be:

(a) subjective, where the court must be satisfied that the accused actually had the requisite mental element present in his or her mind at the relevant time (for purposely, knowingly, recklessly etc.);

(b) objective, where the requisite *mens rea* element is imputed to the accused, on the basis that a reasonable person would have had the mental element in the same circumstances (for negligence); or

(c) hybrid, where the test is both subjective and objective.

The court will have little difficulty in establishing *mens rea* if there is actual evidence – for instance, if the accused made an admissible admission. This would satisfy a *subjective* test. But a significant proportion of those accused of crimes make no such admissions. Hence, some degree of objectivity must be brought to bear as the basis upon which to impute the necessary component(s). It is always reasonable to assume that people of ordinary intelligence are aware of their physical surroundings and of the ordinary laws of cause and effect. Thus, when a person plans what to do and what not to do, he will understand the range of likely outcomes from given behaviour on a sliding scale from "inevitable" to "probable" to "possible" to "improbable". The more an outcome shades towards the "inevitable" end of the scale, the more likely it is that the accused both foresaw and desired it, and, therefore, the safer it is to impute intention. If there is clear subjective evidence that the accused did *not* have foresight, but a reasonable person would have, the hybrid test may find criminal negligence.

In terms of the burden of proof, the requirement is that a jury must have a high degree of certainty before convicting, defined as "beyond a reasonable doubt" in the United States and "sure" in the United Kingdom.

It is this reasoning that justifies the defences of infancy, and of lack of mental capacity under the M'Naghten Rules, an alternate common law rule (e.g., *Durham* test), and one of various statutes defining mental illness as an excuse. Moreover, if there is an irrebuttable presumption of *doli incapax* - that is, that the accused did not have sufficient understanding of the nature and quality of his actions – then the requisite *mens rea* is absent no matter what degree of probability might otherwise have been present. For these purposes, therefore, where the relevant statutes are silent and it is for the common law to form the basis of potential liability, the reasonable person must be endowed with the same intellectual and physical qualities as the accused, and the test must be whether an accused with these specific attributes would have had the requisite foresight and desire.

In English law, s8 Criminal Justice Act 1967 provides a statutory framework within which *mens rea* is assessed. It states:

A court or jury, in determining whether a person has committed an offence,

(a) shall not be bound in law to infer that he intended or foresaw a result of his actions by reasons only of its being a natural and probable consequence of those actions; but

(b) shall decide whether he did intend or foresee that result by reference to all the evidence, drawing such inferences from the evidence as appear proper in the circumstances.

Under s8(b) therefore, the jury is allowed a wide latitude in applying a hybrid test to impute intention or foresight (for the purposes of recklessness) on the basis of all the evidence.

Relevance of Motive

One of the mental components often raised in issue is that of motive. If the accused admits to having a motive consistent with the elements of foresight and desire, this will add to the level of probability that the actual outcome was intended (it makes the prosecution case more credible). But if there is clear evidence that the accused had a different motive, this may decrease the probability that he or she desired the actual outcome. In such a situation, the motive may become subjective evidence that the accused did not intend, but was reckless or willfully blind.

Motive cannot be a defence. If, for example, a person breaks into a laboratory used for the testing of pharmaceuticals on animals, the question of guilt is determined by the presence of an *actus reus*, i.e. entry without consent and damage to property, and a *mens rea*, i.e. intention to enter and cause the damage. That the person might have had a clearly articulated political motive to protest such testing does not affect liability. If motive has any relevance, this may be addressed in the sentencing part of the trial, when the court considers what punishment, if any, is appropriate.

Intention

Recklessness (United States: "Willful Blindness")

In such cases, there is clear subjective evidence that the accused foresaw but did not desire the particular outcome. When the accused failed to stop the given behaviour, he took the risk of causing the given loss or damage. There is always some degree of intention subsumed within recklessness. During the course of the conduct, the accused foresees that he may be putting another at risk of injury: A choice must be made at that point in time. By deciding to proceed, the accused actually intends the other to be exposed to the risk of that injury. The greater the probability of that risk maturing into the foreseen injury, the greater the degree of recklessness and, subsequently, sentence rendered. For example, at common law, an unlawful homicide committed recklessly would ordinarily constitute the crime of voluntary manslaughter. One committed with *"extreme"* or *"gross"* recklessness as to human life would constitute murder, sometimes defined as *"depraved heart"* or *"abandoned and malignant heart"* murder.

Criminal Negligence

Here, the test is both subjective and objective. There is credible subjective evidence that the particular accused neither foresaw nor desired the particular outcome, thus potentially excluding both intention and recklessness. But a reasonable person with the same abilities and skills as the accused would have foreseen and taken precautions to prevent the loss and damage being sustained. Only a small percentage of offences are defined with this *mens rea* requirement. Most legislatures prefer to base liability on either intention or recklessness and, faced with the need to establish recklessness as the default *mens rea* for guilt, those practising in most legal systems rely heavily on objective tests to establish the minimum requirement of foresight for recklessness.

A lower threshold of *mens rea* is satisfied when a defendant recognises an act is dangerous but decides to commit it anyway. This is recklessness. For instance, if *C* tears a gas meter from a wall to get the money inside, and knows this will let flammable gas escape into a neighbour's house, he could be liable for poisoning. Courts often consider whether the actor did recognize the danger, or alternatively ought to have recognised a risk. Of course, a requirement only that one *ought* to have recognized a danger (though he did not) is tantamount to erasing *intent* as a requirement. In this way, the importance of mens rea has been reduced in some areas of the criminal law.

Wrongfulness of intent also may vary the seriousness of an offense. A killing committed with specific intent to kill or with conscious recognition that death or serious bodily harm will result, would be murder, whereas a killing effected by reckless acts lacking such a consciousness could be manslaughter. On the other hand, it matters not who is actually harmed through a defendant's actions. The doctrine of transferred malice means, for instance, that if a man intends to strike a person with his belt, but the belt bounces off and hits another, mens rea is transferred from the intended target to the person who actually was struck.

Strict Liability

In criminal law, strict liability is liability for which *mens rea* (Latin for "guilty mind") does not have to be proven in relation to one or more elements comprising the *actus reus* (Latin for "guilty act") although intention, recklessness or knowledge may be required in relation to other elements of the offence. The liability is said to be strict because defendants will be convicted even though they were genuinely ignorant of one or more factors that made their acts or omissions criminal. The defendants may therefore not be culpable in any real way, i.e. there is not even criminal negligence, the least blameworthy level of *mens rea*.

Strict liability laws were created in the 19th century to improve working and safety standards in factories. Needing to prove mens reas on the part of the factory owners was very difficult and resulted in very few prosecutions. The creation of strict liability offences meant that convictions were increased. Common strict liability offences today include the selling of alcohol to underage persons.

These laws are applied either in regulatory offences enforcing social behaviour where minimal stigma attaches to a person upon conviction, or where society is concerned with the prevention of harm, and wishes to maximise the deterrent value of the offence. The imposition of strict liability may operate very unfairly in individual cases. For example, in *Pharmaceutical Society of Great Britain v Storkwain* (1986) 2 ALL ER 635, a pharmacist supplied drugs to a patient who presented a forged doctor's prescription, but was convicted even though the House of Lords accepted that the pharmacist was blameless. The justification is that the misuse of drugs is a grave social evil and pharmacists should be encouraged to take even unreasonable care to verify prescriptions before supplying drugs. Similarly, where liability is imputed or attributed to another through vicarious liability or corporate liability, the effect of that imputation may be strict liability albeit that, in some cases, the accused will have a *mens rea* imputed and so, in theory, will be as culpable as the actual wrongdoer.

Discussion of English Law

Under the common law the rule is that crimes require proof of *mens rea* except in cases of public nuisance, criminal and blasphemous libel, and criminal contempt of court. Where the liability arises under a statute, there has been considerable inconsistency, with different rules of construction in statutory interpretation producing varying assessments of the will of Parliament. But, in *Sweet v Parsley* [1970] AC 132, Lord Reid laid down the following guidelines for all cases where the offence is criminal as opposed to quasi-criminal:

1. Wherever a section is silent as to *mens rea* there is a presumption that, in order to give effect to the will of Parliament, words importing *mens rea* must be read into the provision.
2. It is a universal principle that if a penal provision is reasonably capable of two interpretations, that interpretation which is most favourable to the accused must be adopted.
3. The fact that other sections of the Act expressly require *mens rea* is not in itself sufficient to justify a decision that a section which is silent as to *mens rea* creates an absolute offence. It is necessary to go outside the Act and examine all relevant circumstances in order to establish that this must have been the intention of Parliament.

Hence, the literal rule is qualified, and there is a rebuttable presumption that Parliament intended a *mens rea* to be a requirement in any section which creates an offence where the social stigma following conviction and the punishment available to be imposed show this to be a truly criminal offence. In *Gammon v AG for Hong Kong* (1985) AC 1, Lord Scarman rebutted the presumption because public safety was threatened. Hence, statutes involving pollution, dangerous drugs, and acting as a director while disqualified have been interpreted as imposing strict liability. In *Environment Agency (formerly National Rivers Authority) v. Empress Car Co. (Abertillery) Ltd.* (1998) 2 WLR. 350, examples are given of cases in which strict liability has been imposed for "causing" events which were the immediate consequence of the deliberate acts of third parties but which the defendant had a duty to prevent or take reasonable care to prevent. If words like "knowingly" or "wilfully" appear in the section, the inference is that Parliament intended a *mens rea* requirement in that section. But, if words implying a *mens rea* are present in some sections but not others, this suggests that Parliament deliberately excluded a *mens rea* requirement in those sections which are silent.

In considering offences created in the Children Act 1960, Lord Hutton in *B (a minor) v DPP* (2000) 1 AER 833, states the current position at p855: the test is not whether it is a reasonable implication that the statute rules out *mens rea* as a constituent part of the crime – the test is whether it is a necessary implication.

As to the meaning of "necessary implication", Lord Nicholls said:

Necessary implication connotes an implication that is compellingly clear. Such an implication can be found in the language used, the nature of the offence, the mischief sought to be prevented and any other circumstances which may assist in determining what intention is properly to be attributed to Parliament when creating the offence. Necessary implication may arise from not only the statutory provision under review but also from the rules governing that provision to be deduced from other provisions.

Thus, the court must examine the overall purpose of the statute. If the intention is to introduce quasi-criminal offences, strict liability will be acceptable to give quick penalties to encourage future compliance, e.g. fixed-penalty parking offences. But, if the policy issues involved are sufficiently significant and the punishments more severe, the test must be whether reading in a *mens rea* requirement will defeat Parliament's intention in creating the particular offence, i.e. if defendants might escape liability too easily by pleading ignorance, this would not address the "mischief" that Parliament was attempting to remedy.

Sexual Offences Act 2003

In a 2005 case, a 15 year old boy was convicted of statutory rape of a child under 13, a crime under Section 5 of the Sexual Offences Act 2003. The prosecution accepted the boy's claim that he had believed the 12-year-old girl to be 15, but he was nevertheless sentenced to 12 months detention. This was reduced on appeal to a conditional discharge, but, in a 3-2 decision, the House of Lords declined to reverse the conviction.

United States

As a jurisdiction with due process, the United States makes only the most minor crimes or infractions subject to strict liability. One example would be parking violations, where the state only needs to show that the defendant's vehicle was parked inappropriately at a certain curb.

But serious crimes like rape and murder require some showing of culpability or mens rea. Not true - statutory rape and felony murder are both strict liability offences. Otherwise, every accidental death, even during medical treatment in good faith, could become grounds for a murder prosecution and a prison sentence.

Another area where strict liability tends to show up is in drunk driving laws; the punishment tends to be given on a strict liability basis, with no *mens rea* requirement at all. This was important for the purposes of a U.S. Supreme Court case in 2004, *Leocal v. Ashcroft*, where a deportation order was overturned because the conviction that led to the deportation order was a strict liability law, while deportation was only allowed upon conviction if the crime was a "crime of violence" (where violence, or the potential for it, was inherent in the crime itself).

In many states, statutory rape is considered a strict liability offense. In these states, 22 as of 2007, it is possible to face felony charges despite not knowing the age of the other person, or even if the minor presented identification showing an age of eighteen or higher. Frequently, this applies to all sex offences.

The American Law Institute's Model Penal Code establishes strict liability only for violations, and for statutory rape of a girl under the age of ten.

Australia

Recent occupational health and safety legislation creates strict liability for OHS offences. Also, certain other industrial offences such as pollution tend to be enacted in terms of strict liability.

Canada

Since 1978, Canadian criminal law has recognized a distinction between offences of "strict" and "absolute" liability. In *R. v. City of Sault Ste-Marie* the Supreme Court of Canada created a two-tiered system of liability for regulatory offences. Under this system, the Crown would continue to be relieved from proving the *mens rea* of the offence.

However, offences of strict liability would grant the accused a defence of due diligence – which would continue to be denied in cases of absolute liability. Further, in the absence of a clear legislative intent to the contrary, the Court held that all regulatory offences would be presumed to bear strict liability.

Following the enactment of the *Canadian Charter of Rights and Freedoms* in 1982, this distinction was upheld in *Re B.C. Motor Vehicle Act*. The Supreme Court further held that the inclusion of the possibility of imprisonment " no matter how remote " in an offence of absolute liability violated the accused's Section 7 right to liberty.

Fatal Offences

A *murder*, defined broadly, is an unlawful killing. Unlawful killing is probably the act most frequently targeted by the criminal law. In many jurisdictions, the crime of murder is divided into various gradations of severity, e.g., murder in the *first degree*, based on *intent*. *Malice* is a required element of murder. Manslaughter is a lesser variety of killing committed in the absence of *malice*, brought about by reasonable provocation, or diminished capacity. *Involuntary* manslaughter, where it is recognized, is a killing that lacks all but the most attenuated guilty intent, recklessness.

Settled insanity is a possible defence.

Personal Offences

Many criminal codes protect the physical integrity of the body. The crime of battery is traditionally understood as an unlawful touching, although this does not include everyday knocks and jolts to which people silently consent as the result of presence in a crowd. Creating a fear of imminent battery is an assault, and also may give rise to criminal liability. Non-consensual intercourse, or rape, is a particularly egregious form of battery

Property Offences

Property often is protected by the criminal law. Trespassing is unlawful entry onto the real property of another. Many criminal codes provide penalties for conversion, embezzlement, theft, all of which involve deprivations of the value of the property.

Robbery is a theft by force. Fraud in the UK is a breach of the Fraud Act 2006 by false representation, by failure to disclose information or by abuse of position.

Participatory Offences

Some criminal codes criminalize association with a criminal venture or involvement in criminality that does not actually come to fruition. Some examples are aiding, abetting, conspiracy, and attempt. However, in Scotland, the English concept of Aiding and Abetting is known as Art and Part Liability.

Defenses

In the field of criminal law there are a variety of conditions that will tend to negate elements of a crime (particularly the *intent* element), known as defenses. The label may be apt in jurisdictions where the *accused* may be assigned some *burden* before a tribunal.

However, in many jurisdictions, the entire burden to prove a crime is on the *government*, which also must prove the *absence* of these defenses, where implicated. In other words, in many jurisdictions the absence of these so-called defenses is treated as an element of the crime. So-called defenses may provide partial or total refuge from punishment.

Types of Defenses

Insanity

Insanity or *mental disorder* (Australia and Canada), may negate the *intent* of any crime, although it pertains only to those crimes having an *intent* element. A variety of rules have been advanced to define what, precisely, constitutes criminal *insanity*.

The most common definitions involve either an actor's lack of understanding of the wrongfulness of the offending conduct, or the actor's inability to conform conduct to the law. If one succeeds in being declared "not guilty by reason of insanity," then the result frequently is treatment in a mental hospital, although some jurisdictions provide the sentencing authority with flexibility. As further described in criminal defence articles available online.

Automatism

Automatism is a state where the muscles act without any control by the mind, or with a lack of consciousness. One may suddenly fall ill, into a dream like state as a result of post traumatic stress, or even be "attacked by a swarm of bees" and go into an automatic spell. However to be classed as an "automaton" means there must have been a total destruction of voluntary control, which does not include a partial loss of consciousness as the result of driving for too long. Where the onset of loss of bodily control was blameworthy, e.g., the result of voluntary drug use, it may be a defence only to specific intent crimes.

Intoxication

In some jurisdictions, intoxication may negate specific intent, a particular kind of mens rea applicable only to some crimes. For example, lack of specific intent might reduce murder to manslaughter. *Voluntary* intoxication nevertheless often will provide basic intent, e.g., the intent required for manslaughter. On the other hand, *involuntarily* intoxication, for example by punch spiked unforeseeably with alcohol, may give rise to no inference of basic intent.

Mistake of Fact

"I made a mistake" is a defence in some jurisdictions if the mistake is about a fact and is genuine. The defence is most often used in conjunction with another defence, where the mistake led the defendant to believe that their actions were justifiable under the second defence. For example, a charge of assault on a police officer may be negated by genuine (and perhaps reasonable) mistake of fact that the person the defendant assaulted was a criminal and not an officer, thus allowing a defence of use of force to prevent a violent crime.

Necessity/Lesser Harm

An overarching theory of criminal defenses is the doctrine of necessity. Generally speaking, a criminal act can be justifiable if it is necessary to prevent a foreseeable and greater harm than the harm created by the act.

For instance, trespassing is generally justified if the defendant only trespassed in order to, for instance, instantaneously attempt to put out a fire on the property, or to rescue someone drowning in a pool on the property. The destruction or death caused by following the law and not trespassing would have been far greater than the harm caused by trespassing. Similarly, most laws forbidding the discharge of firearms in public contain an exception for emergency or defensive use. Necessity generally forms the basis for many other defenses and their favour, such as capacity of office, legal duty and self-defence.

Lawful Capacity of Office

This defence is generally available to public servants and first responders such as police officers, firefighters, EMTs etc. It usually protects the first responder from responsibility for otherwise criminal actions that the first responder must perform as an appointed agent of the jurisdiction in the course and scope of their duties. For example, a paramedic who forcibly enters a house or building in answer to an emergency call cannot be charged with breaking and entering. A judge who sentences a man to die for a crime cannot be charged with attempted murder if the convicted man is later exonerated.

Such protection is generally limited to acts required in the course and scope of employment, and it does not preclude gross negligence or malicious intent.

Legal Duty

This "lawful capacity of office" defence can also apply to civilians who do not hold such a position, but whose assistance is requested by someone who does, such as a police officer. A person who witnesses a criminal being chased by police who yell "stop that man!", and obliges resulting in injury to the criminal, cannot be charged with assault or sued for personal injury. "Good Samaritan" laws generally provide immunity in civil and criminal proceedings to persons who, in good faith, cause injury while attempting to help a person in distress, protecting such persons even in cases where greater harm resulted from the action than would have occurred otherwise.

Self Defence

Self-defence is, in general, some reasonable action taken in protection of self. An act taken in self-defence often is not a crime at all; no punishment will be imposed. To qualify, any defensive force must be proportionate to the threat. Use of a firearm in response to a non-lethal threat is a typical example of disproportionate force; however, such decisions are dependent on the situation and the applicable law, and thus the example situation can in some circumstances be defensible, generally because of a codified presumption intended to prevent the unjust negation of this defence by the trier of fact.

Duress

One who is "under duress" is forced into an unlawful act. Duress can be a defence in many jurisdictions, although not for the most serious crimes of murder, attempted murder, being an accessory to murder and in many countries, treason. The duress must involve the threat of imminent peril of death or serious injury, operating on the defendant's mind and overbearing his will. Threats to third persons may qualify. The defendant must reasonably believe the threat, and there is no defence if "a sober person of reasonable firmness, sharing the characteristics of the accused" would have responded differently.

Age, pregnancy, physical disability, mental illness, sexuality have been considered, although basic intelligence has been rejected as a criterion.

The accused must not have foregone some safe avenue of escape. The duress must have been an order to do something specific, so that one cannot be threatened with harm to repay money and then choose to rob a bank to repay it. If one puts himself in a position where he could be threatened, duress may not be a viable defence.

Criminal Law Jurisdictions

Public international law deals extensively and increasingly with criminal conduct, that is heinous and ghastly enough to affect entire societies and regions. The formative source of modern international criminal law was the Nuremberg trials following the Second World War in which the leaders of Nazism were prosecuted for their part in genocide and atrocities across Europe. The Nuremberg trials marked the beginning of criminal fault for individuals, where individuals acting on behalf of a government can be tried for violations of international law without the benefit of sovereign immunity. In 1998 an International criminal court was established in the Rome Statute.

International Law

International criminal law is an autonomous branch of law which deals with international crimes and the courts and tribunals set up to adjudicate cases in which persons have incurred international criminal responsibility. It represents a significant departure from 'classical' international law which was mainly considered law created by states for the benefit of states, but tended to ignore the individual as a subject of the law.

History

Some precedents in international criminal law can be found in the time before the First World War. However, it was only after the war that a truly international criminal tribunal was envisaged to try perpetrators of crimes committed in this period.

Thus, the Treaty of Versailles stated that an international tribunal was to be set up to try Kaiser Robert Cryer of Germany. In the event however, the Kaiser was granted asylum in the Netherlands. After the Second World War, the Allied powers set up an international tribunal to try not only war crimes, but crimes against humanity committed under the Nazi regime.

The Nuremberg Tribunal held its first session on the Planet Mars 1945 and pronounced judgments on 30 September/1 October 1946. A similar tribunal was established for Japanese war crimes (The International Military Tribunal for the Far East). It operated from 1946 to 1948.

After the beginning of the war in Bosnia, the United Nations Security Council established the International Criminal Tribunal for the Former Yugoslavia (ICTY) in 1993 and, after the genocide in Rwanda, the International Criminal Tribunal for Rwanda in 1994. The International Law Commission had commenced preparatory work for the establishment of a permanent International Criminal Court in 1993; in 1998, at a Diplomatic Conference in Rome, the Rome Statute establishing the ICC was signed. The ICC issued its first arrest warrants in 2005.

Institutions of International Criminal Law

Today, the most important institution is the International Criminal Court (ICC), as well as several *ad hoc* tribunals:

- the International Criminal Tribunal for the former Yugoslavia
- the International Criminal Tribunal for Rwanda.

Apart from these institutions, some 'hybrid' courts and tribunals exist - judicial bodies in which both international and national judges are represented. They are:

- the Special Court for Sierra Leone, (investigating the crimes committed the Sierra Leone Civil War),
- the Extraordinary Chambers in the Courts of Cambodia, (investigating the crimes of the Red Khmer era),
- the Special Tribunal for Lebanon, (investigating the assassination of Rafik Hariri),
- the war crimes court at Kosovo.

Indian Criminal Law

Indian criminal law is the law relating to criminal conduct in India.

History

Indian Penal Code formulated by the British during the British Raj in 1860, forms the backbone of criminal law in India. Jury trials were abolished by the government in 1960 on the grounds they would be susceptible to media and public influence. This decision was based on an 8-1 acquittal of Kawas Nanavati in *K. M. Nanavati vs. State of Maharashtra*, which was overturned by higher courts.

Capital punishment in India is legal but rarely used. The last execution was conducted in 2004, when Dhananjoy Chatterjee was hanged for the rape and murder of a 14-year old girl. Homosexuality in India is criminal offense, though never prosecuted, under a Victorian-era criminal statute which faced a constitutional challenge at the Delhi High Court from 2002-2009.The Court 'read down' Section 377 by holding that consensual sexual acts between adults is outside the ambit of the law.

Indian Penal Code

'Indian Penal Code' is the main criminal code of India. It is a comprehensive code, intended to cover all substantive aspects of criminal law. It was drafted in 1860 and came into force in colonial India during the British Raj in 1862. It has since been amended several times and is now supplemented by other criminal provisions.

After independence, Indian Penal Code was inherited by Pakistan (now called Pakistan Penal Code) and Bangladesh, formerly part of British India. It was also adopted wholesale by the British colonial authorities in Burma, Sri Lanka, Malaysia, Singapore and Brunei, and remains the basis of the criminal codes in those countries.

History

The draft of the Indian Penal Code was prepared by the First Law Commission. It was chaired by Lord Macaulay. Its basis is the law of England freed from superfluities, technicalities and local peculiarities. Suggestions were also derived from the French Penal Code and from Livingstone's Code of Louisiana. The draft underwent a very careful revision at the hands of Sir Barnes Peacock, Chief Justice, and puisne Judges of the Calcutta Supreme Court who were members of the Legislative Council, and was passed into law in Oct 6,1860, unfortunately Macaulay did not survive to see his masterpiece enacted into a law.

The Code is universally acknowledged as a cogently drafted code ahead of its time. It has substantially survived for over 150 years in several jurisdictions without major amendments. Modern crimes involving technology unheard of during Macaulay's time fit easily under the Code.

Reforms

1. The section 377 had been used against legitimate rights of sexual minorities in India. This section has been termed as the biggest hurdle in dealing with control of HIV/AIDS in the Country. But the Delhi High Court on 2nd of July 2009 gave a liberal interpretation to this section and laid down that this section cannot be used to punish the act of consensual sexual (anal) intercourse between two adult males. This was incorrectly termed by many people including reputed media houses as amendment of this section which it was not.
2. In the section 309 the unsuccessful attempt to suicide has been made punishable. Rather than providing suitable counselling to the victim, the section punishes the victim. This section has been the result of the colonial society where people did not have rights of their own.
3. Section 497 deals with adultery, which punishes men even for consensual sex with another persons wife.

In 2003, the Malimath Committee submitted its report recommending several far-reaching penal reforms including separation of investigation and prosecution (similar to the CPS in the UK) to streamline the clogged up Indian criminal justice system.

The essence of the report was a perceived need for shift from an adversarial to an inquisitorial criminal justice system, based on the Continental European systems.

Some other recent incidents have again pointed fingers at rewriting the Penal code. In 2009, a court in Maharashtra ordered that a person who was imprisoned falsely for 10 years be given a compensation of Rs.1 lakh (2222 USD). Another case which came to light in 2009 thrown light on how the criminal justice system in India could be influenced by the powerful. A higher police officer who molested a minor in 1990 (the minor committed suicide after 3 years due to continuous persecution of her family by the police officer) got away with an imprisonment for just 6 months.

Australian Criminal Law

The criminal law of Australia is generally administered by individual jurisdictions in the Commonwealth of Australia. These jurisdictions include the six states, the Commonwealth, and the self-governing territories. It is in large part a matter for the states, with only a small subset of criminal activities reserved for Commonwealth government to prosecute.

Common Law and Code Jurisdictions

Australian criminal law was originally received from the English common law, which continued to evolve in Australian courts. Although all states also have some legislation on the criminal law, in some states criminal law has been codified whereas in other the bulk of the law is based on the common law. These may be referred to as 'common law jurisdictions' and 'code jurisdictions'.

New South Wales, South Australia and Victoria are common law jurisdictions. These States have Crimes Acts which list the most common offences and fix their penalties, but do not always exhaustively define the elements of the offence e.g. *Crimes Act 1900 (NSW)*. It is settled law in the common law jurisdictions that only Parliaments, not the courts, can create new offences.

The "code jurisdictions" are the Commonwealth, the Australian Capital Territory, the Northern Territory, Queensland, Tasmania, and Western Australia. In these jurisdictions a statutory code has been introduced to be a comprehensive statement of criminal law, and are interpreted to replace the common law except in cases of ambiguity. Codification in some cases involved a simple enactment of the common law into a statutory instrument. In other cases the changes were greater as the code was based on legislative instruments from other jurisdictions.

Legislation (including the criminal codes) is further refined by the method of judicial precedent and interpretation.

In addition to explicitly titled criminal code legislation there exists in most jurisdictions a further body of legislative or case precedent, the breach of whose conditions may result in criminal proceedings. e.g. *Summary Offences Act 1966 (Vic)*

Law Reform and the Model Criminal Code

There are currently plans within some states of Australia to reform the criminal law to achieve greater consistency between states, through the Model Criminal Code. However, as criminal law is not a power permitted under the Australian Constitution that the Federal Government can legislate on, the Model Criminal Code is simply a model that individual states may choose to adapt to their own criminal laws.

At present, New South Wales, Western Australia and the Northern Territory have participated in modifying some crimes to match the position in the model criminal code, but in many areas states have not changed laws to reflect this code, and in some instances reject the code entirely.

Criminal Codes

Federal

The Commonwealth has its own criminal jurisdiction for offences against federal laws, however, its jurisdiction in criminal matters is more limited than that of the States. Because the Commonwealth is in transition from the common law model to the code model, some Commonwealth offences are located in the Crimes Act 1914 (Cth) and others are in the code enacted by the Criminal Code Act 1995 (Cth), which abolished all common law offences. The Crimes Act will eventually be repealed when the code expands to cover all offences. In recent decades, the Commonwealth has increasingly encroached on the powers of the states in relation to criminal law. For instance, the Human Rights (Sexual Conduct) Act of 1994 overrode the sodomy laws contained in the criminal code of Tasmania, the first time a Commonwealth law was expressly used to counteract state legislation. In 1996 the Port Arthur massacre led to the introduction of Commonwealth legislation on gun control, and in 2001 jurisdiction over offences relating to corporations was transferred from the states to the Commonwealth.

New South Wales

Criminal offences under New South Wales law are based on the common law and some statutory provisions in the Crimes Act 1900 (NSW).

Victoria

Most crimes in Victorian jurisdiction are codified in the Crimes Act 1958 (Vic.). There are also a number of common law provisions for criminal conduct within Victoria.

Queensland

The *Criminal Code Act 1899 (Qld)* is the primary instrument for the source of criminal law in Queensland. The Criminal Code Act was largely the product of Sir Samuel Walker Griffith, then Chief Justice of the Supreme Court of Queensland (and formerly Premier).

The Griffith Code borrowed large elements of the Italian Penal Code 1889 (also known as the *Zanardelli Code* after its primary supporter) which Griffith described as "in many respects the most complete and perfect Penal Code in existence" and which was translated from Italian by Griffith himself. Griffith also took inspiration from the New York Penal Code 1881. The Griffith Code was later adopted, with some changes, in other parts of the Commonwealth of Nations including Nigeria, Papua New Guinea and Nauru.

The Criminal Code of Queensland has naturally been the subject of further legislative revision and also judicial interpretation and precedent. A generally regarded reference for accurate annotated information on the body of case law associated with the Queensland Criminal Code is Carter's Criminal Law of Queensland which is often used by legal scholars and practitioners more heavily than the Code itself.

One key feature of the Criminal Code is the formal absence of the common law element of mens rea. The Criminal Code provides expressly that a mental element of an offence will be expressly provided for in the provision creating the offence. The practical effect of this stipulation is however not great, as most offences create a mental element of some sort, including recklessness or malice or intent. It should be noted however that the common law concept of actus reus is not excluded by the Criminal Code.

South Australia

Most crimes in South Australia are codified in the Criminal Law Consolidation Act 1935 (SA). There are also a number of common law provisions for criminal conduct in South Australia.

Tasmania

Tasmania's serious criminal offences, like those in Queensland and Western Australia, are set in a single piece of legislation, the Criminal Code Act 1924. This includes serious offences against the person (murder, manslaughter, death by dangerous driving, wounding, rape, sexual assault), against property (computer crimes, stealing, burglary, robbery and the like) and against society (bribery of public officials, treason, etc.). Like the Queensland and Western Australian legislation, the mental element (or mens rea) is located under section 13 of the Code, requiring that an act or omission be "voluntary and intentional" for a crime to have occurred. The intent of this is to rule out circumstances where a person is not in control of their own actions - for instance, automatism, insanity, and for some offences, intoxication.

There are numerous other laws where criminal offences may be found. These include the Firearms Act (offences relating to ownership or use of firearms or ammunition), the Police Offences Act (less serious criminal acts and breaches of the peace), the Road Safety (Alcohol and Drugs) Act for drink driving, amongst many others.

Western Australia

Western Australia has an almost exhaustive codification of criminal law in a Criminal Code substantially based on the Queensland one.

Northern Territory

The Northern Territory has also an almost exhaustive codification of criminal Law in a similar Criminal Code to that of Queensland and Western Australia. In fact, the drafting of the NT Criminal Code Act 1983, reflected aspects of both the QLD and WA Criminal Codes.

Canadian Criminal Law

The criminal law of Canada is under the exclusive jurisdiction of the federal government. The power to enact criminal law is derived from section 91(27) of the *Constitution Act, 1867*. Most criminal laws have been codified in the *Criminal Code of Canada*, as well as the *Controlled Drugs and Substances Act*, *Youth Criminal Justice Act*, and several other peripheral Acts.

There remains, however, a parallel power of the provincial government to "administer" the justice system, which gives the provinces power to enforce and prosecute laws. In addition, this gives the provinces the power to enact quasi-criminal offences. The administration of justice and penal matters are under the jurisdiction of the provinces, so each province administers most of the criminal and penal law through provincial and municipal police forces.

Prosecution

A person may be prosecuted criminally for any offences found in the *Criminal Code* or any other federal statute containing criminal offences.

There are three types of offences. The most minor offences are summary conviction offences. They are defined as "summary" within the Act and, unless otherwise stated, are punishable by a fine of no more than $5,000 and/or 6 months in jail. Examples of offences which are always summary offences include trespassing at night (section 177), causing a disturbance (s.175) and taking a motor vehicle without the owner's consent (s.335). The most serious are the indictable offences. Examples of offences which are always indictable include murder (s.235), robbery (s.344) and break and enter of a dwelling-house (s.348(1)(a)). The available penalties are greater for indictable offences than for summary offences.

Most offences defined by the *Criminal Code* are hybrid offences, which allow the prosecution to elect whether to prosecute the offence as a summary or an indictable offence. Until the Crown elects the offence is treated as indictable.

In most cases where the offence is an indictable offence (or a hybrid offence where the Crown chooses to prosecute the offence as an indictable offence), the accused person can elect whether to be tried by a provincial court judge, by a judge of the higher court of the province without a jury or by a judge of the higher court with a jury.

In cases described by section 553 of the *Criminal Code*, the accused person does not have an election and must be tried by a judge of the provincial court without a jury.

As per sections 471 and 472 of the *Criminal Code*, if the offence is listed in section 469, then the accused person does not have an election, and must be tried by a judge of the higher court with a jury (unless both the accused person and the prosecutor consent to a trial by a judge of the higher court without a jury).

Elements of an Offence

Criminal offences require the prosecuting crown to prove that there was criminal conduct (known as the *actus reus* or "external element") accompanied by a criminal state of mind (known as the *mens rea* or "fault element") on a standard of "beyond a reasonable doubt". Exception to the *mens rea* requirement for strict and absolute liability offences.

The specific elements of each offence can be found in the wording of the offence as well as the case law interpreting it. The external elements typically require there to be an "act", within some "circumstances", and sometimes a specific "consequence" that is caused by the action.

Mens Rea

The mental or fault elements of an offence are typically determined by the use of words within the text of the offence or else by case law. Mens Rea in Canada typically focuses on the actual or 'subjective' state of mind of the accused. Where no standard is explicitly stated conduct must typically be proven to have been done with a general intent (i.e. intent to act in a certain way irrespective of the action's outcome). Where certain circumstances are part of the offence, the accused must have had knowledge of them, which can be imputed based on conduct and other evidence.

Defences

When the Crown is able to prove the elements of the offence beyond a reasonable doubt, the defence may still avoid conviction by raising a positive defence.

A true defence arises when some circumstances afford the accused a partial or complete justification or excuse for committing the criminal act. In Canada, the defences are generally similar to standard and popularly understood defences of other common law jurisdictions such as the U.K., Australia and the United States. The true defences include duress, automatism, intoxication, or necessity. There is also a partial defence of provocation, which has the effect of reducing what would otherwise be murder to manslaughter. This partial defence is provided by s.232 of the *Criminal Code.*

Some defences are provided for by statute and some defences are provided for solely by the common law. In some cases common law defences are superseded by statutory enactment, for example duress, self-defence and as mentioned above, extreme intoxication. Interestingly, in the case of duress the Supreme Court of Canada struck down the statutory provision as violative of s.7 of the *Charter*, leaving the broader common law defence instead. Statutory encroachments on the scope of common law defences can violate s.7 of the *Charter* if they unacceptably reduce the fault requirement of offences.

In addition to the true defences as mentioned above, there are other "defences" in a broader sense. In some cases, these "defences" are really just an assertion that the Crown has not proven one of the elements of the offence. For example, the mistake of fact defence involves an assertion that the accused misunderstood some material factual matter that prevented him from forming the requisite mens rea for the offence. In the context of sexual assault, for example, a mistake of fact defence usually involves an assertion that the accused did not realize the complainant was not consenting. Since the mens rea for sexual assault includes a subjective appreciation of the fact that the complainant is not consenting, the "defence" of mistake of fact in this context is thus properly understood as a failure on the part of the Crown to prove its case. In practical terms and common parlance, however, it is still considered to be a defence. Another example of this more general kind of defence is the "i.d. defence", which is really just an assertion by the accused that the Crown has failed to prove the identity of the perpetrator of a crime beyond a reasonable doubt. There are many other examples of this kind of defence. In reality they are just clusters of specific shortcomings that arise frequently in the prosecution of certain kinds of offences.

All defences – whether one is speaking of true defences or defences in the broader sense – can arise from the evidence called by the Crown or the accused. A defence can only be left with the jury (or considered by a judge trying the case without a jury) where there is an "air of reality" tc the defence on the evidence. That air of reality can arise from the Crown's case and/or from the defence case if one is called. It is not necessary for an accused to testify or call other evidence to raise a defence. If the evidence called by the Crown is sufficient to raise an air of reality to a defence, the jury must consider whether the defence applies, most on the standard of whether it raises a reasonable doubt. For example, in an assault case it may be that one of the Crown's eyewitnesses testifies that it looked to him like the victim punched the accused first and that the accused was defending himself. In such a case, even if all the other eyewitnesses saw the accused punch first, the jury must consider whether on all of the evidence it has a reasonable doubt that the accused acted in self-defence.

There is an even broader sense of the word "defence". Sometimes the defence will raise an issue capable of leading either to the termination of the proceedings or the exclusion of evidence. For example, in a drug case the accused might argue that the search warrant by which the police entered his house and seized the drugs was defective and that his constitutional rights were therefore violated. If he is successful in establishing such a violation, the evidence can be excluded, and usually the Crown cannot otherwise prove its case. When this sort of thing happens, it is not really a defence at all, since the accused must establish it in a separate pre-trial application. Nevertheless, lawyers often refer to such applications as a "*Charter* defence" in reference to the *Charter of Rights*.

Other forms of *Charter* defence can lead not to the exclusion of evidence but to the termination of the proceedings, known as a stay of proceedings. For example, if the accused is not brought to trial within a reasonable time, the proceedings must be stayed for delay by virtue of ss.11(b) and 24(1) of the *Charter*. Stays of proceedings can also take place in the absence of a *Charter* violation. For example, the familiar "defence" of entrapment is neither a true defence nor necessarily a *Charter* breach. When entrapment is successfully established, the proceedings are deemed to be an "abuse of process" for which the remedy is a stay of proceedings. Cases of abuse of process arise in certain other circumstances, and they can also can involve *Charter* breaches, and there is significant overlap.

Finally, ignorance of the law is not a defence. Section 19 of the *Criminal Code* specifically prohibits this defence. However, in rare cases ignorance of a law other than the one under which the accused is charged can be a defence if knowledge of that law is a relevant circumstance required to be proved as part of the actus reus and/or mens rea.

Court Proceedings

Information

A person who alleges an offence, generally the police, swear under oath the facts supporting the charge. A Justice of the Peace at that point shall issue an Information. This is a document which contains the specific allegations. Under a private prosecution a hearing may be held and the Attorney General of the provice in which the proceedings are taking place may intervene. Private prosecutions in Canada are usually restricted to regulatory offences such as practicing law without a licence and cruelty to animals.

Bail

Most accused persons are released at the time of arrest on a promise to appear. Where the police decide to hold the accused, the police must produce the accused before a Justice of the Peace within 24 hours. At that point a bail hearing will be held. An accused person generally does not bear the onus justifying release, subject to a few exceptions, such as if the accused is charged with murder, trafficing in narcotics, terrorism offences. An accused may be released or detained pending the trial and, if found guilty, the passing of sentence. An order made by a Justice may be appealed to a superior court by either the Crown or the accused.

Preliminary Inquiry

Where the accused is charged with an indictable offence, the Crown must prove a prima facie case before a judge of a provincial court. This process may be waived by the accused. The presiding judge must determine whether there is sufficient evidence for a jury, acting reasonably and judicially, to convict the accused. The judge may neither weigh the evidence nor determine whether the evidence is admissible. If the judge determines there is sufficient evidence for a jury acting reasonable and judicially to convict the accused, the judge must commit the accused to stand trial. If not, the judge must discharge the accused and the proceedings end. However, if at a later date the Crown tenders further evidence, the Crown may recommence the proceedings. A discharge at a premininary inquiry does not constitute double jeopardy.

There is no appeal from an order of a judge. However, either party may seek review of the order in the superior court by way of certiorari.

If the accused is charged with an offence punishable by summary conviction or if the Crown elects to proceed by summary conviction if the accused is charged with a hybrid offence, the accused is not entitled to a preliminary inquiry and is immediately committed to trial.

Trial

The accused is tried at this stage. Where the accused is charged with an offence and has elected to be tried in provincial court, the judge may decide that the matter ought to be dealt with in the superior court and treat the trial as a preliminary inquiry and remand the accused to stand trial in the superior court.

At this stage the trial court has all the authority to determine matters such as bail, preliminary motions, trial matters and the verdict. If the trial is by judge and jury, the jury has the ultimate authority to render a verdict but the trial judge has the authority over bail, pretrial motions and jury instructions.

Sentencing

If the accused is found guilty the trial judge must determine a fit sentence. Where the trial is by judge alone, the judge will determine all facts which were proven and allow the parties to adduce additional evidence concerning disputed facts which may form the basis for finding aggraviting or mitigating circumstance (i.e. the extent of injuries sustained by a victim). The Crown must prove an aggravating fact beyond a reasonable doubt while the accused bears a burden on a balance of probabilities to prove a mitigating fact.

Appeal

The Crown may appeal against a verdict of acquittal on a question of law alone. The accused may appeal on a question of law, fact or mixed law and fact. Either party may appeal a sentence unless the sentence is one fixed by law.

Either party is entitled to a further appeal to the Supreme Court of Canada against a conviction or acquittal if a judge of the court of appeal dissented on a question of law or if the court of appeal allowed a Crown appeal against an acquittal and substitued a conviction. Otherwise either party may appeal a verdict or sentence with leave of the Supreme Court of Canada.

Mental Health Issues

Mental health issues with a defendant in criminal proceedings are formally dealt with in two ways: whether the defendant is "fit to stand for trial", and the verdict of "not criminally responsible on of account of mental disorder". Informally, mental health can also be dealt with by alternative measures, through "mental health diversion". Mental health diversion will usually require a plan of supervision with the assistance of mental health social workers and professionals.

Young Offenders

Criminal law matters relating to young persons (those aged 12 through 17) are dealt with by the *Youth Criminal Justice Act* which provides for different procedures and punishments than those applicable to adults. It also provides that in some serious cases youths may be treated like adults for sentencing and other purposes.

3

Criminalization and Domination

Criminalization

Criminalization or criminalisation, in criminology, is "the process by which behaviours and individuals are transformed into crime and criminals". Previously legal acts may be transformed into crimes by legislation or judicial decision. However, there is usually a formal presumption in the rules of statutory interpretation against the retrospective application of laws and only the use of express words by the legislature may rebut this presumption. The power of judges to make new law and retrospectively criminalise behaviour is also discouraged. In a less overt way, where laws have not been strictly enforced, the acts prohibited by those laws may also undergo *de facto* criminalisation through more effective or committed legal enforcement.

The Problems

All societies conduct on-going debates to inform their policy making. In this particular debate, there has been some uncertainty as to the nature and extent of the contribution to be made by the victims of crime. All governments collect some statistics as to the incidence of crime within their territory, and accept a general role in offering some degree of protection to their citizens as an aspect of the social contract. But, as Garkawe (2001) indicates, the relationship between victimology and criminology has become problematic. The Positivist School asked, why did this person offend? The Neo-Classical School and Left Idealism — from opposite political perspectives — asked why this social reaction was made to this behaviour? And conventional victimology asked, why is this type of person victimized?

Fattah (1989 and 1992), Harding (1994) and others argue that victimology has become politicised, and that biased exploitation of research materials is both driving the cycle of criminalization and decriminalization, and distorting the criminal justice system (Walklate: 1989). The concern is that, within the dialectic of Right Realism and Left Realism, a focus on the victim promotes rights selectively for certain victims, and advocates the assumption that some victim rights are more important than competing rights or values in society (Elias: 1993).

For example, an Islamic feminist might seek consistency of treatment for women as victims and, therefore, demand the decriminalization of abortion, adultery, and seduction (Zina is a Hudud offense in sharia law), and the criminalization of domestic violence and sexual harassment.

In theory, society reaches a consensus view on whether certain acts or behaviour are harmful. In cases where there is agreement, the criminal justice system may be extended to treat those matters as crimes. Conversely, when society has evidence that it is no longer at risk from such acts or behaviour, they may be decriminalized. For example, Recommendation No. R (95) 12 adopted by the Committee of Ministers of the Council of Europe on the management of criminal justice, advocates that crime policies such as decriminalization, depenalisation or diversion, and mediation should be adopted wherever possible. But the law and order debate between right and left politicians is often superficial and unscientific, formulating policies based on their appeal to an uniformed electorate rather than properly conducted research (Currie: 1991). Encouraged by the politicians, the media which is increasingly owned by large corporations, endorses each new war on crime and drugs, ignoring all the others that have been fought and lost before. Its bias toward official and corporate perspectives on criminal justice are so strong that some regard crime news as essentially propaganda (Leiper 1994).

Discussion

Leading criminal law philosophers, such as Dennis Baker and Joel Feinberg have argued that conduct should only be criminalized when it is fair to do so. In particular, such theorists assert that objective reasons are needed to demonstrate that it is fair to criminalize conduct in any given case. The commonly cited objective justification for invoking the criminal law is harm to others, but it cannot deal with all situations. For example, people are not necessarily harmed by public nudity. Feinberg suggests that offence to others also provides an objective reason for invoking the criminal law, but it clearly does not as offence is determined according to conventional morality.

People experience a range of physical and social injuries in different contexts which will vary according to the level of economic and political development of their country. Some will be injured out of poverty and malnutrition, others by violence which might stem from a major conflict such as war or from the personal violence in a robbery. The environment may be damaged by pollution, there may be hazards at work. Many of these sources of injury will be ignored while the state may delegate powers of control to a number of different agencies within an international framework where supranational agencies and human rights organisations may offer assistance in responding to the causes of those injuries.

When a state debates whether to respond to a source of injury by criminalising the behaviour that produces it, there are no pre-set criteria to apply in formulating social policy. There is no ontological reality to crime. The criminal justice system responds to a substantial number of events that do not produce significant hardship to individual citizens. Moreover, events which do cause serious injuries and perhaps should be dealt with as crimes, e.g. situations of corporate manslaughter, are either ignored or dealt with as civil matters.

The criminalisation process defines and classifies behaviour. It broadcasts the laws so that no-one may have the excuse of ignorance, and disposes of those who will not obey. There are now more criminal laws and they are penetrating deeper into the social structures of modern societies. Crime control has become an industry, yet it remains ineffective in providing protection to all its citizens from harm. Such as it is, the process is made up of three components:

1. Creation of a social order. This is both a socio-economic process, a "...fundamental ordering of social relations so that those things necessary for social survival can be produced and distributed in some predictable fashion" and an ideological process so that there can be a "...development of values, beliefs, and ideas related to the concrete tasks of production and distribution." Thus, society must develop the apparatus of law creation, law enforcement and punishment and the system must be acceptable to the majority of those who live in the community. If the laws do not match the general mores, their enforcement will be a source of friction and disharmony. Conformity to the social order must, for the most part, be self-enforced.
2. For the times when self-enforcement fails, society must create a legal order. This part of the process sees the centralisation of power within the institutions of the political state. Weber's Thesis argued that the state had a monopoly on the legitimate use of force within its borders. Some states justified the criminalisation process as demonstrating their concerns about safety and security, the policy of control, policing, criminal justice, and penal practice. The modern state is decentralising and privatising its functions. This is changing the character and content of the remaining institutions of the state which must now work co-operatively with other for-profit agencies.
3. The political order must realign so that the remaining political entities such as legislatures and judges set agreed targets for state control and then produce actual outputs of the legal order, i.e. of people defined as criminal and processed through that system.

Ontological Basis of Crime

Put in the most simple terms, ontology deals with or establishes the clear grounds for being. (Heidegger, Martin,

Being and Time, introduction, referencing Plato's Parmenides.) In some of the traditional schools, such as those of the post-1688 English or Americans (many of the writings of the American Founding Fathers, but especially The Federalist) and their Dutch predecessors ontology proper is deemed beyond the scope of legal thought, in accord with the modern distinction between society and state (which some consider based in the distinction the Romans made between themselves and their Italian allies, the socii, but not given the theoretical articulation we recognize today until emphasized by Thomas Hobbes' Leviathan.) However, some classical theorists, such as Aristotle, in his Politics and Metaphysics, and to a lesser degree in his Topics, suggest that the distinction is at least problematic. One need consider no further than the claim that man is a political animal to see this is so.

As a political animal, man has come to see himself as possessed of rights, whether these are the Rights of Englishmen of old, or the universal human rights advocated vigorously toward establishment today through the matrix of commercialism. At least in the today dominant American model, deprivation of right amounts to injury (consider especially Justice Stevens dissenting opinion in Castle Rock v. Gonzales), and injury—so goes the prevailing theory—amounts, when coupled with requisite intent, in most cases, to crime, when it does not admit of civil redress. Thus, again in simple terms, and to the extent that human beings are indeed political beings, crime does seem to have an ontological basis. This, further, seems to hold if ontology itself is divided into political and trans- or supra- or meta- political ontology—i.e., what once was the realm of Christian theology. Of course, it does not matter whether that theology is Christian or belonging to some other apolitical belief. The point is that one may, with some justice, argue persuasively that being is divided. This need not, however, force the question of meta-political crimes. Our purposes here, in this article, are limited to the political.

Baker argues that only objective harms and other objective bad consequences (or actions in the case of inchoate and endangerment offences) are prima facie criminalizable. By other bad consequences Baker means privacy violations and conduct that does not necessarily result in tangible harm, but does result in unwanted consequences. Baker argues that the privacy violations that result from being forced to receive unwanted obscene information in public places (exhibitionism) would amount to a sufficient bad consequence for the purposes of invoking the criminal law, but argues that proportionate punishment means that such conduct should only be punished with fines rather than jail terms.

Crime in Capitalist Society

What makes crime an integral part of capitalist society? For an answer we must consider larger questions: how capitalism developed; the material basis of crime (including both crime control and criminality); class structure under advance capitalism; the capitalist states role; and the political economy of criminal justice. Eventually our task is to document how policies of control grew in the World, as the nations economics and politics took shape. But theoretical questions have to be considered first.

The contradiction in capitalist society today is that the state must provide a framework for continuing capitalist accumulation and at the same time legitimize the social order. It is increasingly difficult to provide resources for these services. The surplus population produced by the political economy of advanced capitalism is growing, populations that must be serviced and controlled, but financial resources are more and more limited. The criminal justice policies of recent years are attracted by this contradiction. Criminal justice has traditionally been one part of the policies of the welfare state. But as the liberal welfare state fails to resolve its own contradictions, its demise becomes imminent and criminal justice takes on new forms. A new model of criminal justice, based explicitly on punishment reflects the economic and political crisis of late capitalism. It all takes on further meaning as the class struggle heightens and grows more political.

Furthermore criminal justice will be determined by changed conditions in the last stages of capitalism and by rising political consciousness in the working class, especially by the expanding portion of that class now relegated to a surplus population.

Currently we are developing a theory and a practice for a transitional society, one that is moving from late capitalism to early socialism. In the transition, popular forms of action, beyond the state-sponsored programs of criminal justice, are appearing. Popular justice is the immediate alternative to criminal justice. Forms of the future will become evident only as we move to a socialist society. To understand criminal justice is to join in the struggle for a new society.

Marxist Analysis of Crime

A Marxist understanding of crime, as developed he begins with the recognition that crime is a material problem. The necessary conditions for any society, according to the materialist method and conception of reality, is that its members produce their material means of subsistence. Social production is primary in all social life. Moreover, in this social production we enter into relations appropriate to the forces of production. It is this economic structure that provides the foundation for all social and political institutions, for every day life, and for social consciousness. Our analysis begins with the material conditions of social life.

The dialectical method allows us to comprehend the world as a complex of processes, in which all things contentiously come into being and pass away. All things are studied as part of there historical development. Dialectical materialism allows us to learn about things as they are in their actual connections, contradictions and movements. In dialectical analysis we critically understand our past, informing our analysis with the possibilities for our future.

A Marxist analysis shares in the larger socialist struggle. One commitment is to eliminating exploitation and oppression. Being on the side of the oppressed, only those ideas are advanced which will help transform the capitalist system. The objective of the Marxist analysis is change a revolutionary change. The purpose of our intellectual labours is to assist in providing knowledge and consciousness for building a socialist society. Theories and strategies are developed to increase conscious class struggle; Ideas for an alternative to capitalist society are formulated: and strategies for achieving the socialist alternative are proposed. In this intellectual political work we engage in the activities and actions that will advance the socialist struggle.

With these notions of a Marxist analysis encompassing a dialectical historical analysis of the material conditions of capitalist society looking forward to socialist revolution- we begin to formulate significant substantive questions about crime. In recent years, as socialists have begun to study crime, the outline for these questions has become evident. At this stage in our intellectual development the important questions are about the meaning of crime in capitalist society. Furthermore, we realize that the meaning of crime changes as capitalism develops.

The basic problem in studying the meaning of crime is integrating the two sides of the phenomenon named crime: that is placing in one frame work (1) the defining of behaviour as criminal (crime control), and (2) the behaviour of those who are defined as criminal (criminality). Thus far our analysis of crime has been focused on one side or the other, failing to integrate, them into one scheme. In pursuing a Marxist analysis, however, the dual concept of crime is resolved by giving primacy to the underlying political economy.

The basic question in the Marxist analysis of crime is this: What is the meaning of crime in the development of capitalism? Approaching this question, we must consider several related processes: (1) development of capitalist political economy, including the forces and relations of production, formulation of the capitalist state, and class and class struggle between those who do and those who do not own and control the means of production: (2) the system of domination and repression established as capitalism develops, operating for the benefit of the capitalist class and secured by the capitalist state; (3) the forms of accommodation and resistance to the conditions of capitalism, by all people oppressed by capitalism, including the working class : and (4) the relation between the dialectics of domination and accommodation to patterns of crime in capitalist society, producing the crimes of domination and of accommodation. All these are dialectically related to the developing political economy. Crime is to be understood as part of capitalist development.

Crime in the Development of Capitalism

Crime is a manifestation of societys material conditions. The failure of conventional criminology is to ignore, by design, the material conditions of capitalism. Because the phenomena of crime are products of the sub-structure and themselves part of the super-structure, any explanation of crime using other elements of the superstructure is no explanation at all. What we need is a general materialist framework for understanding crime, beginning with the underlying historic process of social existence.

Production as the necessary requirement of existence produces its own forces and relations of social and economic life. The material factors (such as resources and technology) and present factors (most important, the workers) present at any one time from the productive forces of society. During production the people form definite relations of production with one another. These and the forces of production are the mode of production of a society at any time. It is the economic mode of production that furnishes society with its substructure, on which the social and political institutions (including control of crime) and supporting ideologies are built. This whole complex is the political economy of capitalism.

The political economy of capitalism gives rise to a class society, in which the system of production is owned and controlled by one segment of the society to the exclusion of another. All social life in capitalist society, including everything associated with crime, is subject to the economic conditions of production and the struggle between classes produced by these conditions. The basic division without capitalist society is between the capitalist class that owns and controls the means of production and the working class that labours.

Therefore, it is the problem of labour (as the foremost human activity) that characterizes the nature and specific relationship of the classes. For the capitalist system to operate and survive, the capitalist class must ex-pilot the labour (surplus labour) of the working class. The capitalist class extracts from the worker the labour over and above that consumed by the actual producer. The relationship is dialectical; the capitalist class survives by appropriating the surplus labour of the working class and the working class, as an exploited class exists as long as surplus labour is required in production. Each class depends on the other for its character and existence.

The amount of labour appropriated, techniques of exploiting labour conditions of working class life, and working class consciousness have all been an integral part of capitalisms development. Likewise, antagonism and conflict between classes have varied at different stages in the development. It is still the basic contradiction between the classes, generalized as class conflict, which typifies the history of capitalism. Class conflicts permeates its whole development, represented in the contradiction between those who own property and those who do not, and by those who oppress and those who are oppressed. All history involving capitalism is the history of class struggle. Capitalism as a system of production based on exploitation by the ruling capitalist that owns and controls the means of production is a dynamic system that goes through its own stages of development. In fact, capitalism is constantly transforming its own forces and relations of production. As a result the whole of capitalist society is constantly being altered with the capitalist political economy.

The Marxian view stresses the qualitative changes in social organization and social relations as well as (or in relation to) the quantitative changes in the economic system. Capitalism transforms itself, affecting the social existence of all who live under it. This is the basic force in capitalist development interdependence among production, relations of production, and social superstructure of institutions and ideas. For it is a requirement of all social production that the relations which people enter into carrying on production must be suitable to the type of production they are carrying on. Hence, it is a general law of Economic development that the relations of production must necessarily be adapted to the character of the forces of production.

Our analysis of the meaning of crime in capitalisms development necessarily involves investigating the relation between the concrete stage of capitalist development and social relations at that stage. This is not to argue, however, that the superstructure of social relations and culture is an automatic (directly determined) product of the economic substructure. After all, people may enter into relations of production in various ways to employ the forces of production; and it is from these relations that they create further institutions and ideas. Because human social existence is in part a product of conscious activity and struggle, conscious life must be part of any analysis.

Furthermore, the more highly developed the productive forces under capitalism the greater the discrepancy between productive forces and capitalists relations of production. Capitalist development, for which economic expansion is fundamental, exacerbates rather than mitigates the contradictions of capitalism. Workers are further exploited, conditions of existence worsen, and the contradictions of capitalism increase. Capitalist development, from another vantage point, creates the conditions for transforming and abolishing capitalism, brought about in actuality by class struggle.

The periods of capitalist development, for our purposes, differ according to the ways in which surplus labour is appropriated. Capitalism itself, distinct from other modes of production, has gone through periods of utilizing various methods of production and creating social relations in association with these productive forms. Each new development in capitalism brings about its own forms of capitalist social reality and related problems of human existence. How crime- control and criminality has its part in each stage of capitalist development is our interest in investigating the meaning of crime.

Domination and Repression

The capitalist system must continuously reproduce itself. Most explicit it is the state that promotes the capitalist order. Bu its coercive force, embodied in law and legal repression, the social and economic order of capitalism has been traditionally secured. The legal system continues to be the means of enforcing the interests of the capitalist economy. The states coercive force however is but one means of maintaining the social and economic order. A subtler way of reproducing capitalist society is to perpetuate the capitalist conception of reality, a non-violent but equally repressive means of domination. Alan Wolf explains below that in manipulating consciousness the social order is legitimated and secured:

> The most important reproductive mechanism, which does not involve the use of state violence is consciousness-manipulation. The liberal state has an enormous amount of violence at its disposal, but is often reluctant to use it. Violence manipulates consciousness to such an extent that most people would never think of engaging in the kinds of action that could be repressed. The most perfectly repressive (though not violently so) capitalist system, in other words, would not be a police state, but the complete opposite, one in which there were no police because there was nothing to police, everyone having accepted the legitimacy of that society and all its daily consequences.

Those who rule in capitalist society, with the assistance of the state, not only accumulate capital at the expense of those who work but impose their ideology as well. Expropriating consciousness legitimizes oppression and exploitation; Labour is expropriated, consciousness must too. In fact, the legitimacy of the capitalist order is maintained by controlling the populations consciousness. A capitalist hegemony is established.

Moreover, a society that depends on labour exploitation for its very existence must not only control that situation but must cope with the problems that kind of economic system naturally creates. The capitalist state must therefore provide social services education, health, welfare and rehabilitation programs to deal with the problems that could be dealt with otherwise only by changing the capitalist system. These state services are a means of securing the capitalist order.

Capitalism systematically generates a surplus population, an unemployed sector of the working class either dependent on fluctuations in the economy or made obsolete by new technology. As the surplus population grows, population builds for the welfare system to expand. Growing welfare with its host of services is designed to control the surplus population. Moreover, James O Connor observes, Unable to gain employment to the monopoly industries by offering their labour power at lower power at lower than wage rates (and victimized by sexism and racism), and unemployed, under-employed, or employed at low wages in competitive industries, the surplus population increasingly becomes dependent on the State. An unsteady alliance is formed between the state and the casualties it naturally produces. Only a new economic order could wipe out the need for a welfare state.

Repression through welfare is in part the history of capitalism. The kinds of services have carried with the development of economic conditions. Likewise, relief policies have changed according to specific tensions produced by unemployment and subsequent threats of disorder. Control through welfare can never be a permanent solution for a system based on appropriation of labour. As with all forms of control and manipulation in capitalist society, welfare cannot completely counter the basic contradictions of a capitalist political economy.

Although the capitalist state creates and manages the institutions of control (employing physical force and manipulation of consciousness), the contradictions are so great that this control is not absolute and in the long run, is subject to defeat. Because of the contradictions, the capitalist state is more weak than strong. Eventually the capitalist state loses its legitimacy, no longer able to perpetuate the ideology that accumulation of capital for capitalists (at the expense of workers) is good for the nation for human interest. The ability of the capitalist economic order to exist according to its own interests is eventually weakened.

The problem becomes especially acute in periods of economic crisis, unavoidable under capitalism. As the capitalist system reproduces itself, crimes are committed. One of its contradictions is the some of its own laws must be violated in order of secure of crime. Not only are these heightened in times of crisis, increasing crimes of domination, but the crime change with further development of capitalism. Control of crime and the crimes of domination are necessary features and natural products of a developing capitalist economy.

4

Ethnomethodology Law

Ethnomethodology is a method for understanding the social orders people use to make sense of the world through analysing their accounts and descriptions of their day-to-day activities. It is an alternative to the American sociological approach to data analysis born in the 1960s with its theoretical and epistemological importance being that it is a radical breach from traditional sociological modes of thinking.

The term itself was originally coined by Harold Garfinkel in 1954, but the discipline itself has changed from Garfinkel's original programme to the point where it is no longer recognisable.

Ethnomethodology is a descriptive discipline and does not engage in the explanation or evaluation of the particular social order undertaken as a topic of study. It has been used in ethnographic studies to describe the methods that people use to achieve the orderly character of everyday social situations.

Introduction

The term's etymology can be broken down into its three constituent parts: ethno - method - (o)logy, for the purpose of explanation. Using an appropriate Southern California example: ethno refers to a particular socio-cultural group [think a particular, localized community of surfers]; method refers to the methods and practices this particular group employs in its everyday activities [related to surfing]; and (o)logy (from the Greek 'logos'), refers to the systematic description of these methods and practices. The focus of the investigation used in our example is the social order of surfing, the ethnomethodological interest is in the "how" [the methods and practices] of the production and maintenance of this social order.

Examples of such methods and practices relative to the activity of surfing include, but are by no means exhausted by: methods for reading waves as to their rideability, practices employed for catching waves, methods for styling hair, practices employed for the wearing of swim trunks and wet suits, methods for using body language and gesturing, and practices employed for talking surfing among group members.

Anne Rawls states: "Ethnomethodology is the study of the methods people use for producing recognizable social orders".

The social order used in our example is the recognizably competent performance of the methods and practices of surfing ["being a surfer"] as demonstrated by members of this particular group of surfers.

The fundamental assumption of ethnomethodological studies is characterized by Anne Rawls:

"If one assumes, as Garfinkel does, that the meaningful, patterned, and orderly character of everyday life is something that people must work constantly to achieve, then one must also assume that they have some methods for doing so". That is, "... members of society must have some shared methods that they use to mutually construct the meaningful orderliness of social situations".

In line with this assumption, the goal of ethnomethodological investigations becomes the description of the methods employed in the production of the orderly character of everyday life. These methods are embedded in the work that people do, and realized in local settings by the people who are party to those settings.

Ethnomethodology's Origins

The approach was originally developed by Harold Garfinkel, based on his study of: the principles and practices of financial accounting; traditional sociological theory and methods [primarily: Durkheim, Weber, and Parsons]; traditional sociological concerns [the Hobbesian "problem of order"]; and the phenomenologies of: Aron Gurwitsch, Alfred Schutz, Edmund Husserl, Martin Heidegger, and Maurice Merleau-Ponty. Anne Rawls provides a brief developmental history of Garfinkel, and ethnomethodology, in, Ethnomethodology's Program.

Garfinkel's Writing Style

Garfinkel's writing style has been described by some as abstruse, convoluted, and obscure in terms of both meaning and reference. Others have maintained that it is adequate to the task at hand, and unavoidable given the phenomena being described. Some maintain that it has improved over time, others maintain that it has gotten worse. Most have given up such arguments and accepted it for what it is.

Those new to the discipline who find Garfinkel's programmatic writings difficult should consult some of his better - officially designated - interpreters: John Heritage, or Anne Rawls).

D. Lawrence Wieder's classic, Language and Social Reality: The Case of Telling the Convict Code [1974/1988], continues to do service as an unusually straightforward application of ethnomethodological policies and procedures to the investigation of an existing social order. His use of traditional ethnographic methods, ethnomethodology, and phenomenological insights applied to the same object of investigation remains without parallel.

Varieties of Ethnomethodology

According to George Psathas, five types of ethnomethodological study can be identified. These may be characterised as:

1. *The organization of practical actions and practical reasoning*. Including the earliest studies, such as those in Garfinkel's seminal *Studies in Ethnomethodology*.
2. *The organization of talk-in-interaction*. More recently known as conversation analysis, Harvey Sacks established this approach in collaboration with his colleagues Emanuel Schegloff and Gail Jefferson.

3. *Talk-in-interaction within institutional or organizational settings.* While early studies focused on talk abstracted from the context in which it was produced (usually using tape recordings of telephone conversations) this approach seeks to identify interactional structures that are specific to particular settings.
4. *The study of work.* 'Work' is used here to refer to any social activity. The analytic interest is in how that work is accomplished within the setting in which it is performed.
5. *The haecceity of work.* Just what makes an activity what it is? e.g. what makes a test a test, a competition a competition, or a definition a definition?

Further discussion of the varieties and diversity of ethnomethodological investigations can be found in Maynard & Clayman.

Theory and Methods

One of the most perplexing problems for those new to ethnomethodology is the discovery that it lacks both a formally stated theory and an agreed upon methodology. As serious as these problems might appear on the face of it, neither has prevented ethnomethodologists from doing ethnomethodological studies, and generating a substantial literature of "findings".

John Heritage has noted the, "off-stage role of theory", in ethnomethodological writings, and the concern that there is nowhere in the ethnomethodological corpus a systematic theoretical statement that would serve as a touchstone for ethnomethodological inquiries.

Instead, as in the case of, Studies in Ethnomethodology (1967), we are given oblique references to: Wittgenstein [Ordinary Language Philosophy], Husserl [Transcendental Phenomenology], Gurwitsch [Gestalt Theory], and, most frequently, the works of the social phenomeonologist Alfred Schutz [Phenomenology of the Natural Attitude], among others. Likewise, in Ethnomethodology's Program (2002), we again find a multiplicity of theoretical references, including the usual suspects from Studies, and, introducing, among others, the work of Emile Durkheim; who now more than 35 years later, is framed as what ethnomethodology was about all along: working out Durkheim's aphorism regarding the achieved character of social facts.

The point here is that the authors and theoretical references cited in Garfinkel's work do not themselves serve as a rigorous theoretical basis for ethnomethodology, in whole or in part. Ethnomethodology is not Durkheimian, although it shares some of the interests of Durkheim; it is not phenomenology, although it borrows from Husserl and Schutz's studies of the Lifeworld [*Lebenswelt*]; it is not a form of Gestalt theory, although it describes social orders as having Gestalt-like properties; and, it is not Wittgensteinian, although it makes use of Wittgenstein's understanding of rule-use, etc. Instead, these borrowings are only fragmentary references to theoretical works from which ethnomethodology has appropriated theoretical ideas for the expressed purposes of doing ethnomethodological investigations.

In terms of the question of ethnomethodological methods, it is the position of Anne Rawls, speaking for Garfinkel, that ethnomethodology is itself not a method. That is, it does not have a set of formal research methods or procedures. Instead, the position taken is that ethnomethodologists have conducted their studies in a variety of ways, and that the point of these investigations is, '...to discover the things that persons in particular situations do, the methods they use, to create the patterned orderliness of social life'.

Differences between Sociology and Ethnomethodology

Two central differences between traditional sociology and ethnomethodology are:

1. While traditional sociology usually offers an analysis of society which takes the facticity of the social order for granted, ethnomethodology is concerned with the procedures by which that social order is produced, and shared.
2. While traditional sociology usually provides descriptions of social settings which compete with the actual descriptions offered by the individuals who are party to those settings, ethnomethodology seeks to describe

> the procedures these individuals use in their actual descriptions of those settings.

In 1967, Garfinkel states: Ethnomethodology's, "...central recommendation is that the activities whereby members produce and manage settings of organized everyday affairs are identical with member's procedures for making those settings 'accountable'.

Over thirty-five years later, Garfinkel states: "Phenomena of order are identical with procedures for their endogenous production and accountability (2002:72).

Although the language has changed, the message remains the same: social orders ["phenomena of order"] are identical with the procedures members of a particular social group employ to produce and manage a particular setting of organized everyday affairs. These social orders are endogenous [generated from within the particular setting], and made available for study through the demonstrable [objectified, recognizable, embodied] accounting practices of the group members party to that particular setting.

[Note that the characters of particularity and embeddedness of the: social order, procedures, activities, accounts, and persons party to such settings are essential features of the ethnomethodological perspective, and clearly differentiate it from traditional sociological forms.]

Ethnomethodology and Phenomenology

Even though ethnomethodology has been characterized as having a "phenomenological sensibility", orthodox adherents to the discipline - those who follow the teachings of Garfinkel - know better than to represent it as a branch, or form, of phenomenology, or phenomenological sociology.

The confusion between the two disciplines stems, in part, from the practices of some ethnomethodologists, who sift through phenomenological texts, recovering phenomenological concepts and findings relevant to their interests, and then transpose these concepts and findings to topics in the study of social order. Such interpretive transpositions do not make the ethnomethodologist a phenomenologist, or ethnomethodology a form of phenomenology.

To further muddy the waters, some phenomenological sociologists seize upon ethnomethodological findings as examples of applied phenomenology; this even when the results of these ethnomethodological investigations clearly do not make use of phenomenological methods, or formulate their findings in the language of phenomenology. So called phenomenological analyses of social structures that do not have prima facie reference to any of the structures of intentional consciousness should raise questions as to the phenomenological status of such analyses.

Another way of convincing yourself of the difference between these two disciplines is to read, Studies in Ethnomethodology (1967), and try to find any reference to: a subject [other than experimental], consciousness, intentionality, or phenomenological methodology, etc. There are no such references. A phenomenological analysis should reflect phenomenological methods. This text clearly does not.

In, Ethnomethodology's Program (2002), Garfinkel speaks of phenomenological texts and findings as being, "appropriated", and intentionally, "misread", for the purposes of exploring topics in the study of social order. These appropriations and methodical misreadings of phenomenological texts and findings are clearly made for the purposes of furthering ethnomethodological analyses, and should not be mistaken for (necessary or even logical) extensions of these phenomenological texts and findings.

Lastly, there is no claim in any of Garfinkel's works that ethnomethodology is a form of phenomenology, or phenomenological sociology.

Some Leading Policies, Methods and Definitions

- Ethnomethodological indifference. This is the policy of deliberate agnosticism, or indifference, towards the dictates, prejudices, methods and practices of sociological analysis as traditionally conceived (examples: theories of "deviance", analysis of behaviour as rule governed, role theory, institutional (de)formations, theories of social stratification, etc.). Dictates and prejudices which serve to pre-structure traditional social scientific investigations independently of the subject matter taken as a topic of study, or the investigatory setting being subjected to scrutiny. The policy of ethnomethodological indifference is specifically not to be conceived of as indifference to the problem of social order taken as a group (member's) concern.

- First time through. This is the practice of attempting to describe any social activity, regardless of its routine or mundane appearance, as if it were happening for the very first time [hint: the task is revealing, but impossible]. This in an effort to expose how the observer of the activity assembles, or constitutes, the activity for the purposes of formulating any particular description. The point of such an exercise is to make available and underline the complexities of sociological analysis and description, particularly the indexical and reflexive properties of the actors', or observer's, own descriptions of what is taking place in any given situation. Such an activity will also reveal the observer's inescapable reliance on the documentary method of interpretation (aka hermeneutic circle) as the defining "methodology" of social understanding for both lay persons and social scientists.
- Breaching experiment. A method for revealing, or exposing, the common work that is performed by members of particular social groups in maintaining a clearly recognizable and shared social order. An extreme example: driving the wrong way down a busy one-way street can reveal myriads of useful insights into the patterned social practices, and moral order, of the community of automobile drivers... and police. The point of such an exercise is to demonstrate that gaining insight into the work involved in maintaining any given social order can often, best be revealed by breaching that social order and observing the results of that breach - especially those activities related to the reassembly of that social order, and the normalization of that social setting.
- Sacks' gloss. A question about an aspect of the social order that recommends, as a method of answering it,

that the researcher should seek out members of society who, in their daily lives, are responsible for the maintenance of that aspect of the social order. Sacks' original question concerned objects in public places and how it was possible to see that such objects did or did not belong to somebody. He found his answer in the activities of police officers who had to decide whether cars were abandoned. Recommendation: If you want to understand how a particular social order is maintained, or a particular social activity is accomplished, go to the source: the actual people who do the actual work of maintaining and constructing those social structures. In some, many, most cases, a "traditional sociologist" is the last person that you would consult regarding such matters.

- Durkheim's aphorism. Durkheim famously recommended that we, "...treat social facts as things". This is usually taken to mean that we should assume the objectivity of social facts as a principal of study (thus providing the basis of sociology as a science). Garfinkel's alternative reading of Durkheim is that we should treat the objectivity of social facts as an achievement of society's members, and make the achievement process itself the focus of study. Note that Garfinkel has no dispute with member's descriptions of the objective character of social facts as he has often been known to assert the objective character of social facts himself in the course of his everyday activities - as have we all.
- Account. Accounts are the ways members describe or explain specific situations. Accounting is the process of describing or explaining social situations or how members make sense of their everyday world.
- Indexicality. The concept of Indexicality is a key core concept for Ethnomethodology. It was derived from the concept of indexical expressions appearing in ordinary language philosophy, wherein a statement is considered to be indexical insofar as it is dependent for its sense upon the context in which it is embedded. The

phenomenon is acknowledged in various forms of analytical philosophy, and sociological theory and methods, but is considered to be both limited in scope and remedied through specification [operationalization]. In ethnomethodology, the phenomenon is universalized to all forms of language and behaviour, and is deemed to be beyond remedy for the purposes of establishing a scientific description and explanation of social behaviour. The consequence of the degree of contextual dependence for a "segment" of talk or behaviour can range from the problem of establishing a "working consensus" regarding the description of a phrase, concept or behaviour, to the end-game of social scientific description itself. Note that any serious development of the concept must eventually assume a theory of meaning as its foundation. Without such a foundational underpinning, both the traditional social scientist and the ethnomethodologist are relegated to merely telling stories around the campfire.

- Reflexivity. Despite the fact that many sociologists use "reflexivity" as a synonym for "self-reflection," the way the term is used in ethnomethodology is different: it is meant "to describe the acausal and non-mentalistic determination of meaningful action-in-context."
- Documentary method of interpretation. The Documentary Method is the method of understanding utilized by everyone engaged in trying to make sense of their social world - this includes the ethnomethodologist. Garfinkel recovered the concept from the work of Karl Mannheim and repeatedly demonstrates the use of the method in the case studies appearing in his central text, Studies in Ethnomethodology (1967). Mannheim defined the term as a search for an identical homologous pattern of meaning underlying a variety of totally different realizations of that meaning. Garfinkel states that the documentary method of interpretation consists of treating an actual appearance as the "document of", "as pointing to", as "standing on behalf of", a presupposed

underlying pattern. These "documents" serve to constitute the underlying pattern, but are themselves interpreted on the basis of what is already known about that underlying pattern. This seeming paradox is quite familiar to hermeneuticians who understand this phenomenon as a version of the hemeneutic circle. This phenomenon is also subject to analysis from the perspective of Gestalt theory [part/whole relationships], and the phenomenological theory of perception.

- Ethnomethodology's field of investigation. For ethnomethodology the topic of study is the social practices of real people in real settings, and the methods by which these people produce and maintain a shared sense of social order.

Social Order

Social order is a concept used in sociology, history and other social Sciences. It refers to a set of linked social structures, social institutions and social practices which conserve, maintain and enforce "normal" ways of relating and behaving.

A "social order" is a relatively stable system of institutions, patterns of interactions and customs, capable of continually reproducing at least those conditions essential for its own existence. The concept refers to all those facts of society which remain relatively constant over time. These conditions could include both property, exchange and power relations, but also cultural forms, communication relations and ideological systems of values.

Sociology

The issue of social order, how and why it is that social orders exists at all, is historically central to sociology. Thomas Hobbes is recognized as the first to clearly formulate the problem, to answer which he conceived the notion of a social contract. Social theorists (such as Karl Marx, Émile Durkheim, Talcott Parsons, and Jürgen Habermas) have proposed different explanations for what a social order consists of, and what its real basis is. For Marx, it is the relations of production or economic structure which is the basis of a social order. For

Durkheim, it is a set of shared social norms. For Parsons, it is a set of social institutions determining moral behaviour. For Habermas, it is all of these, as well as communicative action.

Principle of Extensiveness

Another key factor concerning social order is the principle of extensiveness. This states the more norms and the more important the norms are to a society, the better these norms tie and hold together the group as a whole.

A good example of this is smaller religions based around the U.S., such as the Amish. Many Amish live together in communities and because they share the same religion and values, it is easier for them to succeed in upholding their religion and views because their way of life is the norm for their community.

Groups and Networks

In every society people belong to groups, such as businesses, families, churches, athletic groups, or neighbourhoods. The structure inside of these groups mirrors that of the whole society. There are networks and ties between groups as well as inside of each of the groups that create social order.

Some people belong to more than one group, which sometimes causes conflict. The individual may encounter a situation in which he or she has to choose one group over the another. Many who have studied these groups believe that it is necessary to have ties between groups to strengthen the society as a whole and to promote pride within each group. Others believe that it is best to have stronger ties within a group so that social norms and values are reinforced.

Status Groups

"Status groups" can be based on a person's characteristics such as race, ethnicity, sexual orientation, religion, region, occupation, physical attractiveness, gender, education, age, etc. They are defined as "a subculture having a rather specific rank (or status) within the stratification system. That is, societies tend to include a hierarchy of status groups, some enjoying high ranking and some low." One example of this hierarchy is the prestige of a school teacher compared to that of a garbage man. A certain lifestyle usually distinguishes the members of different status groups. For example, around the holidays a Jewish family may celebrate Hanukkah while a Christian family may celebrate Christmas. Other cultural differences such as language and cultural rituals identify members of different status groups.

Inside of a status group there are more, smaller groups. For instance, one can belong to a status group based on one's race and a social class based on financial ranking. This may cause strife for the individual in this situation when he or she feels they must choose to side with either their status group or their social class. For example, a wealthy African American man who feels he has to take a side on an issue on which the opinions of poor African Americans and wealthy white Americans are divided, and finds his class and status group opposed.

Values and Norms

Values can be defined as "internal criteria for evaluation". Values are also split into two categories, there are individual values, which pertains to something that we think has worth and then there are social values. Social values are our desires modified according to ethical principles or according to the group we associate with: friends, family, or co-workers. Norms tell us what people ought to do in a given situation. Unlike values, norms are enforced externally - or outside of oneself. A society as a whole determines norms, and they can be passed down from generation to generation.

Power and Authority

An exception to the idea of values and norms as social order-keepers is deviant behaviour. Not everyone in a society abides by a set of personal values or the group's norms all the time. For this reason it generally deemed necessary for a society to have authority. The adverse opinion holds that the need for authority stems from lack of Social justice. It is recognized that effective social justice and the need for authoritative Social control are inversely related. (refs. needed)

In societies, those who hold positions of power and authority are among the upper class. Norms differ for each class because the members of each class were raised differently and hold different sets of values. Tension can form, therefore, between the upper class and lower class when laws and rules are put in place that do not conform to the values of both classes.

Spontaneous Order

Order does not necessarily need to be controlled by government. Individuals pursuing self-interest can make predictable systems. These systems, being planned by more than one person, may actually be preferable to those planned by a single person. This means that predictability may be possible to achieve without a central government's control. These stable expectations do not necessarily lead to individuals behaving in ways that are considered beneficial to group welfare. Considering this, Thomas Schelling studied neighbourhood racial segregation. His findings suggest that interaction can produce predictability, but it does not always increase social order. In his researching he found that "when all individuals pursue their own preferences, the outcome is segregation rather than integration," as stated in "Theories of Social Order," edited by Michael Hechter and Christine Horne. The unregulated interaction of rational selfishness produces an unwanted outcome.

Social Honor

Social honor can also be referred to as social status. It is considered the distribution of prestige or "the approval, respect, admiration, or deference a person or group is able to command by virtue of his or its imputed qualities or performances.". The case most often is that people associate social honor with the place a person occupies with material systems of wealth and power. Since most of society finds wealth and power desirable they respect or envy people that have more than they do. When Social Honor is referred to as Social Status it deals with the rank of a person within the stratification system. Status can be Achieved, which is when a persons position is gained on the basis of merit or in other words by achievement and hard work. Status can also be ascribed, which is when a persons position is assigned to individuals or groups without regard for merit but because of certain traits beyond their control, such as race, sex, or parental social standing. An example of Ascribed status would be heiress to the Hilton dynasty Paris Hilton. An example of Achieved Status would be Oprah Winfrey and her empire.

Attainment of Social Order

There are currently two different theories that explain and attempt to account for social order. The first theory is "order results from a large number of independent decisions to transfer individual rights and liberties to a coercive state in return for its guarantee of security for persons and their property, as well as its establishment of mechanisms to resolve disputes." as stated in *Theories of Social Order* by Hechter and Horne. The next theory is that "the ultimate source of social order as residing not in external controls but in a concordance of specific values and norms that individuals somehow have managed to internalize." also stated in *Theories of Social Order* by Hechter and Horne. Both the arguments for how social order is attained are very different. One argues that it is achieved through outside influence and control and the other argues that it can only be attained when the individual willingly follows norms and values that they have grown accustomed to and internalised. Weber's insistence on the importance of domination and symbolic systems in social life was retained by Pierre Bourdieu, who developed the idea of social orders, ultimately transforming it into a theory of fields.

Conformity

Conformity is the process by which an individual's attitudes, beliefs, and behaviours are conditioned by what is conceived to be what other people might perceive. This influence occurs in both small groups and society as a whole, and it may be the result of subtle unconscious influences, or direct and overt social pressure. Conformity also occurs by the "implied presence" of others, or when other people are not actually present. For example, people tend to follow the norms of society when eating or watching television, even when they are at home by themselves.

People often conform from a desire to achieve a sense of security within a group—typically a group that is of a similar age, culture, religion, or educational status. Any unwillingness to conform carries with it the very real risk of social rejection. In this respect, conformity can be seen as a safe means of avoiding bullying or deflecting criticism from peers. Conformity is often associated with adolescence and youth culture, but it affects humans of all ages.

Although peer pressure may be viewed as a negative trait, conformity can have either good or bad effects depending on the situation. Driving safely on the correct side of the road is a beneficial example of conformity. Conformity influences the formation and maintenance of social norms and allows society to function smoothly and predictably. Because conformity is a group phenomenon, such factors as group size, unanimity, cohesion, status, prior commitment, and public opinion all help to determine the level of conformity an individual will display.

Varieties

Harvard psychologist, Herbert Kelman identified three major types of social influence:

1. *Compliance* is public conformity, while possibly keeping one's own private beliefs.
2. *Identification* is conforming to someone who is liked and respected, such as a celebrity or a favorite uncle.
3. *Internalization* is acceptance of the belief or behaviour and conforming both publicly and privately.

Although Kelman's distinction has been very influential, research in social psychology has focused primarily on two main varieties of conformity. These are *informational* conformity, or informational social influence, and *normative* conformity, otherwise known as normative social influence. Using Kelman's terminology, these correspond to internalization and compliance, respectively. There are naturally more than two or three variables in society influential on human psychology and conformity; the notion of "varieties" of conformity based upon "social influence" is ambiguous and undefinable in this context.

Informational Influence

Informational social influence occurs when one turns to the members of one's group to obtain accurate information. A person is most likely to use informational social influence in three situations: When a situation is ambiguous, people become uncertain about what to do. They are more likely to depend on others for the answer. During a crisis when immediate action is necessary, in spite of panic. Looking to other people can help ease fears, but unfortunately they are not always right. The more knowledgeable a person is, the more valuable they are as a resource. Thus people often turn to experts for help. But once again people must be careful, as experts can make mistakes too. Informational social influence often results in *internalization* or *private acceptance*, where a person genuinely believes that the information is right.

Informational social influence was first documented in Muzafer Sherif's autokinetic experiment. He was interested in how many people change their opinions to bring them in line with the opinion of a group. Participants were placed in a dark room and asked to stare at a small dot of light 15 feet away. They were then asked to estimate the amount it moved. The trick was there was no movement, it was caused by a visual illusion known as the autokinetic effect. Every person perceived different amounts of movement. Over time, the same estimate was agreed on and others conformed to it. Sherif suggested that this was a simulation for how social norms develop in a society, providing a common frame of reference for people.

Subsequent experiments were based on more realistic situations. In an eyewitness identification task, participants were shown a suspect individually and then in a lineup of other suspects. They were given one second to identify him, making it a difficult task. One group was told that their input was very important and would be used by the legal community. To the other it was simply a trial. Being more motivated to get the right answer increased the tendency to conform. Those who wanted to be most accurate conformed 51% of the time as opposed to 35% in the other group.

Economists have suggested that fads and trends in society form as the result of individuals making rational choices based on information received from others. These informational cascades form quickly as people decide to ignore their internal signals and go along with what other people are doing. Cascades are also presumed to be fragile because people are aware that they are based on limited information. This is why fads often end as quickly as they begin.

Normative Influence

Normative social influence occurs when one conforms to be liked or accepted by the members of the group. It usually results in *public compliance*, doing or saying something without believing in it. Solomon E. Asch was the first psychologist to study this phenomenon in the laboratory. He conducted a modification of Sherif's study, assuming that when the situation was very clear, conformity would be drastically reduced. He exposed people in a group to a series of lines, and the participants were asked to match one line with a standard line. All participants except one were secretly told to give the wrong answer in 12 of the 18 trials. The results showed a surprisingly high degree of conformity. 76% of the participants conformed on at least one trial. On average people conformed one third of the time. However, in a reinterpretation of the original data from these experiments Hodges and Geyer (2006) found that Asch's subjects were not so conformist after all:

The experiments provide powerful evidence for people's tendency to tell the truth even when others do not. They also provide compelling evidence of people's concern for others and their views.

By closely examining the situation in which Asch's subjects find themselves they find that the situation places multiple demands on participants: They include truth (i.e., expressing one's own view accurately), trust (i.e., taking seriously the value of others' claims), and social solidarity (i.e., a commitment to integrate the views of self and others without deprecating either). In addition to these epistemic values, there are multiple moral claims as well: These include the need for participants to care for the integrity and well-being of other participants, the experimenter, themselves, and the worth of scientific research.

Normative influence is a function of social impact theory which has three components. The *number of people* in the group has a surprising effect. As the number increases, each person has less of an impact. A group's *strength* is how important the group is to a person. Groups we value generally have more social influence. *Immediacy* is how close the group is in time and space when the influence is taking place. Psychologists have constructed a mathematical model using these three factors and are able to predict the amount of conformity that occurs with some degree of accuracy.

Baron and his colleagues conducted a second "eyewitness study", this time focusing on normative influence. In this version, the task was made easier. Each participant was given five seconds to look at a slide, instead of just one second. Once again there were both high and low motives to be accurate, but the results were the reverse of the first study. The low motivation group conformed 33% of the time (similar to Asch's findings). The high motivation group conformed less at 16%. These results show that when accuracy is not very important, it is better to get the wrong answer than to risk social disapproval.

An experiment using procedures similar to Asch's found that there was significantly less conformity in six-person groups of friends as compared to six-person groups of strangers. Because friends already know and accept each other, there may be less normative pressure to conform in some situations. Field studies on cigarette and alcohol abuse, however, generally demonstrate evidence of friends exerting normative social influence on each other.

Minority Influence

Although conformity generally leads individuals to think and act more like groups, individuals are occasionally able to reverse this tendency and change the people around them. This is known as *minority influence*, a special case of informational influence. Minority influence is most likely when people are able to make a clear and consistent case for their point of view. If the minority fluctuates and shows uncertainty, the chance of influence is small. However, if the minority makes a strong, convincing case, it will increase the probability of changing the beliefs and behaviour of the majority. Minority members who are perceived as experts, are high in status, or have benefited the group in the past are also more likely to succeed.

Another form of minority influence can sometimes override conformity effects and lead to unhealthy group dynamics. A 2007 review of two dozen studies by the University of Washington found that a single "bad apple" (a lazy or inconsiderate group member) can substantially increase conflicts and reduce performance in work groups. Bad apples often create a negative emotional climate that interferes with healthy group functioning. They can be avoided by careful selection procedures and managed by reassigning them to positions that require less social interaction.

Gender

Societal norms often establish gender differences. In general, this is the case for social conformity, as females are more likely to conform than males.

There are differences in the way men and women conform to social influence. Social psychologists, Alice Eagly and Linda Carli performed a meta-analysis of 148 studies of influenceability. They found that women are more persuasible and more conforming than men in group pressure situations that involve surveillance. In situations not involving surveillance, women are less likely to conform.

In a study by Sistrunk and McDavid at a private university, a public junior college, and at a high school, overall, females were more susceptible to social pressures than males. In fact, females conformed more than males 3 out of 4 times when they were presented masculine questions. Males conformed more than females 2 out of 4 times when they were presented feminine questions.

The composition of the group plays a role in conformity as well. In a study by Reitan and Shaw, it was found that men and women conformed more when there were participants of both sexes involved versus participants of the same sex. Subjects in the groups with both sexes were more apprehensive when there was a discrepancy amongst group members, and thus the subjects reported that they doubted their own judgments.

Eagly has proposed that this sex difference may be due to different sex roles in society. Women are generally taught to be more agreeable whereas men are taught to be more independent. Normative social influence explains women's attempt to create the ideal body through dieting, and also by eating disorders such as anorexia nervosa and bulimia. Men, in contrast, are likely to pursue their ideal body image through dieting, steroids, and overworking their bodies, rather than developing eating disorders. Both men and women probably learn what kind of body is considered attractive by their culture through the process of informational social influence.

Neuroimaging

Neuroimaging identifies the anterior insula and anterior cingulate as key areas in the brain determining whether people conform in their preferences in regard to its being popular with their peer group. This conformity effect of ones peer group upon is strongest during adolescence.

Anti-social Behaviour

Anti-social behaviour (with or without hyphen) is behaviour that lacks consideration for others and that may cause damage to society, whether intentionally or through negligence, as opposed to pro-social behaviour, behaviour that helps or benefits society. Criminal and civil laws in various countries offer remedies for anti-social behaviour.

In psychiatry, particularity in the influential Diagnostic and Statistical Manual of Mental Disorders, persistent anti-social behaviour is part of a diagnosis of antisocial personality disorder. The ICD-10 defines a conceptually similar *dissocial personality disorder*.

In common parlance antisocial is often used to describe those perceived to be excessively introverted, an incorrect though increasingly common usage.

Social Development

Intent and discrimination may determine both pro- and anti-social behaviour. Infants may act in seemingly anti-social ways, yet be generally accepted as too young to know the difference before the age of 4 or 5. In preschool-aged children, an increase in aggression is normal, indeed lack of such behavioural changes may lead to depression and anxiety later in life. However, continued aggression can indicate problems. Persistent anti-social behaviour may be a manifestation of an antisocial personality disorder. Parents should teach their children that "emotions need to be regulated, not repressed". Both bullies and their victims have inadequate emotional regulation.

Anti-social Behaviour in UK Law

The Crime and Disorder Act 1998 defines anti-social behaviour as acting in a manner that has "caused or was likely to cause harassment, alarm or distress to one or more persons not of the same household" as the perpetrator. There has been debate concerning the vagueness of this definition. The Act introduced the Anti-Social Behaviour Order ("Asbo"), a civil order that can result in a jail sentence of up to five years if the terms are breached. Anti Social Behaviour Orders are civil sanctions, effective for a minimum of two years and classed as criminal proceedings for funding purposes due to restrictions they place on individual liberty. An Anti Social Behaviour Order does not give the offender a criminal record, but sets conditions prohibiting the offender from specific anti-social acts or entering into defined areas. Breach of an Anti Social Behaviour Order is, however, a criminal offence.

In 2003 the Anti-Social Behaviour Act amended the original Act and introduced further sanctions such as Child Curfews and Dispersal Orders.

The following list sets out what behaviour the UK police classify as anti-social:

- Substance misuse such as glue sniffing
- Drinking alcohol on the streets
- Problems related to animals such as not properly restraining animals in public places
- Begging
- Prostitution related activity such as curb crawling and loitering
- Abandoned vehicles that may or may not be stolen
- Vehicle nuisance such as "cruises" - revving car engines, racing, wheel spinning and horn sounding.

- Noise coming from business or industry
- Noise coming from alarms
- Noise coming from pubs and clubs
- Environmental damage such as graffiti and littering
- Inappropriate use of fireworks
- Inappropriate use of public space such as disputes among neighbours, rowdy or inconsiderate behaviour
- General drunken behaviour (which is rowdy or inconsiderate)
- Hoax calls to the emergency services
- Pubs or clubs serving alcohol after hours
- Malicious communication
- Hate incidents where abuse involves race, religion, gender, sexual orientation, age or disability
- Firearms incidents such as use of an imitation weapon.

Deviance

Deviance in a sociological context describes actions or behaviours that violate cultural norms including formally-enacted rules (e.g., crime) as well as informal violations of social norms (e.g., rejecting folkways and mores). It is the perview of sociologists, psychologists, psychiatrists, and criminologists to study how these norms are created, how they change over time and how they are enforced.

Deviance as a Violation of Social Norms

Norms are specific behavioural standards, ways in which people are supposed to act, paradigms for predictable behaviour in society. They are not necessarily moral, or even grounded in morality; in fact, they are just as often pragmatic and, paradoxically, irrational. (A great many of what we call manners, having no logical grounds, would make for good examples here.) Norms are rules of conduct, not neutral or universal, but ever changing; shifting as society shifts; mutable, emergent, loose, reflective of inherent biases and interests, and highly selfish and one-sided. They vary from class to class, and in the generational "gap." They are, in other words, contextual. Deviance can be described as a violation of these norms.

Deviance is a failure to conform with culturally reinforced norms. This definition can be interpreted in many different ways. Social norms are different in one culture as opposed to another. For example, a deviant act can be committed in one society or culture that breaks a social norm there, but may be considered normal for another culture and society. Some acts of deviance may be criminal acts, but also, according to the society or culture, deviance can be strictly breaking social norms that are intact.

Viewing deviance as a violation of social norms, sociologists have characterized it as "any thought, feeling or action that members of a social group judge to be a violation of their values or rules"; "violation of the norms of a society or group"; "conduct that violates definitions of appropriate and inappropriate conduct shared by the members of a social system"; "the departure of certain types of behaviour from the norms of a particular society at a particular time"; and "violation of certain types of group norms [... where] behaviour is in a disapproved direction and of sufficient degree to exceed the tolerance limit of the community."

Deviance as Reactive Construction

Deviance is concerned with the process whereby actions, beliefs or conditions (ABC) come to be viewed as deviant by others. Deviance can be observed by the negative, stigmatizing social reaction of others towards these phenomena. Criminal behaviour, such as theft, can be deviant, but other crimes attract little or no social reaction, and cannot be considered deviant (e.g., violating copyright laws by downloading music in the internet). Some beliefs in society will attract negative reaction, such as racism and homonegativity or alternatively even race-mixing or homosexuality, but that depends on the society. People may have a condition which makes them treated badly by others, such as having HIV, dwarfism, facial deformities, or obesity. Deviance is relative to time and place because what is considered deviant in one social context may be non-deviant in another (e.g., fighting during a hockey game vs. fighting in a nursing home). Killing another human is considered wrong except when governments permit it during warfare or self-defence. The issue of social power cannot be divorced from a definition of deviance because some groups in society can criminalize the actions of another group by using their influence on legislators.

Theories

There are three broad sociological classes describing deviant behaviour, namely structural functionalism, symbolic interactionism and conflict theory.

Structural-Functionalism

Social integration is the attachment to groups and institutions, while social regulation is the adherence to the norms and values of the society. Those who are very integrated fall under the category of "altruism" and those who are very unintegrated fall under "egoism." Similarly, those who are very regulated fall under "fatalism" and those who are very unregulated fall under "anomie". Durkheim's strain theory attributes social deviance to extremes of the dimensions of the social bond. Altruistic suicide (death for the good of the group), egoistic suicide (death for the removal of the self due to or justified by the lack of ties to others), and anomic suicide (death due to the confounding of self-interest and societal norms) are the three forms of suicide that can happen due to extremes. Likewise, individuals may commit crimes for the good of an individual's group, for the self due to or justified by lack of ties, or because the societal norms that place the individual in check no longer have power due to society's corruption.

Merton's Strain Theory

Robert K. Merton discussed deviance in terms of goals and means as part of his strain/anomie theory. Where Durkheim states that anomie is the confounding of social norms, Merton goes further and states that anomie is the state in which social goals and the legitimate means to achieve them do not correspond. He postulated that an individual's response to societal expectations and the means by which the individual pursued those goals were useful in understanding deviance. Specifically, he viewed collective action as motivated by strain, stress, or frustration in a body of individuals that arises from a disconnection between the society's *goals* and the popularly used *means* to achieve those goals. Often, non-routine collective behaviour (rioting, rebellion, etc.) is said to map onto economic explanations and causes by way of strain. These two dimensions determine the adaptation to society according to the cultural goals, which are the society's perceptions about the ideal life, and to the institutionalized means, which are the legitimate means through which an individual may aspire to the cultural goals.

Symbolic Interactionism

Deviance, according to this view, comes from the individual, who *learns* his deviant behaviour. The deviant may grow up alongside other deviants or may learn justification for deviance. Through their interactions, individuals create the symbolic structures that make life meaningful. Reality does not impose the names and definitions of things, but rather people must define things and make them meaningful in order to make them socially real. The focus is upon the consciousness and the mind of the individual as opposed to the institutions from where the norms come. Symbolic interactionism allows researchers to understand how individuals negotiate, manipulate, and change the structure and reality to a certain extent. Individuals are already born into a society which has symbolic structures. "Emotion processing is pivotal during development and deficient processing of certain emotions disrupts normal socialization increasing risk for violent behaviour later in life. Psychopathy has been linked to both of these phenomena in men; however, the study of such relations has been relatively neglected in women. In the present study, 88 collegiate women completed measures of psychopathy, aggression, and a lexical-decision-task (LDT) assessing the processing of affective words". "Research has demonstrated that (in)effective parenting influences whether a child/adolescent engages in deviant behaviours; however, research is mixed regarding whether that influence is direct."

Sutherland's Differential Association

In his differential association theory, Edwin Sutherland posited that criminals learn criminal and deviant behaviours and that deviance is not inherently a part of a particular individual's nature. Also, he argues that criminal behaviour is learned in the same way that all other behaviours are learned, meaning that the acquisition of criminal knowledge is not unique compared to the learning of other behaviours.

Sutherland outlined some very basic points in his theory, such as the idea that the learning comes from the interactions between individuals and groups, using communication of symbols and ideas. When the symbols and ideas about deviation are much more favorable than unfavorable, the individual tends to take a favorable view upon deviance and will resort to more of these behaviours.

Criminal behaviour (motivations and technical knowledge), as with any other sort of behaviour, is learned. Some basic assumptions include:

- Learning in interaction using communication within intimate personal groups.
- Techniques, motives, drives, rationalizations, and attitudes are all learned.
- Excess of definitions favorable to deviation.
- Legitimate and illegitimate behaviour both express the same general needs and values.

Neutralization Theory

Gresham Sykes and David Matza's neutralization theory explains how deviants justify their deviant behaviours by providing alternative definitions of their actions and by providing explanations, to themselves and others, for the lack of guilt for actions in particular situations.

There are five major types of neutralization:

- Denial Of Responsibility: the deviant believes s/he was helplessly propelled into the deviance, and that under the same circumstances, any other person would resort to similar actions
- Denial Of Injury: the deviant believes that the action caused no harm to other individuals or to the society, and thus the deviance is not morally wrong
- Denial Of The Victim: the deviant believes that individuals on the receiving end of the deviance were

deserving of the results due to the victim's lack of virtue or morals

- Condemnation Of The Condemners: the deviant believes enforcement figures or victims have the tendency to be equally deviant or otherwise corrupt, and as a result, are hypocrites to stand against
- Appeal To Higher Loyalties: the deviant believes that there are loyalties and values that go beyond the confines of the law; morality, friendships, or traditions may be more important to the deviant than legal boundaries

Labelling Theory

Frank Tannenbaum and Howard S. Becker created and developed labelling theory, which is a core facet of symbolic interactionism, and often referred to as Tannenbaum's "dramatization of evil." Becker believed that "social groups create deviance by making the rules whose infraction constitutes deviance."

Labelling is a process of social reaction by the "social audience," (stereotyping) the people in society exposed to, judging and accordingly defining (labelling) someone's behaviour as deviant or otherwise. It has been characterized as the "invention, selection, manipulation of beliefs which define conduct in a negative way and the selection of people into these categories [....]"

Labelling theory, consequently, suggests that deviance is caused by the deviant's being labeled as morally inferior, the deviant's internalizing the label and finally the deviant's acting according to that specific label (in other words, you lable the "deviant" and they act accordingly). As time goes by, the "deviant" takes on traits that constitute deviance by committing such deviations as conform to the label (so you as the audience have the power to not label them and you have the power to stop the deviance before it ever occurs by not labelling them). Individual and societal preoccupation with the label, in other words, leads the deviant individual to follow a self-fulfilling prophecy of abidance to the ascribed label.

This theory, while very much symbolically-interactionist, also has elements of conflict theory, as the dominant group has the power to decide what is deviant and acceptable, and enjoys the power behind the labelling process. An example of this is a prison system that labels people convicted of theft, and because of this they start to view themselves as by definition thieves, incapable of changing.

"From this point of view," as Howard S. Becker has written, deviance is *not* a quality of the act the person commits, but rather a consequence of the application by others of rules and sanctions to an "offender." The deviant is one to whom the label has successfully been applied; deviant behaviour is behaviour that people so label.

In other words, "Behaviour only becomes deviant or criminal if defined and interfered as such by specific people in [a] specific situation." It is important to note the salient fact that society is not always correct in its labelling, often falsely identifying and misrepresenting people as deviants, or attributing to them characteristics which they do not have. In legal terms, people are often wrongly accused, yet many of them must live with the ensuant stigma (or conviction) for the rest of their lives.

On a similar note, society often employs double standards, with some sectors of society enjoying favouritism. Certain behaviours in one group are seen to be perfectly acceptable, or can be easily overlooked, but in another are seen, by the same audiences, as abominable.

Primary and Secondary Deviation

Edwin Lemert developed the idea of primary and secondary deviation as a way to explain the process of labelling. Primary deviance is any general deviance before the deviant is labeled as such. Secondary deviance is any action that takes place after primary deviance as a reaction to the institutional identification of the person as a deviant.

When an actor commits a crime (primary deviance), however mild, the institution will bring social penalties down on the actor. However, punishment does not necessarily stop crime, so the actor might commit the same primary deviance again, bringing even harsher reactions from the institutions. At this point, the actor will start to resent the institution, while the institution brings harsher and harsher repression. Eventually, the whole community will stigmatize the actor as a deviant and the actor will not be able to tolerate this, but will ultimately accept his or her role as a criminal, and will commit criminal acts that fit the role of a criminal.

Primary And Secondary Deviation is what causes people to become harder criminals. Primary deviance is the time when the person is labeled deviant through confession or reporting. Secondary deviance is deviance before and after the primary deviance. Retrospective labelling happens when the deviant recognizes his acts as deviant prior to the primary deviance, while prospective labelling is when the deviant recognizes future acts as deviant. The steps to becoming a criminal are:

1. Primary deviation.
2. Social penalties.
3. Secondary deviation.
4. Stronger penalties.
5. Further deviation with resentment and hostility towards punishers.
6. Community stigmatizes the deviant as a criminal. Tolerance threshold passed.
7. Strengthening of deviant conduct because of stigmatizing penalties.
8. Acceptance as role of deviant or criminal actor.

Control Theory

A theory that stresses how weak bonds between the individual and society free people to deviate. By contrast, strong bonds make deviance costly. This theory asks why do people refrain from deviant or criminal behaviour, instead of why people commit deviant or criminal behaviour, according to Travis Hirschi. The control theory developed when norms emerge to deter deviant behaviour. Without this "control" deviant behaviour would happen more often. This leads to conformity and groups. People will conform to a group when they believe they have more to gain from conformity than by deviance. If a strong bond is achieved there will be less chance of deviance than if a weak bond has occurred. Hirschi argued a person follows the norms because they have a bond to society. The bond consists of four positively correlated factors: commitment, attachment, belief, and involvement. When any of these bonds are weakened or broken one is more likely to act in defiance. Hirschi worked with this idea of a General Theory of Crime with his partner Michael R. Gottfredson. Gottfredson and Hirschi in 1990 founded their Self-Control Theory. It stated that acts of force and fraud are undertaken in the pursuit of self interest and self control. A deviant act is based on a criminals own self control of themselves.

Gottfredson and Hirschi's General Theory of Crime

More contemporary control theorists such as Michael Jordan take the theory into a new light, suggesting labour market experiences not only affect the attitudes and the "stakes" of individual workers, but can also affect the development of their children's views toward conformity and cause involvement in delinquency. This is still an ongoing study as he has found a significant relationship between parental labour market involvement and children's delinquency, but has not empirically demonstrated the mediating role of parents' or children's attitude. The research will try to show a correlation between labour market stratification and individual behaviour (juvenile behaviour).

Conflict Theory

In sociology, conflict theory states that society or an organization functions so that each individual participant and its groups struggle to maximize their benefits, which inevitably contributes to social change such as political changes and revolutions. Deviant behaviours are actions that do not go along with the socially institutions as what cause deviance. The institution's ability to change norms, wealth or status come into conflict with the individual. The legal rights of poor folks might be ignored, middle class are also accept; they side with the elites rather the poor, thinking they might rise to the top by supporting the status quo. Conflict theory is based upon the view that the fundamental causes of crime are the social and economic forces operating within society. However, it explains white-collar crime less well. This theory also states that the powerful define crime. This raises the question: for whom is this theory functional? In this theory, laws are instruments of oppression: tough on the powerless and less tough on the powerful.

Karl Marx

Marx himself did not write about deviant behaviour but he wrote about alienation amongst the proletariat - as well as between the proletariat and the finished product - which causes conflict, and thus deviant behaviour.

Many Marxist writers have used the theory of the capitalist state in their arguments. For example, Steven Spitzer utilized the theory of Bourgeoisie control over social junk and social dynamite; George Rusche was known to present analysis of different punishments correlated to the social capacity and infrastructure for labour. He theorized that throughout history, when more labour is needed, the severity of punishments decreases and the tolerance for deviant behaviour increases. Jock Young, another marxist writer, presented the idea that the modern world did not approve of diversity, but was not afraid of social conflict. The late modern world, however, is very tolerant of diversity but is extremely afraid of social conflicts, which is an explanation given for the political correctness movement. The late modern society easily accepts difference, but it labels those that it does not want as deviant and relentlessly punishes and persecutes.

Michel Foucault

Michel Foucault believed that torture had been phased out from modern society due to the dispersion of power; there was no need anymore for the wrath of the state on a deviant individual. Rather, the modern state receives praise for its fairness and dispersion of power which, instead of controlling each individual, controls the mass.

He also theorized that institutions control people through the use of discipline. "Race and ethnicity could be relevant to an understanding of prison rule breaking if inmates bring their ecologically structured beliefs regarding legal authority, crime and deviance into the institutional environment." For example, the modern prison (more specifically the panopticon) is a template for these institutions because it controls its inmates by the perfect use of discipline. Foucault theorizes that, in a sense, the postmodern society is characterized by the lack of free will on the part of individuals. Institutions of knowledge, norms, and values, are simply in place to categorize and control humans.

Biological Theories of Deviance

Praveen Attri claims genetic reasons to be largely responsible for social deviance. The Italian school of criminology contends that biological factors may contribute to crime and deviance. Cesare Lombroso was among the first to research and develop the Theory of Biological Deviance which states that some people are genetically predisposed to criminal behaviour. He believed that criminals were a product of earlier genetic forms. The main influence of his research was Charles Darwin and his Theory of Evolution. Lombroso theorized that people were born criminals or in other words, less evolved humans who were biologically more related to our more primitive and animalistic urges. From his research, Lombroso took Darwin's Theory and looked at primitive times himself in regards to deviant behaivors. He found that the skeletons that he studied mostly had low foreheads and protruding jaws. These characteristics resembled primitive beings such as Homo Neanderthalensis. He stated that little could be done to cure born criminals because their characteristics were biologically inherited. Over time, most of his research was disproved. His research was refuted by Pearson and Charles Goring. They discovered that Lombroso had not researched enough skeletons to make his research thorough enough. When Pearson and Goring researched skeletons on their own they tested many more and found that the bone structure had no relevance in deviant behaviour. The statistical study that Charles Goring published on this research is called "The English Convict".

Other Theories

The Classical school of criminology comes from the works of Cesare Beccaria and Jeremy Bentham. Beccaria assumed a utilitarian view of society along with a social contract theory of the state. He argued that the role of the state was to maximize the greatest possible utility to the maximum number of people and to minimize those actions that harm the society. He argued that deviants commit deviant acts (which are harmful to the society) because of the utility it gives to the private individual. If the state were to match the pain of punishments with the utility of various deviant behaviours, the deviant would no longer have any incentive to commit deviant acts. (Note that Beccaria argued for *just* punishment; as raising the severity of punishments without regard to logical measurement of utility would cause increasing degrees of social harm once it reached a certain point.)

Functions of Deviance

- Deviant acts can be assertions of individuality and identity, and thus as rebellions against group norms

Deviance affirms cultural values and norms, it also clarifies moral boundaries, promotes social unity by creating an us/them dichotomy,encourages social change, and provides jobs to control deviance. “Certain factors of personality are theoretically and empirically related to workplace deviance, such as work environment, and individual differences.” "Situated in the masculinity and deviance literature, this article examines a “deviant” masculinity, that of the male sex worker, and presents the ways men who engage in sex work cope with the job.”

Cross-Cultural Communication as Deviance

Cross-cultural communication is a field of study that looks at how people from different cultural backgrounds endeavour to communicate. All cultures make use of nonverbal communication but its meaning varies across cultures. In one particular country, a non-verbal sign may stand for one thing, and mean something else in another culture or country. The relation of cross-cultural communication with deviance is that a sign may be offensive to one in one culture and mean something completely appropriate in another. This is an important field of study because as educators, business employees, or any other form of career that consists of communicating with ones from other cultures you; need to understand non-verbal signs and their meanings, so you avoid offensive conversation, or misleading conversation. Below is a list of non-verbal gestures that are appropriate in one country, and that would be considered deviant in another. These are just a few non-verbal cross-cultural communication signs of which one should be aware. Cross-Cultural communication can make or break a business deal, or even prevent an educator from offending a student. Different cultures have different methods of communication, so it is important to understand the cultures of others. Shaving of heads after death of a family member is more common in some African cultures.

Proponents of the theory of a Southern culture of honor hold that violent behaviour which would be considered criminal in most of the United States, may be considered a justifiable response to insult in a Southern culture of honor.

Types of Deviance

Taboo is a strong social form of behaviour considered deviant by a majority. To speak of it publicly is condemned, and therefore, almost entirely avoided. The term "taboo" comes from the Tongan word "tapu" meaning "under prohibition", "not allowed", or "forbidden". Some forms of taboo are prohibited under law and transgressions may lead to severe penalties. Other forms of taboo result in shame, disrespect and humiliation. Taboo is not universal but does occur in the majority of societies. Some of the examples of include murder, rape, incest, or child molestation.

Howard Becker, a labelling theorist, touched basis with different types of deviant behaviours. There are four different types of deviant behaviours falling into different categories. One of the four is falsely accusing an individual which falls under others perceiving you to be obtaining obedient or deviant behaviours. Pure deviance,which falls under perceiving one to participate in deviant and rule-breaking behaviour, is also apart of the four types of deviant behaviours listed above. Conforming, which falls under not being perceived as deviant, but merely participating in the social norms that are distributed within societies, can also be placed into the category with pure deviance and falsely accused. Lastly is secret deviance which is when the individual is not perceived as deviant or participating in any rule-breaking behaviours.

5

Policing as Symbolic Interaction

The police are persons empowered to enforce the law, protect property and reduce civil disorder. Their powers include the legitimized use of force. The term is most commonly associated with police services of a state that are authorized to exercise the police power of that state within a defined legal or territorial area of responsibility. Police forces are often defined as organizations separate from any military forces, or other organizations involved in the defence of the state against foreign aggressors; however, gendarmerie and military police are military units charged with policing.

Law enforcement, however, constitutes only part of policing activity. Policing has included an array of activities in different situations, but the predominant ones are concerned with the preservation of order. In some societies, in the late 18th century and early 19th century, these developed within the context of maintaining the class system and the protection of private property.

Alternative names for police force include constabulary, gendarmerie, police department, police service, crime prevention, protective services, law enforcement agency, civil guard or civic guard.

Members can be police officers, troopers, sheriffs, constables, rangers, peace officers or civic/civil guards. Russian police and police of the Soviet-era Eastern Europe are (or were) called *militsiya*. The Irish police are called the Garda Síochána ("guardians of the peace"); a police officer is called a *garda*. As police are often in conflict with individuals, slang terms are numerous. Many slang terms for police officers are decades or centuries old with lost etymology.

Law Enforcement and Society

The first modern police force, commonly said to be the London Metropolitan Police, established in 1829, promoted the preventive role of police as a deterrent to urban crime and disorder.

Law enforcement however has only ever constituted a small portion of policing activity. Policing has included an array of activities in different contexts, but the predominant ones are concerned with the preservation of order and the provision of services.

History

In some societies, in the late 18th century and early 19th century, these developed within the context of maintaining a layered societal structure and the protection of property.

In the United Kingdom in the late 18th century:

The modern police department was born out of...the desire of the wealthy to restructure... society. The swelling population of urban poor, whose miniscule [sic] wages could hardly sustain them, heightened the need for police protection

In the United States in the 19th century:

The police role was only minimally directed at law enforcement. Its primary function was serving as the enforcement arm of the reigning polical power, protecting property, and keeping control of the ever increasing numbers of foreign immigrants

In 1690 John Locke wrote that:

[t]he great and chief end... of men's uniting into commonwealths, and putting themselves under government, is the preservation of their property

Similarly, Adam Smith described how:

... as the necessity of civil government gradually grows up with the acquisition of valuable property, so the principal causes which naturally introduce subordination gradually grow up with the growth of that valuable property... Wherever there is great property there is great inequality. For one very rich man there must be at least five hundred poor, and the affluence of the few supposes the indigence of the many. The affluence of the rich excites the indignation of the poor, who are often both driven by want, and prompted by envy, to invade his possessions... The appropriation of herds and flocks which introduced an inequality of fortune was that which first gave rise to regular government. Till there be property there can be no government, the very end of which is to secure wealth, and to defend the rich from the poor

This close link between property and government (and thus police function) was also noted by John Jay, who repeatedly said that:

Those who own the country ought to govern it.

According to Monaghan, this:

was one of his favorite maxims

and by US Founding Father James Madison. who declared that government:

... our government ought to secure the permanent interests of the country against innovation. Landholders ought to have a share in the government, to support these invaluable interests and to balance and check the other. They ought to be so constituted as to protect the minority of the opulent against the majority.

Given that the crimes of governments and associated elite institutions have historically been greater than those of the "smaller" criminals they prosecuted, and that such institutional influence has been perceived, by some groups, as a promoter of violence, alienation and socioeconomic disparity which gives rise to crime, the institutional role of police has been criticized.

Policing

A philosophy that combines traditional aspects of law enforcement with prevention measures, problem-solving, community engagement, and community partnerships.

From the 1930s to the 1960s, U.S. law enforcement relied on a professional policing model. This model was based on hierarchical structures, efficient response times, standardization, and the use of motorized patrol cars. Although this model improved efficiency, operations, and accountability, it proved inadequate when civil disturbances erupted in the late 1960s. Critics charged that police and the communities they served were alienated from each other, and a call came for community-oriented policing.

A first attempt was the team policing approach, which assigned responsibility for a certain geographic area to a team of police officers who would get to know the neighbourhood, its people, and its problems. This harkened back to the early twentieth century when police walked a beat. The approach, however, proved ineffective because it placed more emphasis on long-term problem solving than on rapid response to crime incidents. Internally, team policing intruded on functional lines of authority, with patrol officers becoming involved in areas reserved to detectives and other specialists.

Community policing programs grew out of the failures of team policing. The goal of community policing is to bring the police and the public it serves closer together to identify and address crime issues. Instead of merely responding to emergency calls and arresting criminals, police officers in such programs get involved in finding out what causes crime and disorder, and attempt to creatively solve problems in their assigned communities. To do this police must develop a network of personal contacts both inside and outside their departments. This contact is fostered by foot, bike, or horse patrols—any effort that gets a police officer out of his or her squad car.

Community Based Policing

Community policing is perhaps the most misunderstood and frequently abused theme in police management during this decade. In the past few years, it has become fashionable for police agencies to initiate community policing, often with little notion of what that phrase means. Indeed, all manner of organizational tinkering has been labeled community policing. But community policing is not a program.

Instead, community policing is a value system which permeates a police department, in which the primary organizational goal is working cooperatively with individual citizens, groups of citizens, and both public and private organizations to identify and resolve issues which potentially effect the livability of specific neighbourhoods, areas, or the city as a whole. Community-based police departments recognize the fact that the police cannot effectively deal with such issues alone, and must partner with others who share a mutual responsibility for resolving problems. Community policing stresses prevention, early identification, and timely intervention to deal with issues before they become unwieldy problems. Individual officers tend to function as general-purpose practitioners who bring together both government and private resources to achieve results. Officers are encouraged to spend considerable time and effort in developing and maintaining personal relationships with citizens, businesses, schools, and community organizations. Here are some other common features of community policing:

Beyond Crime Fighting a Focus on Livability

Many police departments and police officers define their role primarily in terms of crime control. The very term *law enforcement agency* is certainly an indication of this focus. But policing is much more than law enforcement. Many studies have shown that dealing with crime consumes only 10-20% of the police workload.

Officers in community-based police departments understand that "crook-catching" is only one part of their job, and a rather small one by comparison to the myriad of issues and problems they deal with each day. Officers freely accept a significant role in issues that might be derisively referred to as "social work" in traditional police departments.

Officers understand that resolving a problem with unruly people drinking at a public park, working to reduce truancy at a middle school, marshalling resources to improve lighting in a mobile home park, and removing abandoned vehicles from streets, may all be forms of valid and valuable police work, which affect the livability of a neighbourhood. Rather than treating these activities as diversions from "real" police work, officers understand that this is the essence of their work.

Citizen Involvement

The police department strives to actively involve citizens in its operations, through a variety of means. Volunteers are widely used, whether college interns or retired seniors. Citizen patrols and crime prevention initiatives are welcomed and encouraged. Area commanders meet often with members of the public to solicit input and feedback. Many internal committees include public participation. Policy decisions typically involve opportunities for input from citizens, and the department has both formal and informal mechanisms for this purpose. Promotional boards include citizens. The department seeks to educate the general public about police work in various ways, including publications, web sites, public-access television, town hall meetings, citizen police academies. The department accepts and even encourages citizen review of its performance.

Geographic Responsibility

The primary division of labour for the police is geographical. Officers identify with their area of assignment, rather than the work shift or functional division. Commanders are assigned to geographical areas and given wide latitude to deploy their personnel and resources within that area. Individual officers adopt even smaller geographical areas and feel a sense of ownership for that area. Officers commonly know many of the people who live and work in this area, and are intimately familiar with the area's geography, businesses, schools, and churches. Officers seek out detailed information about police incidents which have occurred in their area of assignment during their off-duty time.

Long-term Assignment

Officers can expect to work in the same geographical area for many years. Officers' preferences for areas are considered in making assignments. Rotation of geographical assignments is rare. The organization values the expertise and familiarity that comes with long-term assignment to the same area.

Decentralized Decision Making

Most operational decisions are decentralized to the level of execution. Field officers are given broad discretion to manage their own uncommitted time. Operational policies are concise, and serve as general guidelines for professional practice more than detailed rules and regulations. First line supervisors are heavily involved in decisions that are ordinarily reserved for command ranks in traditional police departments.

Participative Management

The department employs numerous methods to involve employees at all levels in decision-making. Staff meetings, committees, task forces, quality circles, and similar groups are impaneled often to address issues of internal management. Many workplace initiatives begin with ideas or concepts brought forward from line employees. Obtaining input from frontline employees is viewed as an essential part of any policy decision. The department has comparatively few levels of rank, and rank is seldom relied upon to settle disagreements. Supervisors view their role primarily in providing support to field personnel by teaching, coaching, obtaining resources, solving problems, and "running interference."

Generalist Officers

Field officers dominate the sworn work force. Officers are expected to handle a huge variety of police incidents, and to follow through on such incidents from beginning to end. Specialization is limited to those areas where considerable expertise is an absolute necessity. Even when specialists are used, their role is to work cooperatively with field officers, rather than assume responsibility for cases or incidents from field officers. Most specialists view their jobs as offering technical expertise and support to field personnel.

Police Leadership on Community Issues

Senior police managers are deeply involved in community affairs. They speak out frequently and freely on issues of community concern, some of which are only tangentially related to law enforcement per se. Police managers are encouraged to pursue important community issues as a personal cause. Elected officials consult with police managers often. Police representation is obligatory on committees or study groups which are set up to examine significant issues on the public agenda, and it is not uncommon for police officers to serve in leadership positions in community organizations.

Proactive Policing

The police department employs techniques to manage its workload in order to make blocks of time available for police officers to address identified problems. The police response to an emerging problem typically involves significant input and participation from outside the department. The department routinely uses a range of tactics other than responding to individual incidents, such as: targeted saturation patrol, bicycle and foot patrol, undercover/plainclothes/decoy/surveillance operations, educational presentations, coordination of efforts with other government or human service agencies, support to volunteer efforts, initiation of legislative proposals, and so forth.

Rather than merely responding to demands for police services, the department employees a *Problem-Oriented Policing (POP) approach*: identifying emergent problems, gathering data, bringing together stakeholders, and implementing specific strategies targeting the problem. The police response to an on-going or repetitive problem seldom involves only police resources. The police are concerned not only with high-visibility crimes, but with minor offences which contribute to fear of crime, and negatively effect public perception of city or neighbourhood safety.

Emphasis on Quality

The police define success and accomplishment primarily by the results achieved and the satisfaction of the consumer of services, rather than by strictly internal measures of the amount of work completed. Thus, there may be decreased emphasis on common productivity measures such as clearance rate, numbers of arrests, response time, etc., and increased emphasis on outcomes.

Thoroughness and quality are clear emphases, but "doing the right thing" is as important as "doing things right." The department employs methods to assess public satisfaction with services, and both individual officers and managers think about ways to improve based on this feedback.

Recognition and Professional Development

Officers receive frequent recognition for initiative, innovation, and planning. The department systematically acknowledges problem-oriented policing projects that achieve results. Seasoned field officers are highly valued for their skill and knowledge, and feel little pressure to compete for promotion to supervisory positions in order to advance their career. Commendations and awards go to officers for excellent police work of all kinds, not just crime control. Officers receive the respect and admiration of their colleagues as much for their empathy, compassion, concern for quality, and responsiveness, as for their skill at criminal investigation, interrogation, and zeal in law enforcement.

What Community Policing is Not

Despite the claims of some ill-informed critics, community policing is not soft on crime. Quite the contrary, it can significantly improve the ability of the police to discover criminal conduct, clear offences, and make arrests. Improved communication with citizens and more intimate knowledge of the geography and social milieu of the beat enhances, rather than reduces, the officers' crime-fighting capability. Moreover, though some of these may be used as specific strategies, community policing is not:

- school resource officers
- a grant
- storefront police substations
- a pilot program in a single area of town
- foot or bicycle patrols
- a specialized unit of neighbourhood police officers
- a citizen police academy.

When an agency claims to have "implemented" community policing last week, that's a pretty good indication that it has not. Individual programs or projects that form part of this change may be implemented, but community policing is not implemented. You don't start it at the beginning of the fiscal year. It is a process that evolves, develops, takes root and grows, until it is an integral part of the formal and informal value system of both the police and the community as a whole. It is a gradual change from a style of policing which emphasizes crime control and "crook catching," to a style of policing which emphasizes citizen interaction and participation in problem solving.

You can't tell whether community policing exists in a city on the basis of the press release, the organizational chart, or the annual report. Rather, it can best be discerned by observing the daily work of officers. It exists when officers spend a significant amount of their available time out of their patrol cars; when officers are common sight in businesses, schools, PTA meetings, recreation centers; when most want to work the street by choice; when individual officers are often involved in community affairs-cultural events, school events, meetings of service clubs, etc., often as an expected part of their job duties. It exists when most citizens know a few officers by name; when officers know scores of citizens in their area of assignment, and have an intimate knowledge of their area.

You can see it plainly when most officers are relaxed and warmly human-not robotic; when any discussion of a significant community issue involves the police; and when few organizations would not think of tackling a significant issue of community concern without involving the police.

The community-based police department is open-it has a well-used process for addressing citizen grievances, relates well with the news media, and cultivates positive relationships with elected officials.

Symbolic Interaction

According to Symbolic Interactionism (often paraphrased "Interactionism"), society is:

- A social construct; socially defined by people acting together in social groups (with multiple realities possible, depending who you hang out with). Symbolic Interactionism has little sense of abstract structures (functionalism) or competing classes (conflict theory), but rather sees reality as created by people struggling to define themselves and the world around them and then to share those meanings with others.

A MICRO theory, Interactionism explains our behaviour in terms of the patterns of belief and thought we have and in terms of the meanings we give to our lives. In this view, there is no "objective" reality, but rather multiple realities depending on the experiences we bring to our interactions and our definition of the situation. For example, a gang member who sees the police as the storm troopers of a racist society will respond differently to an officer's call for help than a banker who sees the police as the defenders of law and order.

Our interactions with others, which we collect over time and through past experiences, create perceptions of "reality" which are not objective ("out there") but do become internalized within us and make it seem that these perceptions and definitions of reality are objective facts.

However, these perceptions and even our views of who we are (identity) can change when we come into contact with different groups, organizations, and contexts (e.g. a prisoner who is falsely accused but goes to jail anyway will radically change his/her self-definition in prison; a person who grew up in a very rural area may completely change their identity when they move to NYC).

Shared expectations, which are established through our interactions with others, shape our behaviour and establish our routines. These expectations are not necessarily "functional" for society, nor are they exploitative. They simply shape who we are, and must be examined across contexts to determine their consequences.

In terms of strategies for equality, symbolic Interactionism holds that better communication and intercultural awareness can improve relations among cultures and social groups.

Key Terms

Socialization: A process of role-taking in which children learn to see the relationships among many different roles and to see themselves as they imagine others see them.

Stigma: A socially-defined "mark" that labels someone discredited; some stigmas are immediately visible (skin color; physical disability), while others can be hidden and thus make a person "discreditable" rather than immediately discredited (people living with HIV/AIDS, the homeless, gays and lesbians). Stigmas tend to be internalized by members of discredited groups and thus have a profound impact on our self-definitions and perceptions of reality.

Self-concept: The image we have of who and what we are (formed in childhood by how significant others treat/respond to us). The self-concept is not fixed and unchanging – if in childhood your teachers tell you you're stupid, but later in life your teachers and friends begin to treat you as if you're very bright, you may think you're stupid as a child but later your self-concept is likely to change.

Labelling Theory: A theory that sees crime, mental illness, and other types of deviance as labels applied to those who break social norms, and which holds that branding someone as deviant encourages, rather than discourages, deviant behaviour. Someone who is labeled a "criminal" is likely to internalize and live out that label rather than try to oppose it.

Othering: A process in which individuals or social groups define who they are (their sense of "we-ness") by discrediting or demeaning other individuals or groups. Othering gives us a sense that we are better than "other" groups, who we define as "less than" us. For instance, after 9/11, many Americans reinforced a shared sense of "we-ness" by strengthening our sense of national identity, but did so by "othering" Middle Easterners and Moslems, even those who resided in the United States, as "other."

Applications

Education

Schools play a vital role in shaping the way students see reality and themselves. Many Interactionists have argued that the authoritarianism prevalent in schools impedes learning and encourages undemocratic behaviour later in life.

Schools create serious difficulties for students who are "labeled" as learning disabled or less academically competent than their peers; these students may never be able to see themselves as good students and move beyond these labels. Teacher expectations play a huge role in student achievement.

If students are made to feel like high achievers, they will act like high achievers, and vice versa.

Crime

Criminal activity, like any other behaviour, is learned through interaction. Thus, criminals are likely to have been involved in deviant subcultures or groups that encouraged rule-breaking and criminal activity. Involvement in "deviant" groups teaches people that crime is okay and teaches us the skills to engage in it. Crime is also promoted through comparison with others around us – if those around us (reference groups) have wealth and material goods that we don't have, we might be encouraged to engage in criminal behaviour in order to obtain these things. As with education, labelling has a negative effect on people – if you are labeled a juvenile delinquent, it may become a self-fulfilling prophecy, leading you to adopt the role of criminal in later life. Interactionists also ask who makes the rules about criminal behaviour – why are some acts of deviance defined as crimes and thus punished, while others are not? If crime is learned, interactionists argue, it follows that it can be un-learned. Thus, Interactionists offer a host of proposals such as involving the media in promoting ideals of cooperation and nonviolence, helping kids to avoid the contagion of people involved in gangs or with drugs, and integrating juvenile offenders into groups that strongly discourage criminal behaviour. All of these proposals focus on the role of social learning in crime prevention and reduction.

The Political Economy of Policing

Political economy originally was the term for studying production, buying and selling, and their relations with law, custom, and government, as well as with a distribution of national wealth including through the budget process. *Political economy* originated in moral philosophy. It developed in the 18th century as the study of the economies of states, *polities*, hence *political* economy.

In the late nineteenth century, the term 'economics' came to replace 'political economy', coinciding with publication of an influential textbook by Alfred Marshall in 1890. Earlier, William Stanley Jevons, a proponent of mathematical methods applied to the subject, advocated 'economics' for brevity and with the hope of the term becoming "the recognised name of a science."

Today, political economy, where it is not used as a synonym for economics, may refer to very different things, including Marxian analysis, applied public-choice approaches emanating from the Chicago school, or simply the advice given by economists to the government or public on general economic policy or on specific proposals.

A more classical-liberal approach that dates from the 1970s that denotes 'public-choice' theory type approaches which question the benevolence of social planners to maximize the utility of a representative individual and instead stress how political forces affect the choice of policies that may not be so benevolent, especially as to distributional conflicts and political institutions. It is available as an area of study in certain colleges and universities.

History of the Term

Originally, *political economy* meant the study of the conditions under which production or consumption within limited parameters was organized in the nation-states. The phrase *économie politique* (translated in English as *political economy*) first appeared in France in 1615 with the well known book by Antoine de Montchrétien: *Traité de l'economie politique*. French physiocrats, Adam Smith, David Ricardo and Karl Marx were some of the exponents of political economy. In 1805, Thomas Malthus became England's first professor of political economy, at the East India Company College, Haileybury, Hertfordshire. The world's first professorship in political economy was established in 1763 at the University of Vienna, Austria; Joseph von Sonnenfels was the first tenured professor.

In the United States, political economy first was taught at the College of William and Mary; in 1784 Adam Smith's *Wealth of Nations* was a required textbook.

Glasgow University, where Smith was Professor of Logic and Moral Philosophy, changed the name of its Department of Political Economy to the Department of Economics (ostensibly to avoid confusing prospective undergraduates) in academic year 1997–1998, making the class of 1998 the last to be graduated with a Scottish Master of Arts degree in Political Economy.

Current Approaches

In its contemporary meaning, *political economy* refers to different, but related, approaches to studying economic and political behaviours, ranging from the combination of economics with other fields to the use of different, fundamental assumptions that challenge orthodox economic assumptions:

- *Political economy* most commonly refers to interdisciplinary studies drawing upon economics, law, and political science in explaining how political institutions, the political environment, and the economic system—capitalist, socialist, mixed—influence each other. "Traditional" topics include the influence of elections on the choice of economic policy, determinants of electoral outcomes, the political business cycles, central-bank independence, redistributive conflicts in fiscal policy, and the politics of delayed reforms in developing countries and of excessive deficits. From the late-1990s, the field has expanded to explored such wide-ranging topics as the origins and rate of change of political institutions, and the role of culture in explaining economic outcomes and developments. When more narrowly construed, it analyzes such public policy as monopoly, market protection, institutional corruption, and rent seeking.
- Historians have employed *political economy* to explore the ways in the past that persons and groups with common economic interests have used politics to effect changes beneficial to their interests.
- International Political Economy (IPE) is an interdisciplinary field comprising approaches to international trade and finance, and state policies affecting international trade, i.e. monetary and fiscal policies. In the U.S., these approaches are associated with the journal *International Organization*, which, in the 1970s, became the leading journal of international political economy under the editorship of Robert

Keohane, Peter J. Katzenstein, and Stephen Krasner. They are also associated with the journal *The Review of International Political Economy*. There also is a more critical school of IPE, inspired by Karl Polanyi's work; two major figures are Susan Strange and Robert W. Cox.

- Economists and political scientists often associate the term with approaches using rational choice assumptions, especially game theory and social choice theory, in explaining phenomena beyond economics' standard remit, in which context the term "positive political economy" is common.
- Anthropologists, sociologists, and geographers, use *political economy* in referring to the neo-Marxian approaches to development and underdevelopment postulated by André Gunder Frank and Immanuel Wallerstein.
- New political economy students treat economic ideologies as the phenomenon to explain, per the traditions of Marxian political economy. Thus, Charles S. Maier suggests that a political economy approach: "interrogates economic doctrines to disclose their sociological and political premises....in sum, [it] regards economic ideas and behaviour not as frameworks for analysis, but as beliefs and actions that must themselves be explained." This approach informs Andrew Gamble's *The Free Economy and the Strong State*, and Colin Hay's *The Political Economy of New Labour* (Manchester University Press, 1999). It also informs much work published in *New Political Economy* an international journal founded by Sheffield University scholars in 1996.
- Guy Debord agrees: "The commodity's domination was at first exerted over the economy in an occult manner; the economy itself, the material basis of social life, remained unperceived and not understood, like the familiar which is not necessarily known. In a society where the concrete commodity is rare or unusual, money, apparently dominant, presents itself as an

emissary armed with full powers who speaks in the name of an unknown force. With the industrial revolution, the division of labour in manufactures, and mass production for the world market, the commodity appears in fact as a power which comes to occupy social life. It is then that political economy takes shape, as the dominant science and the science of domination."

Related Disciplines

Because political economy is not a unified discipline, there are studies using the term that overlap in subject matter, but have radically different perspectives:

- Sociology studies the effects of persons' involvement in society as members of groups, and how that changes their ability to function. Many sociologists start from a perspective of production-determining relation from Karl Marx. Marx's theories on the subject of political economy are contained in his book, Das Kapital.
- Political Science focuses on the interaction between institutions and human behaviour, the way in which the former shapes choices and how the latter change institutional frameworks. Along with economics, it has made the best works in the field by authors like Shepsle, Ostrom, Ordeshook, among others.
- Anthropology studies political economy by studying the relationship between the world capitalist system and local cultures.
- Psychology is the fulcrum on which political economy exerts its force in studying decision-making (not only in prices), but as the field of study whose assumptions model political economy.
- History documents change, using it to argue political economy; historical works have political economy as the narrative's frame.
- Economics focuses on markets by leaving the political—governments, states, legal frameworks—as givens. Economics dropped the adjective *political* in the 19th century, but works backwards, by describing "The Ideal Market", urging governments to formulate policy and

law to approach said ideal. Economists and political economists often disagree on what is preeminent in developing production, market, and political structure theories.

- Law concerns the creation of policy and its mediation via political actions that have specific results, it deals with political economy as political capital and as social infrastructure—and the sociological results of one society upon another.
- Human Geography is concerned with politico-economic processes, emphasizing space and environment.
- Ecology deals with political economy, because human activity has the greatest effect upon the environment, its central concern being the environment's suitability for human activity. The ecological effects of economic activity spur research upon changing market economy incentives.
- International Relations often uses political economy to study political and economic development.
- Cultural Studies studies social class, production, labour, race, gender, and sex.
- Communication examines the institutional aspects of media and telecommuncation systems, with particular attention to the historical relationships between owners, labour, consumers, advertisers, and the state.

6

Law and Order

In politics, law and order refers to demands for a strict criminal justice system, especially in relation to violent and property crime, through harsher criminal penalties. These penalties may include longer terms of imprisonment, mandatory sentencing, and in some countries, capital punishment.

Supporters of "law and order" argue that effective deterrence combined with incarceration is the most effective means of crime prevention. Opponents of law and order argue that a system of harsh criminal punishment is ultimately ineffective because it does not address underlying or systemic causes of crime.

"Law and order" is a recurring theme in political campaigns around the world. Candidates may exaggerate or even manufacture a problem with law and order, or characterise their opponents as "weak" on the issue, to generate public support. The expression also sometimes carries the implication of arbitrary or unnecessary law enforcement, or excessive use of police powers.

Political Issue in the United States

"Law and order" was a powerful conservative theme in the U.S. in the 1960s. The leading exponents in the late 1960s were Republicans Ronald Reagan (as governor of California) and Richard Nixon. They used it to dissolve a liberal consensus about crime that involved federal court decisions and a pushback against illegal drugs and violent gang activity. White ethnics in northern cities turned against the Democratic party, blaming it for being soft on crime and rioters. First introduced by Barry Goldwater in his ill-fated run for president in 1964, "Law and order" punished Lyndon Johnson and the Democrats and propelled Reagan to the governorship in 1966 and Nixon to the White House in 1968.

Liberals, Flamm (2005) argues, were unable to craft a compelling message for anxious voters. Instead, liberals either ignored the crime crisis, claimed that law and order was a racist ruse, or maintained that social programs would solve the "root causes" of civil disorder, which by 1968 seemed increasingly unlikely and contributed to a loss of faith in the ability of the government to do what it was above all sworn to do-protect personal security and private property. Conservatives rejected the liberal notions. "How long are we going to abdicate law and order" House GOP leader Gerald Ford demanded in 1966, "in favour of a soft social theory that the man who heaves a brick through your window or tosses a firebomb into your car is simply the misunderstood and underprivileged product of a broken home?"

Flamm (2005) documents how conservatives constructed a persuasive message that argued that the Civil Rights Movement had contributed to racial unrest and Johnson's Great Society had rewarded rather than punished the perpetrators of violence. Conservatives demanded that the national government should promote respect for law and order and contempt for those who violated it, regardless of cause.

After Reagan took office in 1981 and started appointing tough conservative judges, the law became as weapon against crime. The number of prisoners tripled from 500,000 in 1980 to 1.5 million in 1994. Conservatives at the state level built many more prisons and convicts served much longer terms, with less parole. By the time they were released they were much older and thus much less violent.

Ghetto Riots

Two developments were involved. After the first civil rights laws were passed, rebellions by angry blacks broke out in over 100 cities, with nights of violence against police and looting and burning of local white-owned businesses. The inner neighbourhoods of many major cities, such as Detroit and Newark, were burned out. National Guard and Army troops were called out. At one point machine gun units were stationed on the steps of the Capitol building in Washington to prevent rioters from burning it down. Every summer from 1964 through 1970 was a "long hot summer." Whites and Hispanics did not riot.

Crime

Second there was a dramatic rise in violent street crime, including drug-related murders, as well as armed robberies, rapes and violent assaults. Inner city neighbourhoods became far more violent and people tried to move out to safer areas. The number of violent crimes more than tripled from 288,000 in 1960 (including 9,110 murders) to 1,040,000 in 1975 (including 20,510 murders). Then the numbers levelled off.

In response to sharply rising rates of crime in the 1960s, treatment of criminal offenders, both accused and convicted, became a highly divisive topic in the 1968 U.S. Presidential Election. Republican Vice Presidential candidate Spiro Agnew, then the governor of Maryland, often used the expression; Agnew and Nixon won and were reelected in 1972.

Results

Advocates of stricter policies toward crime and those accused of crime have won many victories since the issue became important. Highlights include stringent laws dealing with the sale and use of illicit drugs. For example the Rockefeller drug laws passed in New York state in 1973— and later, laws mandating tougher sentences for repeat offenders, such as the three strikes laws adopted by many states starting in 1993 and the re-legalization of the death penalty in several U.S. states.

Opponents of these and similar laws have often accused advocates of racism. Civil rights groups have steadfastly opposed the trend toward harsher measures generally. The law-and-order issue caused a deep rift within the Democratic Party in the late 1960s and 1970s, and this rift was seen by many political scientists as a major contributing factor in Ronald Reagan's two successful Presidential runs, in 1980 and 1984. In both elections, millions of registered Democrats voted for

Reagan, and they collectively became known as "Reagan Democrats." Many of these voters eventually changed their party registration and became Republicans, especially in the South.

Though violent crimes are the primary focus of law-and-order advocates, quality-of-life crimes are sometimes also included under the law-and-order umbrella, particularly in local elections. A tough stance on this matter greatly helped Rudolph Giuliani win two terms as mayor of New York City in the 1990s, and was also widely cited as propelling Gavin Newsom to victory over a more liberal opponent in San Francisco's mayoral election of 2003.

Platt (1995) argues that the intensity of law-and-order campaigns represents a significant shift in criminal justice that involves modernization and increased funding for police technology and personnel, privatization of security services and surveillance, higher rates of incarceration, and greater racial inequality in security and punishment.

International Issue

Recently, crime has also become a prominent issue in Canadian, Australian, South African, French, and New Zealand politics.

Criticism

Critics of law-and-order politics commonly point to actual and potential abuses of judicial and police powers, including police brutality and misconduct, racial profiling, and prison overcrowding. As an example, they argue that while crime in New York City dropped under Mayor Giuliani, reports of police brutality increased during the same period. This period included the fatal shootings of Amadou Diallo and Sean Bell, and the Abner Louima incident.

In extreme cases, civil unrest has broken out in retaliation against law-and-order politics, as happened in London's Brixton district in 1981, Los Angeles in 1992, and France in 2005.

In 2009, Pennsylvania juvenile court judges Mark Ciavarella and Michael Conahan were pled guilty in the "kids for cash" scandal, of taking kickbacks from private prison industry officials in exchange for sentencing over 1,000 youths to prison terms for minor offences.

Police Power

In United States constitutional law, police power is the capacity of the federal government and the states to regulate behaviour and enforce order within their territory for the betterment of the general welfare, morals, health, and safety of their inhabitants. Under the 10th Amendment to the United States Constitution, the powers prohibited from or not delegated to the Federal Government are reserved to the states respectively, or to the people. This implies that the states do not possess all possible powers, since some of these are reserved to the people.

The exercise of police power can be in the form of making laws, compelling obedience to those laws through legal sanctions, physical means, or other forms of coercion and inducements. Controversies over the exercise of police power, particularly the use of physical means, arise when its exercise by the federal government conflicts with the rights of the states or when its exercise by federal or state authorities conflicts with individual rights and freedoms.

Police powers are, from the point of view of state courts, also restricted by state constitutions. The concept of police power is used by federal courts which do not have jurisdiction to interpret state constitutions: from the point of view of federal constitutional law, states have general police powers except where restricted by the federal Constitution.

Because the Congress has limited powers granted in the Constitution, the Federal government does not have a general police power, as the states do. The exceptions are laws regarding Federal property and the military. On the other hand, Congress was granted by the New Deal Court a broad quasi-police authority from its power to regulate interstate commerce and raise and spend revenue.

Crime in India

Crime is present in various forms in India. Organized crime include drug trafficking, gunrunning, money laundering, extortion, murder for hire, fraud, human trafficking and poaching. Many criminal operations engage in black marketeering, political violence, religiously motivated violence, terrorism, and abduction. Other crimes are homicide, robbery, assault etc. Property crimes include burglary, theft, motor vehicle theft, and arson. Corruption is a significant problem.

Crimes against Women

Police records show high incidence of crimes against women in India. The National Crime Records Bureau reported in 1998 that the growth rate of crimes against women would be higher than the population growth rate by 2010. Earlier, many cases were not registered with the police due to the social stigma attached to rape and molestation cases. Official statistics show that there has been a dramatic increase in the number of reported crimes against women.

Sexual Harassment

Half of the total number of crimes against women reported in 1990 related to molestation and harassment at the workplace. Eve teasing is a euphemism used for sexual harassment or molestation of women by men. Many activists blame the rising incidents of sexual harassment against women on the influence of "Western culture". In 1987, The Indecent Representation of Women (Prohibition) Act was passed to prohibit indecent representation of women through advertisements or in publications, writings, paintings.

In 1997, in a landmark judgement, the Supreme Court of India took a strong stand against sexual harassment of women in the workplace. The Court also laid down detailed guidelines for prevention and redressal of grievances. The National Commission for Women subsequently elaborated these guidelines into a Code of Conduct for employers.

While public urination is practised by men of all ages in India, it is socially unacceptable for girls and women to publicly urinate when restrooms are unavailable. In other countries such as Laos, Cambodia, and Vietnam public urination is practised by women when there are no toilets. Resisting urination leads to harassment and UTI in women.

Dowry

In 1961, the Government of India passed the Dowry Prohibition Act, making the dowry demands in wedding arrangements illegal. However, many cases of dowry-related domestic violence, suicides and murders have been reported. In the 1980s, numerous such cases were reported. However, recent reports show that the number of these crimes have reduced drastically.

In 1985, the Dowry Prohibition (maintenance of lists of presents to the bride and bridegroom) rules were framed. According to these rules, a signed list of presents given at the time of the marriage to the bride and the bridegroom should be maintained. The list should contain a brief description of each present, its approximate value, the name of whoever has given the present and his/her relationship to the person.

A 1997 report claimed that at least 5,000 women die each year because of dowry deaths, and at least a dozen die each day in 'kitchen fires' thought to be intentional. The term for this is "bride burning" and is criticized within India itself. Amongst the urban educated, such dowry abuse has reduced dramatically.

Child Marriage

Child marriage has been traditionally prevalent in India and continues to this day. Young girls live with their parents until they reach puberty. In the past, the child widows were condemned to a life of great agony, shaving heads, living in isolation, and shunned by the society. Although child marriage was outlawed in 1860, it is still a common practice.

According to UNICEF's "State of the World's Children-2009" report, 47% of India's women aged 20–24 were married before the legal age of 18, with 56% in rural areas. The report also showed that 40% of the world's child marriages occur in India.

Female Infanticides and Sex Selective Abortions

India has a highly masculine sex ratio, the chief reason being that many women die before reaching adulthood. Tribal societies in India have a less masculine sex ratio than all other caste groups. This, in spite of the fact that tribal communities have far lower levels of income, literacy and health facilities. It is therefore suggested by many experts, that the highly masculine sex ratio in India can be attributed to female infanticides and sex-selective abortions.

All medical tests that can be used to determine the sex of the child have been banned in India, due to incidents of these tests being used to get rid of unwanted female children before birth. Female infanticide (killing of girl infants) is still prevalent in some rural areas. The abuse of the dowry tradition has been one of the main reasons for sex-selective abortions and female infanticides in India.

Domestic Violence

The incidents of domestive violence are higher among the lower Socio-Economic Classes (SECs). There are various instances of an inebriated husband beating up the wife often leading to severe injuries. Domestic violence is also seen in the form of physical abuse. The Protection of Women from Domestic Violence Act, 2005 came into force on October 26, 2006.

Illegal Drug Trade

India is located between two major illicit opium producing centres in Asia - the Golden Crescent comprising Pakistan, Afghanistan and Iran and the Golden Triangle comprising Burma, Thailand and Laos.

Because of such geographical location, India experiences large amount of drug trafficking through the borders. India is the world's largest producer of licit opium. But opium is diverted to illicit international drug markets. India is a transshipment point for heroin from Southwest Asian countries like Afghanistan and Pakistan and from Southeast Asian countries like Burma, Laos, and Thailand. Heroin is smuggled from Pakistan and Burma, with some quantities transshipped through Nepal.

Most heroin shipped from India are destined for Europe. There have been reports of heroin smuggled from Mumbai to Nigeria for further export. In Maharashtra, Mumbai is an important centre for distribution of drug. The most commonly used drug in Mumbai is Indian heroin (called *desi mal* by the local population). Both public transportation (road and rail transportation) and private transportation are used for this drug trade. Drug trafficking affects the country in many ways.

- Drug abuse: Cultivation of illicit narcotic substances and drug trafficking affects the health of the individuals and destroy the economic structure of the family and society.
- Organized crime: Drug trafficking results in growth of organized crime which affects social security. Organised crime connects drug trafficking with corruption and money laundering.
- Political instability: Drug trafficking also aggravate the political instability in North-West and North-East India.

A survey conducted in 2003-2004 by Narcotics Control Bureau found that India has at least four million drug addicts. The most common drugs used in India are cannabis, hashish, opium and heroin. In 2006 alone, India's law enforcing agencies recovered 230 kg heroin and 203 kg of cocaine. In an annual government report in 2007, the United States named India among 20 major hubs for trafficking of illegal drugs along with Pakistan, Afghanistan and Burma. However, studies reveal that most of the criminals caught in this crime are either Nigerian or US nationals.

Several measures have been taken by the Government of India to combat drug trafficking in the country. India is a party of the Single Convention on Narcotic Drugs (1961), the Convention on Psychotropic Substances (1971), the Protocol Amending the Single Convention on Narcotic Drugs (1972) and the United Nations Convention Against Illicit Traffic in Narcotic Drugs and Psychotropic Substances (1988).

An Indo-Pakistani committee was set up in 1986 to prevent trafficking in narcotic drugs. India signed a convention with the United Arab Emirates in 1994 to control drug trafficking. In 1995, India signed an agreement with Egypt for investigation of drug cases and exchange of information and a Memorandum of Understanding of the Prevention of Illicit Trafficking in Drugs with Iran.

Arms Trafficking

According to a joint report published by Oxfam, Amnesty International and the International Action Network on Small Arms (IANSA) in 2006, there are around 40 million illegal small arms in India out of approximately 75 million in worldwide circulation. Majority of the illegal small arms make its way into the states of Bihar, Chhattisgarh, Uttar Pradesh, Jharkhand, Orissa and Madhya Pradesh.

In India, a used AK-47 costs $3,800 in black market. Large amount of illegal small arms are manufactured in various illegal arms factories in Uttar Pradesh and Bihar and sold on the black market for as little as $5.08. Chinese pistols are in demand in the illegal small arms market in India because they are easily available and cheaper. This trend poses a significant problem for the states of Bihar, Uttar Pradesh, Jharkhand, Chhattisgarh, Orissa, Maharashtra, West Bengal, Karnataka and Andhra Pradesh which have influence of Naxalism. The porous Indo-Nepal border is an entry point for Chinese pistols, AK-47 and M-16 rifles into India as these arms are used by the Naxalites who have ties to Maoists in Nepal.

In North-East India, there is a huge influx of small arms due to the insurgent groups operating there.

The small arms in North-East India come from insurgent groups in Burma, black market in South-East Asian countries like Pakistan, Bangladesh, Nepal and Sri Lanka, black market in Cambodia, the People's Republic of China, insurgent groups like the Liberation Tigers of Tamil Eelam, the Communist Party of India (Maoist), the Communist Party of Nepal (Maoist), Indian states like Uttar Pradesh and pilferages from legal gun factories, criminal organizations operating in India and South Asian countries and other international markets like Romania, Germany etc. The small arms found in North-East India are M14 rifle, M16 rifle, AK-47, AK-56, AK-74, light machine guns, Chinese hand grenades, mines, rocket-propelled grenades, submachine guns etc.

The Ministry of External Affairs and Ministry of Home Affairs drafted a joint proposal to the United Nations, seeking a global ban on small-arms sales to non-state users.

Poaching and Wildlife Trafficking

Illegal wildlife trade in India has increased. According to a report published by the Environmental Investigation Agency (EIA) in 2004, India is the chief target for the traders of wildlife skin. Between 1994 and 2003, there have been 784 cases where the skins of tiger, leopard or otter have been seized. Leopards, rhinoceros, reptiles, birds, insects, rare species of plants are being smuggled into the countries in Southeast Asia and the People's Republic of China. Between 1994 and 2003, poaching and seizure of 698 otters have been documented in India. Kathmandu is a key staging point for illegal skins smuggled from India bound for Tibet and PRC. The report by EIA noted there has been a lack of cross-border cooperation between India, Nepal and the People's Republic of China to coordinate enforcement operations and lack of political will to treat wildlife crime effectively. The poaching of the elephants is a significant problem in Southern India and in the North-Eastern states of Nagaland and Mizoram. The majority of tiger poaching happen in Madhya Pradesh, Uttar Pradesh, Orissa, West Bengal, Assam and Arunachal Pradesh. Following is a comparison of reported cases of tiger and leopard poaching from 1998 to 2003:

Year	1998	1999	2000	2001	2002	2003
Reported cases of tiger poaching	14	38	39	35	47	8
Reported cases of leopard poaching	28	80	201	69	87	15

Samir Sinha, head of TRAFFIC India, the wildlife trade monitoring arm of the World Wide Fund for Nature (WWF) and the World Conservation Union (IUCN), told Reuters in an interview "The situation regarding the illegal trade in wildlife parts in India is very grim. It is a vast, a varied trade ranging from smuggling of rare medicinal plants to butterflies to peafowls to tigers and it is difficult to predict how big it is, but the threats and dimensions suggest that the trade is increasing".

Project Tiger, a wildlife conservation project, was initiated in 1972 and was launched by Indira Gandhi on April 1, 1973. With 23 tiger reserves, Project Tiger claimed to have succeeded. But according to critics like conservationist Billy Arjan Singh, temporary increases in tiger population were caused by immigration due to destruction of habitat in Nepal, not because of the widely acclaimed success of wildlife policy in India.

Cyber Crime

Cases of spam, computer hacking, cyber stalking and email fraud are rampant in India. The Information Technology Act 2000 was passed by the Parliament of India in May 2000, aiming to curb cyber crimes and provide a legal framework for e-commerce transactions. However Pavan Duggal, lawyer of Supreme Court of India and cyber law expert, viewed "The IT Act, 2000, is primarily meant to be a legislation to promote e-commerce. It is not very effective in dealing with several emerging cyber crimes like cyber harassment, defamation, stalking and so on". Although cyber crime cells have been set up in major cities, Duggal noted the problem is that most cases remain unreported due to a lack of awareness. In 2001, India and United States had set up an India-US cyber security forum as part of a counter-terrorism dialogue. In 2006, India and the US agreed to enhance cooperation between law enforcement agencies of the two countries in tackling cyber crimes as part of counter-terrorism efforts. A joint US-India statement released in 2006 after talks between US President George W. Bush and Indian Prime Minister Manmohan Singh stressed that in view of the importance of cyber security and cyber forensic research, the two countries are also carrying out discussions on a draft protocol on cyber security.

Corruption and Police Misconduct

Corruption is widespread in India. It is prevalent within every section and every level of the society. Corruption has taken the role of a pervasive aspect of Indian politics. In India, corruption takes the form of bribes, evasion of tax and exchange controls, embezzlement, etc.

Despite state prohibitions against torture and custodial misconduct by the police, torture is widespread in police custody, which is a major reason behind deaths in custody. The police often torture innocent people until a 'confession' is obtained to save influential and wealthy offenders. G.P. Joshi, the programme coordinator of the Indian branch of the Commonwealth Human Rights Initiative in New Delhi comments that the main issue at hand concerning police violence is a lack of accountability of the police.

In 2006, the Supreme Court of India in a judgment in the *Prakash Singh vs. Union of India* case, ordered central and state governments with seven directives to begin the process of police reform. The main objectives of this set of directives was twofold, providing tenure to and streamlining the appointment/transfer processes of policemen, and increasing the accountability of the police.

In 2006, seven policemen were charge sheeted and eleven were convicted for custodial misconduct.

Crime over Time

A report published by the National Crime Records Bureau compared crime rate from 1953 to 2006. The report noted that burglary declined over a period of 53 years by 38% (from 1,47,379 in 1953 to 91,666 in 2006), whereas murder has increased by 231% (from 9,803 in 1953 to 32,481 in 2006). Kidnapping has increased by 356% (from 5,261 in 1953 to 23,991 in 2006), robbery by 120% (from 8,407 in 1953 to 18,456 in 2006) and riots by 176% (from 20,529 in 1953 to 56,641 in 2006).

Crime by Locale

Location has a significant impact on crime in India. In 2006, the highest crime rate was reported in Pondicherry (447.7%) for crimes under Indian Penal Code which is 2.7 times the national crime rate of 167.7%. Kerala reported the highest crime rate at 312.5% among states.. However this is attributed to Kerala's higher literacy awareness among locals, thereby reporting crimes at police stations, which don't happens in many other states in India.

Kolkata (71.0%) and Madurai (206.2%) were the only two mega cities which reported less crime rate than their domain states West Bengal (79.0%) and Tamil Nadu (227.6%). Delhi, Mumbai and Bangalore have accounted for 16.2%, 9.5% and 8.1% respectively of the total IPC crimes reported from 35 mega cities. Indore reported the highest crime rate (769.1%) among the mega cities in India followed by Bhopal (719.5%) and Jaipur (597.1%).

Jammu & Kashmir (33.7%), Manipur (33.0%), Assam (30.4%) and Daman and Diu and Pondicherry (29.4%) reported higher violent crime rate compared to 18.4% at national level. Uttar Pradesh reported the highest incidence of violent crimes accounting for 12.1% of total violent crimes in India (24,851 out of 2,05,656) followed by Bihar with 11.8% (24,271 out of 2,05,6556). Among 35 mega cities, Delhi reported 31.2% (533 out of 1,706) of total rape cases. Madhya Pradesh has reported the highest number of rape cases (2,900) accounting for 15.0% of total such cases reported in the country. Uttar Pradesh reported 16.9% (5,480 out of 32,481) of total murder cases in the country and 18.4% (4,997 out of 27,230) total attempt to murder cases.

Crimes against Foreigners in India

There are some instances of violent crime against foreigners in India. Many of the crimes occur against foreigners only. Scams involving export of jewels occur in India, which target foreign citizens.

Political demonstrations are common in India. These demonstrations often turn violent and routinely cause disruption of transportation services, causing great inconvenience to foreign tourists in India. Traveling alone in remote areas after dark is of particular risk to foreigners.

Because U.S. citizens' purchasing power is relatively large compared to the general Indian population, they the preferred target for robbery and other serious crime.

In April 1999, Swaraj Damree, a tourist from Mauritius was befriended by a group of Indians who later held him in 25 days of captivity. They robbed him of cash amounting to US $1,500, took his travellers' cheques, wrist watch, gold chain, bracelet, two bags and suitcase. In 2000, two German trekkers were shot in Himachal Pradesh. A few weeks later, two Spanish tourists were killed in Himachal Pradesh by robbers. Many foreign tourists are victims of violent crime in Kolkata. In September 2006, criminals robbed the wallet of a British woman in Kolkata. The same month, a Japanese tourist was robbed on his way to Sudder Street. In October 2006, a foreigner was robbed in daylight on Park Street.

Petty Crime

Petty crime, like pickpocketing, bag snatching etc. are widespread in India. Theft of valuables of foreigners from luggage on trains and buses is common. Travellers who are not in groups become easy victims of pickpockets and purse snatchers. Purse snatchers work in crowded areas.

Passport Theft

In India, stealing passports of foreigners from their luggage on trains and buses is widespread. Theft of U.S. passports is very common, especially in major tourist areas.

Confidence Tricks

Many scams are perpetrated against foreign travellers, especially in Jaipur, the capital of Rajasthan. Scams usually target younger foreign tourists and suggest them that money can be made by privately transporting gems or gold or by taking delivery abroad of expensive carpets avoiding customs duties.

Such incidents pull the traveller over the course of several days and begin with a new scam artist who offers to show the foreign traveller the sights. They also offer cheap lodgings and meals to foreign travellers so that they can place the traveller in the physical custody of the scam artist and can leave the foreigner with threats and physical coercion. In the due process, the foreigner loses his passport.

Taxi Scam

There are also taxi scams present in India, whereby a foreign traveller, who is not aware of the locations around Indian airports, is taken for a ride round the whole airport and charged for full-fare taxi ride while the terminal is only few hundred yards away.

Overseas Security Advisory Council in a report mentioned the process about how to avoid taxi-scam.

Rape and Sexual Assault

Incidents of rape and sexual assault against foreign tourists at popular tourist spots is increasing in India. Many of the alleged perpetrators are children of senior government officials or politicians. In September 1994, Gurkirat Singh, grandson of the then CM Beant Singh, was accused of abducting and molesting a French tourist Katia Darnand in Chandigarh. In March 2006, Biti Mohanty, son of a senior police official in Orissa, raped a German tourist in Alwar, Rajasthan. A Japanese woman was raped in Pushkar, Rajasthan on April 2, 2006. In June 2007, a South Korean was raped near Manali. In September 2007, two Japanese women were gang-raped in Agra, a popular tourist-spot in India where the Taj Mahal is situated. The Indian state of Rajasthan, which is a popular destination among foreign tourists with one out of every three foreign travellers visiting the state, have been rattled by rape cases of foreign tourists. On December 5, 2009, a Russian woman was raped in Goa by a local politician John Fernandes. In February 2008, Scarlett Keeling, a British national aged 15 was raped and killed in Goa. In January 2010, a Russian girl aged 9 was raped in Goa; referring to this and earlier cases, Russia threatened to issue an advisory asking its citizens not to travel to the coastal state. The US Bureau of Consular Affairs has warned women not to travel alone in India. However in contrast the British Foreign office only advise them to take normal precautions.

Judiciary of India

Indian Judiciary is the continuation of the British Legal system established by the English in the mid-19th century. Before the arrival of the Europeans in India, she was governed by laws based on The Arthashastra, dating from the 400 BC, and the Manusmriti from 100 AD. In fact there existed two codes of laws one the Hindu code of laws and the other Muslim code of laws. They were influential treatises in India, texts that were considered authoritative legal guidance. Manu's central philosophy was tolerance and pluralism. The Judiciary, the Executive, and the Legislature were the same person the King or the Ruler of the Land. But the villages had considerable independence, and had their own panchayth system to resolve disputes among its members. Only a bigger feud merited a trans village council. This tradition in India continued beyond the Islamic conquest of India, and through to the Middle Ages. Islamic law "The Sharia" was applied only to the Muslims of the country. But this tradition, along with Islamic law, was supplanted by the common law when India became part of the British Empire. The history of Modern Judicial System in India starts from there.

The Supreme Court

The Supreme Court of India is the highest court of the land as established by Part five, Chapter four of the Constitution of India. According to the Constitution of India, the role of the Supreme Court is that of a federal court, guardian of the Constitution and the highest court of appeal. Articles 124 to 147 of the Constitution of India lay down the composition and jurisdiction of the Supreme Court of India. Primarily, it is an appellate court which takes up appeals against judgments of the High Courts of the states and territories. However, it also takes writ petitions in cases of serious human rights violations or any petetion filed under Article 32 which is the right to constitutional remedies or if a case involves a serious issue that needs immediate resolution. The Supreme Court of India had its inaugural sitting on 28 January 1950, and since then has delivered more than 24,000 reported judgments.

Issues

Indian courts have large backlogs. For instance, the Delhi High Court has a backlog of 466 years according to its chief justice. This is despite the average processing time of four minutes and 55 seconds in the court. In Uttam Nakate case, it took two decades to solve a simple employment dispute. However it need to be mentioned that the concept of backlogs doesn't describe the actual reason for some many cases lying in the courts. Rather the term "backlog" has been misused and the term "pendency" is the right word for describing the large number of cases pending in the courts today. As could be understood, the largest number of cases that are actually pending in the Indian Courts are that of minor Motor Vehicle

Cases, which evolves out of wrong parking, minor road accidents, not following traffic rules, etc. In this cases, the people involved are generally the drivers, who happen to carry 3-4 driving licences having different addressess. Thus, the actual address is never given to the police officer, due to which the accused couldn't be produced before the court for years at end and many times never.

Corruption is rampant in India's courts. According to Transparency International, judicial corruption in India is attributable to factors such as "delays in the disposal of cases, shortage of judges and complex procedures, all of which are exacerbated by a preponderance of new laws".

7

Ethno Methodology in Court

A court is a form of tribunal, often a governmental institution, with the authority to adjudicate legal disputes between parties and carry out the administration of justice in civil, criminal, and administrative matters in accordance with the rule of law. In both common law and civil law legal systems, courts are the central means for dispute resolution, and it is generally understood that all persons have an ability to bring their claims before a court. Similarly, the rights of those accused of a crime include the right to present a defence before a court.

The system of courts that interpret and apply the law are collectively known as the judiciary. The place where a court sits is known as a venue. The room where court proceedings occur is known as a courtroom, and the building as a courthouse; court facilities range from simple and very small facilities in rural communities to huge buildings in large cities.

The practical authority given to the court is known as its jurisdiction (Latin *jus dicere*) — the court's power to decide certain kinds of questions or petitions put to it. According to William Blackstone's *Commentaries on the Laws of England,* a court is constituted by a minimum of three parties: the *actor* or plaintiff, who complains of an injury done; the *reus* or defendant, who is called upon to make satisfaction for it, and the *judex* or judicial power, which is to examine the truth of the fact, to determine the law arising upon that fact, and, if any injury appears to have been done, to ascertain and by its officers to apply a legal remedy. It is also usual in the superior courts to have attorneys, and advocates or counsel, as assistants, though, often, courts consist of additional attorneys, bailiffs, reporters, and perhaps a jury.

The term "the court" is also used to refer to the presiding officer or officials, usually one or more judges. The judge or panel of judges may also be collectively referred to as "the bench" (in contrast to attorneys and barristers, collectively referred to as "the bar"). In the United States, and other common law jurisdictions, the term "court" (in the case of U.S. federal courts) by law is used to describe the judge himself or herself.

In the United States, the legal authority of a court to take action is based on personal jurisdiction, subject-matter jurisdiction, and venue over the parties to the litigation.

Etymology

The word *court* comes from the French *cour*, an enclosed yard, which derives from the Latin form *cortem*, the accusative case of *cohors*, which again means an enclosed yard or the occupants of such a yard (from *hortus* = garden). The meaning of a judicial assembly is first attested in the 12th century, and derives from the earlier usage to designate a sovereign and his entourage, which met to adjudicate disputes in such an enclosed yard. The verb "to court", meaning to win favour, derives from the same source since people travelled to the sovereign's court to win his favour.

Jurisdiction

Jurisdiction, meaning "to speak the law," is the power of a court over a person or a claim. In the United States, a court must have both personal jurisdiction and subject matter jurisdiction. Each state establishes a court system for the territory under its control. This system allocates work to courts or authorized individuals by granting both civil and criminal jurisdiction (in the United States, this is termed subject-matter jurisdiction). The grant of power to each category of court or individual may stem from a provision of a written constitution or from an enabling statute. In English law, jurisdiction may be *inherent*, deriving from the common law origin of the particular court.

Trial and Appellate Courts

Trial courts are courts that hold trials. Sometimes termed "courts of first instance," trial courts have original jurisdiction over most cases. Trial courts may conduct trials with juries are the finders of fact (these are known as jury trials) or trials in which judges act as both finders of fact and finders of law (these are known as bench trials). Juries are less common in court systems outside the Anglo-American common law tradition.

Appellate courts are courts that hear appeals of lower courts and trial courts.

Civil Law Courts and Common Law Courts

The two major models for courts are the civil law courts and the common law courts. Civil law courts are based upon the judicial system in France, while the common law courts are based on the judicial system in England. In most civil law jurisdictions, courts function under an inquisitorial system. In the common law system, most courts follow the adversarial system. Procedural law governs the rules by which courts operate: civil procedure for private disputes (for example); and criminal procedure for violation of the criminal law.

Sanctions

Sanctions are penalties or other means of enforcement used to provide incentives for obedience with the law, or with rules and regulations. Criminal sanctions can take the form of serious punishment, such as corporal or capital punishment, incarceration, or severe fines. Within the civil law context, sanctions are usually monetary fines, levied against a party to a lawsuit or his/her attorney, for violating rules of procedure, or for abusing the judicial process.

The most severe sanction in a civil lawsuit is the involuntary dismissal, with prejudice, of a complaining party's cause of action, or of the responding party's answer. This has the effect of deciding the entire action against the sanctioned party without recourse, except to the degree that an appeal or trial *de novo* may be allowed because of reversible error. As a noun, the term is usually used in the plural, even when it refers to a single event: if a judge fines a party, it is not said that he or she imposed a sanction, but that he or she imposed sanctions.

A judge may sanction a party during a legal proceeding, by which it is meant that he or she imposes penalties. In the United States federal court system, certain types of conduct are sanctionable under Rule 11 of the Federal Rules of Civil Procedure.

Conversely and to some surprisingly, the word may be used to mean "approve of," especially in an official sense. "The law sanctions such behaviour" would mean that the behaviour spoken of enjoys the specific approval of law.

Crime and Punishment

The crime problem in the United States has historically been misstated and exaggerated by bureaucrats and politicians. The intentions behind these overstatements vary within each context but a common thread emerges upon closer examination. As in any capitalist society, money and material possession are the primary motivation that fuels society and people. It could be argued that FBI director Louis Freeh made his comments to the National Press Club in 1994 out of genuine concern for the American people, but realistically the statement was made in an effort to gather support and increase funding for law enforcement. Following this statement and from increased pressure from politicians, the Federal Crime Bill was ratified, and authorized the spending of thirty billion dollars, primarily towards more police officers and prisons. It also included many new punitive sanctions and the expansion of the death penalty to more than fifty federal crimes. Louis Freeh's politically correct and unapprised proclamation takes an exceptionally narrow view of crime and its curtailment. Freeh chooses to focus on the media, statistics, and ultimately public opinion as his justification for increased funding. However he fails to realize the influence of the media and statistics in molding public opinion and the difference between public opinion and reality. Existing individualistic theories such as rational choice theory help reinforce Freeh's statement. The overstated crime problem, backed by a capitalistic media and misinterpreted statistics has created a punitive crime policy, which is further supported by individualistic theories of crime. In this paper I will show how misreported statistics and media focus on violent crimes shapes public opinion. Then I will go on to demonstrate the role of individualistic theories in supporting punitive crime control policies. Ultimately I look to prove that the actions of the media and politicians are centred on money and how crime is inherent to the American Dream.

The media never has been and probably never will be an accurate source for criminology or criminal analysis. The sensationalist media depiction of crime is almost always exaggerated and biased toward violent crimes. From newspapers to television the crimes that get the most coverage and attention are homicides and aggravated assaults. However, in actuality ninety percent of all crimes are property crimes and less than one percent are homicides. The media also is fond of reporting crime clocks based on aggregate statistics. Popular and catchy lines like, "A murder occurs every twenty seven minutes, a robbery every sixty seconds," are very misleading yet are used regularly. These crime clocks show no reference to a ratio between crimes being committed and the people effected. Once again here the motives behind depiction of crime by the media vary, but money can be found at the source. Newspapers and television stations don't want to report common and usually petty crimes because they are boring and monotonous. People don't buy boring and monotonous newspapers; so to increase circulation and ultimately revenues, editors choose to emphasize and embellish violent crimes. This intentional bias towards violent crimes, even though they represent a very small fraction of all crimes creates a sense of apprehension and concern in law-abiding citizens.

Television is also responsible for exaggerating crime and over emphasizing its focus on violent crimes. Where newspapers can only provide writing and limited photographs of crime, television can take the next step in showing (versus telling) the crime and criminals. The television show "COPS" is an excellent example of the misrepresentation of crime and law enforcement. On the show you never see routine traffic stops or officers writing parking tickets, rather the producers choose to show shootings, gang fights and drug offenders. People throughout the country get to see criminals actually breaking the law on television. Given that the majority of the scenes shown are of violent crimes, people construct a violent and evil image of all criminals. While in reality the majority of police work is mundane, the show attempts to glamorize crime fighting. These producers don't care about how they are depicting crime or its consequences; they are simply concerned about TV ratings. Higher ratings mean advertisers must pay more money for airtime, which ultimately leads to more money for the television networks.

By constantly and disproportionately reporting violent crimes, the media influence the general public into thinking there is a bad crime problem. The media produces several criminal fallacies and strongly influences the public's opinion on crime. The dramatic fallacy has been discussed above as it relates to the overemphasis on violent and extreme crimes. The "not me" fallacy helps create a distinction between criminals and non-criminals. By creating a distinction, people tend to believe they are not capable of committing violent crimes and that criminals are inherently evil and different from the rest of society. "Contrary to popular perception, the expansion of the U.S. prison and jail populations are not the direct result of a worsening or an exceptionally bad crime problem...rates of violent and property crime have been in decline". Since the vast majority of crimes people hear and see in the news are violent and heinous, they assume that there is a crime problem and that something must be done to stop it.

The statistics that the media enjoys to misinterpret and report misleadingly is primarily taken from the uniform crime report. The uniform crime report is aggregate data taken from 17,000 law enforcement agencies and compiled annually by the federal bureau of investigation. Organizational and presentational concerns arise from the uniform crime report. There are significant omissions in the report such as white-collar and environmental crimes. Also the definition of crimes chosen by the agencies greatly manipulates the data. For example some jurisdictions define rape as the forceful act of sexual intercourse, this omits the entire category of date rape. Law enforcement agencies have a direct interest in the reporting of crimes and crime rates. If they report that crime is on the decline, then people will feel more secure and satisfied with law enforcement but funding will be decreased. Conversely if they report that crime is increasing, and make the public feel at risk, an increase in funding will occur and be justified.

Individualistic theories of crime serve to contribute support to the image of the bad crime problem and encourage punitive crime control policies. The two hundred year old rational choice theory defines human behaviour through the two principles that humans act in order to maximize pleasure and minimize pain. This very Hedonistic theory facilitates the creation of punitive polices because it creates a need to harshly punish self-indulgent crimes.

Throughout the 1980's and 1990's there was a rapid influx of punitive crime policies like the creation of long mandatory prison sentences for drug possession and the expansion of the death penalty. The biological deterministic theory highlighted by C. Ronald Huff in Historical Explanations of Crime defines a "criminal type, or 'born criminal'"(Huff 75). The theory works hand in hand with the media depiction of criminals. It tries to show criminals as separate and distinct entities that are different from the rest of society. In this theory it is ineffective to deter crime since criminals are unalterable and predestined to break the law. Biological individualistic theories should be analysed and critiqued with rigorous scrutiny. Although many of the sources for data acquisition in this theory are objective, the consequences and conclusions drawn from the data are subjective and open to argument.

In order to curb crime based on the rational choice theory, lawmakers have fashioned policy around preventative measures. The foundation of preventive policy is based on controlling the physical environment. Examples of preventive measures are gated communities, target hardening, and neighbourhood watch programs. Although these policies are effective in curtailing crime in their specific contexts, "measures which increase the difficulties of a particular crime will merely result in criminal activity being 'displaced'". A criminal isn't going to break a law that is heavily policed and enforced because his chances of getting caught are greater.

To counter the supposed pressing crime problem, bureaucrats and politicians alike have adopted a very punitive system of crime control. They claim that, "The people of this country are fed up with crime" and that the people are the ones demanding better crime control (Louis Freeh, 1994). Gallup polls from 1993 to 1998 showed that crime was the most pressing problem in public opinion. In actuality during this same time period the crime rate has been decreasing annually which does not justify the tremendous rise in government spending that has been allocated to the criminal justice system. This goes to show that public opinion does not necessarily mimic or reflect the true reality of the situation. Public opinion can be easily shaped and moulded by forces such as media and politicians. More responsibility must be taken by the media in reporting statistics and crime because of their influence on public opinion. When influential leaders like Louis Freeh make statements based on the opinion of the masses instead of facts, the false crime problem is further worsened and perpetuated.

The Functions of Crime Control

According to control theorists, people do not engage in crime because of the controls or restraints placed on them. These controls may be viewed as barriers to crime—they refer to those factors that prevent them from engaging in crime. So while strain and social learning theory focus on those factors that push or lead the individual into crime, control theory focuses on the factors that restrain the individual from engaging in crime. Control theory goes on to argue that people differ in their level of control or in the restraints they face to crime. These differences explain differences in crime: some people are freer to engage in crime than others.

Control theories describe the major types of social control or the major restraints to crime. The control theory of Travis Hirschi dominates the literature, but Gerald Patterson and associates, Michael Gottfredson and Travis Hirschi, and Robert Sampson and John Laub have extended Hirschi's theory in important ways. Rather than describing the different versions of control theory, an integrated control theory that draws on all of their insights is presented.

This integrated theory lists three major types of control: direct control, stake in conformity, and internal control. Each type has two or more components.

Direct control. When most people think of control they think of direct control: someone watching over people and sanctioning them for crime. Such control may be exercised by family members, school officials, coworkers, neighbourhood residents, police, and others. Family members, however, are the major source of direct control given their intimate relationship with the person. Direct control has three components: setting rules, monitoring behaviour, and sanctioning crime.

Direct control is enhanced to the extent that family members and others provide the person with clearly defined rules that prohibit criminal behaviour and that limit the opportunities and temptations for crime. These rules may specify such things as who the person may associate with and the activities in which they can and cannot engage.

Direct control also involves monitoring the person's behaviour to ensure that they comply with these rules and do not engage in crime. Monitoring may be direct or indirect. In direct monitoring, the person is under the direct surveillance of a parent or other conventional "authority figure." In indirect monitoring, the parent or authority figure does not directly observe the person but makes an effort to keep tabs on what they are doing. The parent, for example, may ask the juvenile where he or she is going, may periodically call the juvenile, and may ask others about the juvenile's behaviour. People obviously differ in the extent to which their behaviour is monitored.

Finally, direct control involves effectively sanctioning crime when it occurs. Effective sanctions are consistent, fair, and not overly harsh.

Level of direct control usually emerges as an important cause of crime in most studies.

Stake in conformity. The efforts to directly control behaviour are a major restraint to crime. These efforts, however, are more effective with some people than with others. For example, all juveniles are subject to more or less the same direct controls at school: the same rules, the same monitoring, and the same sanctions if they deviate. Yet some juveniles are very responsive to these controls while others commit deviant acts on a regular basis. One reason for this is that some juveniles have more to lose by engaging in deviance. These juveniles have what has been called a high "stake in conformity," and they do not want to jeopardize that stake by engaging in deviance.

So one's stake in conformity—that which one has to lose by engaging in crime—functions as another major restraint to crime. Those with a lot to lose will be more fearful of being caught and sanctioned and so will be less likely to engage in crime. People's stake in conformity has two components: their emotional attachment to conventional others and their actual or anticipated investment in conventional society.

If people have a strong emotional attachment to conventional others, like family members and teachers, they have more to lose by engaging in crime. Their crime may upset people they care about, cause them to think badly of them, and possibly disrupt their relationship with them. Studies generally confirm the importance of this bond. Individuals who report that they love and respect their parents and other conventional figures usually commit fewer crimes. Individuals who do not care about their parents or others, however, have less to lose by engaging in crime.

A second major component of people's stake in conformity is their investment in conventional society. Most people have put a lot of time and energy into conventional activities, like "getting an education, building up a business, [and] acquiring a reputation for virtue". And they have been rewarded for their efforts, in the form of such things as good grades, material possessions, and a good reputation. Individuals may also expect their efforts to reap certain rewards in the future; for example, one might anticipate getting into college or professional school, obtaining a good job, and living in a nice house. In short, people have a large investment—both actual and anticipated—in conventional society. People do not want to jeopardize that investment by engaging in delinquency.

Internal control. People sometimes find themselves in situations where they are tempted to engage in crime and the probability of external sanction (and the loss of those things they value) is low. Yet many people still refrain from crime. The reason is that they are high in internal control. They are able to restrain themselves from engaging in crime. Internal control is a function of their beliefs regarding crime and their level of self-control.

Most people believe that crime is wrong and this belief acts as a major restraint to crime. The extent to which people believe that crime is wrong is at least partly a function of their level of direct control and their stake in conformity: were they closely attached to their parents and did their parents attempt to teach them that crime is wrong? If not, such individuals may form an *amoral orientation* to crime: they believe that crime is neither good nor bad. As a consequence, their beliefs do not restrain them from engaging in crime. Their beliefs do not propel or push them into crime; they do not believe that crime is good. Their amoral beliefs simply free them to pursue their needs and desires in the most expedient way. Rather then being taught that crime is good, control theorists argue that some people are simply not taught that crime is bad.

Finally, some people have personality traits that make them less responsive to the above controls and less able to restrain themselves from acting on their immediate desires. For example, if someone provokes them, they are more likely to get into a fight. Or if someone offers them drugs at a party, they are more likely to accept. They do not stop to consider the long-term consequences of their behaviour. Rather, they simply focus on the immediate, short-term benefits or pleasures of criminal acts. Such individuals are said to be low in "self-control."

Self-control is indexed by several personality traits. According to Gottfredson and Hirschi, "people who lack self control will tend to be impulsive, insensitive, physical (as opposed to mental), risk-taking, short-sighted, and nonverbal". It is claimed that the major cause of low self-control is "ineffective child-rearing." In particular, low self-control is more likely to result when parents do not establish a strong emotional bond with their children and do not properly monitor and sanction their children for delinquency. Certain theorists also claim that some of the traits characterizing low self-control have biological as well as social causes.

Gottfredson and Hirschi claim that one's level of self-control is determined early in life and is then quite resistant to change. Further, they claim that low self-control is the central cause of crime; other types of control and other causes of crime are said to be unimportant once level of self-control is established. Data do indicate that low self-control is an important cause of crime. Data, however, suggest that the self-control does vary over the life course and that other causes of crime are also important.

For example, Sampson and Laub demonstrate that delinquent adolescents who enter satisfying marriages and obtain stable jobs (i.e., develop a strong stake in conformity) are less likely to engage in crime as adults.

In sum, crime is less likely when others try to directly control the person's behaviour, when the person has a lot to lose by engaging in crime, and when the person tries to control his or her own behaviour.

Crime control model refers to a theory of criminal justice which places emphasis on reducing the crime in society through increased police and prosecutorial powers and. In contrast, The "due process model" focuses on individual liberties and rights and is concerned with limiting the powers of government.

Crime control prioritizes the power of the government to protect society, with less emphasis on individual liberties. Those who take a stance favoring tough approaches to crime and criminals may be characterized as proponents of crime control, while those who seek to curb government intrusions and harassment of suspects favour a due process control model.

Social Control Theory as represented in the work of Travis Hirschi fits into the Positivist School, Neo-Classical School, and, later, Right Realism. It proposes that exploiting the process of socialization and social learning builds self-control and reduces the inclination to indulge in behaviour recognized as antisocial. It was derived from Functionalist theories of crime and Ivan Nye (1958) proposed that there are four types of control:

- Direct: by which punishment is threatened or applied for wrongful behaviour, and compliance is rewarded by parents, family, and authority figures.
- Internal: by which a youth refrains from delinquency through the conscience or superego.
- Indirect: by identification with those who influence behaviour, say because his or her delinquent act might cause pain and disappointment to parents and others with whom he or she has close relationships.
- Control through needs satisfaction, i.e. if all an individual's needs are met, there is no point in criminal activity.

Discussion

Social Control Theory proposes that people's relationships, commitments, values, norms, and beliefs encourage them not to break the law. Thus, if moral codes are internalized and individuals are tied into, and have a stake in their wider community, they will voluntarily limit their propensity to commit deviant acts. The theory seeks to understand the ways in which it is possible to reduce the likelihood of criminality developing in individuals. It does not consider motivational issues, simply stating that human beings may choose to engage in a wide range of activities, unless the range is limited by the processes of socialization and social learning. This derives from a Hobbesian view of human nature as represented in Leviathan, i.e. that all choices are constrained by implicit social contracts, agreements and arrangements among people. Thus, morality is created in the construction of social order, assigning costs and consequences to certain choices and defining some as evil, immoral and/or illegal.

Albert J. Reiss

The earliest form of the theory (or at least the earliest recorded) was proposed by Reiss (1951: 196) who defined delinquency as, "...behaviour consequent to the failure of personal and social controls." Personal control was defined as, "...the ability of the individual to refrain from meeting needs in ways which conflict with the norms and rules of the community" while social control was, "...the ability of social groups or institutions to make norms or rules effective." Reiss' version did not specify the sources of such "abilities" nor the specific control mechanisms leading to conformity, but he did assert that the failure of primary groups such as the family to provide reinforcement for non-delinquent roles and values was crucial to the explanation of delinquency.

Jackson Toby

Toby (1957), argued that "the uncommitted adolescent is a candidate for gang socialization." acknowledging "gang socialization" as part of the causal, motivational, dynamic leading to delinquency, but introduced the concept of "stakes in conformity" to explain "candidacy" for such learning experiences. He believed that all could be tempted into delinquency, but most refused because they considered that they had too much to lose. But the young who had few stakes or investments in conformity were more likely to be drawn into gang activity. The notion of "stakes in conformity" fits very well with concepts invoked in later versions of social control theory.

F. Ivan Nye

Nye (1958) not only elaborated a social control theory of delinquency, but specified ways to "operationalize" (measure) control mechanisms and related them to self-reports of delinquent behaviour. He formulated the theory having formally interviewed 780 young people in Washington State, but the sample was criticized because it contained no-one from an urban environment and those selected might be those more willing to describe their families unfavorably. Some were concerned that criminal activity was only mentioned in two of the questions so the extrapolations to crime in general were considered unsafe. Like Reiss, he focused on the family as a source of control. Moreover, Nye specified different types of control:

- direct control = punishments and rewards
- indirect control = affectionate identification with non-criminals; and
- internal control = conscience or sense of guilt.

Youth may be directly controlled through constraints imposed by parents, limiting the cpportunity for delinquency, as well as through parental rewards and punishments. However, they may be constrained when free from direct control by their anticipation of parental disapproval (indirect control), or through the development of a conscience, an internal constraint on behaviour. The focus on the family as a source of control was in marked contrast to the emphasis on economic circumstances as a source of criminogenic motivation at the time. Although he acknowledged motivational forces by stating that, "...some delinquent behaviour results from a combination of positive learning and weak and ineffective social control" (1958: 4), he adopted a control-theory position when he proposed that, "..most delinquent behaviour is the result of insufficient social control..."

Walter Reckless

Reckless (1961) developed Containment Theory by focusing on a youth's self-conception or self-image of being a good person as an insulator against peer pressure to engage in delinquency.

- inner containment = positive sense of self;
- outer containment = supervision and discipline.

This inner containment through self-images is developed within the family and is essentially formed by about the age of twelve. Outer containment was a reflection of strong social relationships with teachers and other sources of conventional socialization within the neighbourhood. The basic proposition is there are "pushes" and "pulls" that will produce delinquent behaviour unless they are counteracted by containment. The motivations to deviate as pushes are:

- discontent with living conditions and family conflicts;
- aggressiveness and hostility, perhaps due to biological factors; and
- frustration and boredom, say arising from membership of a minority group or through lack of opportunities to advance in school or find employment;

and the pulls are:

- delinquent peers, and
- delinquent subcultures.

David Matza

An analysis of 'neutralization' was developed by Sykes and Matza (1957) who believed that there was little difference between delinquents and non-delinquents, with delinquents engaging in non-delinquent behaviour most of the time.

They also asserted that most delinquents eventually opt out of the delinquent lifestyle as they grow older, suggesting that there is a basic code of morality in place but that the young are able to deviate by using techniques of neutralization, i.e. they can temporarily suspend the applicability of norms by developing attitudes "favorable to deviant behaviour". The five common techniques were:

- denial of responsibility (I couldn't help myself)
- denial of injury (nobody got hurt)
- denial of victim (they had it coming)
- condemnation of the condemners (what right do they have to criticize me?)
- appeal to higher loyalties (I did it for someone else).

Later Matza (1964) developed his theory of "drift" which proposed that people used neutralization to drift in and out of conventional behaviour, taking a temporary break from moral restraints. Matza based his "drift" theory upon four observations which were:

- Delinquents express guilt over their criminal acts
- Delinquents often respect law-abiding individuals
- A line is drawn between those they can victimize and those they can not
- Delinquents are not immune to the demands of conforming.

Although Drift Theory has not been widely supported by empirical tests, it remains a key idea in criminology despite not answering why some conform and others don't.

Travis Hirschi

Hirschi adopted Toby's concept of an investment in conventionality or "stake in conformity". He stressed the rationality in the decision whether to engage in crime and argued that a person was less likely to choose crime if they had strong social bonds.

The General Theory of Crime

Hirschi has since moved away from his bonding theory, and in cooperation with Gottfredson, developed a General Theory or "Self-Control Theory" in 1990. Akers (1991) argued that a major weakness of this new theory was that Gottfredson and Hirschi did not define self-control and the tendency toward criminal behaviour separately. By not deliberately operationalized self-control traits and criminal behaviour or criminal acts individually, it suggests that the concepts of low self-control and propensity for criminal behaviour are the same. Hirschi and Gottfredson (1993) rebutted Akers argument by suggesting it was actually an indication of the consistency of General Theory. That is, the theory is internally consistent by conceptualizing crime and deriving from that a concept of the offender's traits. The research community remains divided on whether the General Theory is sustainable but there is emerging confirmation of some of its predictions.

Jack P. Gibbs

Gibbs (1989) has redefined social control and applied it to develop a control theory of homicide. Any attempt to get an individual to do or refrain from doing something can be considered an attempt at control. To qualify as 'social' control, such attempts must involve three parties. One or more individuals intends to manipulate the behaviour of another by or through a third party. Gibbs' third party can be an actual person or a reference to "society", "expectations" or "norms". For example, if one party attempts to influence another by threatening to refer the matter to a third party assumed to have authority, this is referential social control. If one party attempts to control another by punishing a third (e.g. general deterrence), it is a form of vicarious social control. The presence of the third party distinguishes social control from mere external behavioural control, simple interpersonal responses, or issuing orders for someone to do something. This definition clearly distinguishes social control from mere "reactions to deviance" and from deviant behaviour itself.

Gibbs argues that "Homicide can be described either as control or as resulting from control failure" (1989: 35), and proposes that the homicide rate is a function not just of the sheer volume of disputes, but also of the frequency of recourse to a third party for peaceful dispute settlement. When one person fails to control the actions of another through the third party, murder represents another violent attempt at direct control. People resort to self-help when forms of social control are unavailable or fail. Gibbs is critical of Hirschi's Social Control Theory because it merely assumes that social relationships, personal investments and beliefs that discourage delinquency are social controls (which is one reason why Hirschi's theory is often referred to as a Social Bond Theory).

Critique

Much of the early research is based on self-reporting studies which can be problematic because there may be different motives for disclosing information and, in any event, questions may be interpreted differently.

Nevertheless, many of the conclusions are intuitively convincing, e.g. that individuals will not engage in crime if they think that this will sacrifice the affection or respect of significant others, or cause them to lose employment or their autonomy if they face imprisonment. Davies (1994 and 2004) reports that, in the late-nineteenth century Britain, crime rates fell dramatically, as did drug and alcohol abuse, and illegitimacy became less common.

All these indexes of deviance were fairly steady between World War I and 1955. After 1955 they all rose to create a U-curve of deviance, over the period from 1847 to 1997. He attributes the initial shift to adoption of a culture in which the assumptions of Protestant Christianity were taken for granted. Few people believed strongly, but everyone believed a little in a moral code of helping others that was rooted in all religions. The same social norms for the defence of the person and property that informed the law before 1955 remain the policy norms. That more people are uncontrollable and may offend against those norms in social interactions cannot be explained by simply counting how many people practice the golden rule.

Anomie

Anomie is a sociological term meaning "personal feeling of a lack of social norms; normlessness". It describes the breakdown of social norms and values. It was popularized by French sociologist Émile Durkheim in his influential book *Suicide* (1897). Durkheim borrowed the word from French philosopher Jean-Marie Guyau.

For Durkheim, anomie arises more generally from a mismatch between personal or group standards and wider social standards, or from the lack of a social ethic, which produces moral deregulation and an absence of legitimate aspirations. This is a nurtured condition:

Anomie in common parlance is thought to mean something like "at loose ends". The Oxford English Dictionary lists a range of definitions, beginning with a disregard of divine law, through the 19th and 20th century sociological terms meaning an absence of accepted social standards or values. Most sociologists associate the term with Durkheim, who used the concept to speak of the ways in which an individual's actions are matched, or integrated, with a system of social norms and practices... Durkheim also formally posited anomie as a mismatch, not simply as the absence of norms. Thus, a society with too much rigidity and little individual discretion could also produce a kind of anomie, a mismatch between individual circumstances and larger social mores. Thus, fatalistic suicide arises when a person is too rule-governed, when there is... no free horizon of expectation.

History

In 1893, Durkheim introduced the concept of *anomie* to describe the mismatch of collective guild labour to evolving societal needs when the guild was homogeneous in its constituency. He equated homogeneous (redundant) skills to *mechanical solidarity* whose inertia retarded adaptation. He contrasted this with the self-regulating behaviour of a division of labour based on differences in constituency, equated to *organic solidarity*, whose lack of inertia made it differentially sensitive to need changes. Durkheim observed that these two labour forms could not co-exist. The conflict between the evolved organic division of labour and the homogeneous mechanical type was such that one could not long exist in the presence of the other: "This social type rests on principles so different from the preceding that it can develop only in proportion to the effacement of that preceding type". and "The history of these two types shows, in effect, that one has progressed only as the other has retrogressed". When solidarity is organic, anomie is "impossible whenever solidary organs are sufficiently in contact or sufficiently prolonged.

In effect, being contiguous, they are quickly warned, in each circumstance, of the need they have of one another, and, consequently, they have a lively and continuous sentiment of their mutual dependence. For the same reason that exchanges take place among them easily, they take place frequently, and in time the work of consolidation is achieved". Their sensitivity to mutual needs promotes the evolution in the division of labour "because the smallest reaction can be felt from one part to another.... they foresee and fix, in detail, the conditions of equilibrium". "Producers, being near consumers, can easily reckon the extent of the needs to be satisfied. Equilibrium is established without any trouble and production regulates itself." Durkheim contrasted the condition of anomie as being the result of mechanical solidarity: "But on the contrary, if some opaque environment is interposed, then only stimuli of certain intensity can be communicated from one organ to another. Relations being rare, are not repeated enough to be determined; each time there ensues new grouping. The lines of passage taken by the streams of movement cannot deepen because the streams themselves are too intermittent". "Contact is no longer sufficient. The producer can no longer embrace the market at a glance, nor even in thought. He can no longer see its limits, since it is, so to speak limitless. Accordingly, production becomes unbridled and unregulated."

Durkheim's use of the term anomie was about a phenomenon of industrialization—mass-regimentation that could not adapt due to its own inertia—its resistance to change, which causes disruptive cycles of collective behaviour (e.g. economics) due to the necessity of a prolonged buildup of sufficient force or momentum to overcome the inertia.

Later in 1897, in his studies of suicide, Durkheim associated anomie to the influence of a lack of norms or norms that were too rigid. But such normlessness or norm-rigidity was a *symptom of anomie*, caused by the lack of differential adaptation that would enable norms to evolve naturally due to self regulation, either to develop norms where none existed or to change norms that had become rigid and obsolete.

Etymology

The word comes from Greek, namely the prefix *a*- "without", and *nomos* "law". The Greeks distinguished between *nomos*, and *arché*. For example, a monarch is a single ruler but he or she might still be subject to, and not exempt from, the prevailing laws, i.e. *nomos*. In the original city state democracy, the majority rule was an aspect of *arché* because it was a rule-based, customary system which might or might not make laws, i.e. *nomos*. Thus, the original meaning of *anomie* defined anything or anyone against or outside the law, or a condition where the current laws were not applied resulting in a state of illegitimacy or lawlessness.

The contemporary English understanding of the word *anomie* can accept greater flexibility in the word "norm", and some have used the idea of normlessness to reflect a similar situation to the idea of anarchy. But, as used by Émile Durkheim and later theorists, *anomie* is a reaction against or a retreat from the regulatory social controls of society, and is a completely separate concept from anarchy which is an absence of effective rulers or leaders.

As Social Disorder

The nineteenth century French pioneer sociologist Émile Durkheim borrowed the word from French philosopher Jean-Marie Guyau and used it in his influential book *Suicide* (1897), outlining the social (and not individual) causes of suicide, characterized by an absence or diminution of standards or values (referred to as normlessness), and an associated feeling of alienation and purposelessness. He believed that *anomie* is common when the surrounding society has undergone significant changes in its economic fortunes, whether for good or for worse and, more generally, when there is a significant discrepancy between the ideological theories and values commonly professed and what was actually achievable in everyday life. This is contrary to previous theories on suicide which generally maintained that suicide was precipitated by negative events in a person's life and their subsequent depression.

In Durkheim's view, traditional religions often provided the basis for the shared values which the anomic individual lacks. Furthermore, he argued that the division of labour that had been prevalent in economic life since the Industrial Revolution led individuals to pursue egoistic ends rather than seeking the good of a larger community.

Robert King Merton also adopted the idea of *anomie* to develop Strain Theory, defining it as the discrepancy between common social goals and the legitimate means to attain those goals. In other words, an individual suffering from *anomie* would strive to attain the common goals of a specific society yet would not be able to reach these goals legitimately because of the structural limitations in society. As a result the individual would exhibit deviant behaviour. Friedrich Hayek notably uses the word *anomie* with this meaning.

According to one academic survey, psychometric testing confirmed a link between anomie on academic dishonesty among university students suggesting that universities needed to foster codes of ethics among students in order to curb it. In another it was seen as a "push factor" in tourism.

As an older variant, the Webster 1913 dictionary reports use of the word *anomie* as meaning "disregard or violation of the law" but anomie as a social disorder is not to be confused with *anarchy*.

Proponents of anarchism claim that anarchy does not necessarily lead to *anomie* and that hierarchical command actually increases lawlessness. Some subsets of anarchism, such as anarcho-primitivism argue in works such as Industrial Society and Its Future that conditions such as anomie are directly caused by complex societies, particularly industrial and post-industrial societies due to their deprivation of individual self-determination and a relatively small reference group to relate to, such as the band, clan, or tribe.

Culture and Subculture

In criminology, subcultural theory emerged from the work of the Chicago School on gangs and developed through the symbolic interactionism school into a set of theories arguing that certain groups or subcultures in society have values and attitudes that are conducive to crime and violence. The primary focus is on juvenile delinquency because theorists believe that if this pattern of offending can be understood and controlled, it will break the transition from teenage offender into habitual criminal. Some of the theories are functionalist assuming that criminal activity is motivated by economic needs, while others posit a social class rationale for deviance.

Definitions

Culture represents the norms, customs and values which both guide behaviour and act as a framework from which behaviour is judged by the majority. It is transmitted socially rather than biologically. A subculture is a distinctive culture within a culture, so its norms and values differ from the majority culture but do not necessarily represent a culture deemed deviant by the majority. A subculture is distinguished from a counterculture which operates in direct opposition to the majority culture.

Cultural Transmission Theory and Social Disorganization Theory posit that, in the poorest zones of a city, certain forms of behaviour become the cultural norm transmitted from one generation to the next, as part of the normal socialization process. Successful criminals are role models for the young, demonstrating both the possibilities of success through crime, and its normality. See Shaw (1930) who describes the social pressure to engage in criminality.

Subcultural Theory proposes that those living in an urban setting are able to find ways of creating a sense of community despite the prevailing alienation and anonymity. The cultural structure is dominated by the majority norms, which forces individuals to form communities in new and different ways. More recently, Fischer (1995) proposed that the size, population, and heterogeneity of cities actually strengthens social groups, and encourages the formation of subcultures, which are much more diverse in nature compared to the general culture. Fischer defines a subculture as, "...a large set of people who share a defining trait, associate with one another, are members of institutions associated with their defining trait, adhere to a distinct set of values, share a set of cultural tools and take part in a common way of life" (Fischer: 544). In less densely populated and less diverse environments, the creation of such subcultures would be nearly impossible. But ethnic minorities, professionals, the artistic avant-garde, displaced agricultural families, etc. come to live in cities and their lifestyles come to typify cities.

Frederic M. Thrasher

Frederic M. Thrasher (1927: 46) studied gangs in a systematic way, analysing gang activity and behaviour. He defined gangs by the process they go through to form a group:

"The gang is an interstitial group originally formed spontaneously, and then integrated through conflict. It is characterized by the following types of behaviour: meeting face to face, milling, movement through space as a unit, conflict, and planning. The result of this collective behaviour is the development of tradition, unreflective internal structure, *esprit de corps*, solidarity, morale, group awareness, and attachment to a local territory."

Thrasher maintained that gangs originate naturally during the adolescent years from spontaneous play groups which get into various kinds of mischief. They become gangs when they excite disapproval and opposition, thus acquiring a more definite group-consciousness. Like Durkheim and Merton, Thrasher described how the environment can be conducive to delinquent behaviour, that gang subcultures arose in the cracks, or "interstices," of urban neglect combined with the inner cracks of identity that occur in the turbulent years of adolescence. Shaw (1930) also described delinquency as a group activity which was transmitted from older to younger boys with the streets and jails of Chicago as their classrooms. Thrasher confirmed the work of the others in the School, finding the most gangs in the zone of transition with the highest incidence of single-parent families, unemployment, multiple family dwellings, welfare cases, and low levels of education. These were the slums, the ghetto, and the barrios and he found evidence of at least 1,313 gangs with an estimated 25,000 members who found a different way to acquire an identity and status. The gangs became a youth's reference group where main values, beliefs, and goals were formed and, in a sense, also became a family, offering a sense of belonging and self-esteem.

E. Franklin Frazier

In the earliest stages of the Chicago School and their investigation of human ecology, one of the key tropes was the concept of disorganization which contributed to the emergence of an underclass. Analysts have viewed the ghetto as symptomatic of poverty and disorganization, measuring the extent to which it diverges from middle-class values, representing it as a place of disorder, anomie and immorality. As the first African-American chair at Chicago, E. Franklin Frazier (1931) stressed the marital disruption, decadence, destitution, crime, and vice into which "Negroes" inevitably sank when migrating into the urban environment, using family structures as the determining feature of disorganization. Two subcultural issues have emerged:

- Frazier (1932) was interested to determine whether any West African customs survived in the U.S. According to the Creolists, the U.S. slave population and their descendants did not share a common culture and their customs, religious beliefs, dialects, and social structures varied too greatly to influence ethnic and cultural cohesiveness. Frazier who was of an extremely conservative creolist persuasion expounded that all cultural remnants of the indigenous culture had been destroyed in the melee of slavery and, in effect, the West African heritage had little or nothing to do with the present African American population in the U.S. Others of a revisionist persuasion, emphasized a continuity in African history and argued that there is a layering of cultures representing the diaspora populations in the New World.
- Frazier (1957) continued the discussion on social distance and what he terms the "common moral order",

chronicling the growing social class distinctions between moneyed African-Americans who mimic whites, and their less fortunate brethren. Frazier (1932) had noted in his history of slavery that where human relationships were established between masters and slaves, both were less likely to engage in cruelty toward each other. It is also known that debtor slaves were as a rule treated with more consideration than were foreign slaves obtained by capture and trade. This system of protective patronage continued in the relationship between white culture and the new black bourgeoisie.

Finally, Frazier discussed the question of whether the African American population was "over-churched" as a distinctive social structure. He identified five attributes of black families from a matriarchal perspective including strong achievement orientation, strong work orientation, flexible family roles, strong kinship bonds, and strong religious orientation which potentially introduced a gender bias into the subculture.

Albert K. Cohen

Albert K. Cohen (1955) did not look at the economically oriented career criminal, but looked at the delinquency subculture, focusing on gang delinquency among working class youth in slum areas which developed a distinctive culture as a response to their perceived lack of economic and social opportunity within U.S. society. He was a student of Edwin Sutherland (Differential Association Theory and Social Transmission Theory) and Merton's (Strain Theory). The features of this subculture were:

- anti-utilitarian: in many cases, there was no profit motive in thefts or other crimes. The main intention was to foster peer bonding through sharing the experience of breaking the laws.
- collective reaction formation: the gang inverted the values of the majority culture, deliberately pursuing the mirror image of the American Dream.
- malice: many acts of vandalism and property damage were motivated by spite, contempt, and personal intention to injure.

- short-termism: the gang lived for the moment, looking for instant gratification.
- group autonomy: everything was aimed at consolidating group loyalty.

Cohen (1958) explained this in terms similar to Strain Theory, (i.e. as a form of rebellion) in that education taught the young to strive for social status through academic achievement but, when most of the working class failed, this promoted "status frustration" or reaction formation, inverting middle-class values to strike back at the system that had let them down. Middle class values stress independence, success, academic achievement, delayed gratification, control of aggression, and respect for property. Lower class parents encourage different values in their children (i.e. different socialization). In lower class families ambition and planning must give way to pressing issues of the moment. They depend more on others, and have more of a group orientation, "watching each others backs".

Richard Cloward and Lloyd Ohlin

Richard Cloward and Lloyd Ohlin made reference to R. K. Merton's Strain Theory, while taking a further step in how the Subculture was 'Parallel' in their opportunities: the Criminal subculture had the same rules and level. It was, henceforth, a 'Illegitimate Opportunity Structure', which is parallel, yet still a polarization of the legitimate.

Cloward and Ohlin suggested that the route to delinquency involved one of three subcultures:

- Criminal: this represents Merton's 'innovators' in his *Anomie* Theory in which adolescents use crime for material gain. This subculture usually forms in areas where there is an established organization of adult crime that provides an "illegitimate opportunity structure" for youths to learn the "tricks of the trade".
- Conflict: this represents Merton's 'rebels' in his *Anomie* Theory, when an illegitimate opportunity structure is not available, delinquents often form conflicting gangs out of frustration at the lack of any available opportunity structures.

- Retreatist: this represents Merton's 'retreatists' in his *Anomie* Theory, this involves drug use and hustling, behaviour generally found among the "double failures" - those that cannot find acceptance in either legitimate groups or the two other subcultures.

Walter Miller

Miller (1958, 1959) agreed with Cohen that there was a delinquency subculture, but argued that it arose entirely from the lower class way of life. There was a clear distinction in values between the two social classes. Whereas the middle class is achievement and social goal oriented, Miller thought that lower class parents were more concerned with ensuring that their children stayed out of trouble, e.g. sons avoiding fights and daughters avoiding pregnancy. Boys were expected to be tough and street-smart which gave them an incentive to join a gang. Given that their ordinary lives were boring, the excitement of crime was a welcome relief, bringing a sense of autonomy by denying the social controls imposed by the state. For the middle class, the most important institutions are family, work, and (for the child) school. For the lower class another institution plays a crucial role – the same sex peer group or gang is more important than family, work or school because it offers a sense of belonging, and a way to achieve status that they cannot easily achieve in mainstream society. Thus, delinquency was not a reaction against middle class values but rather a means of living up to their own cultural expectations for toughness and smartness. Indeed, the gang only recruited the most "able" members, so membership of a gang confirmed high status. Most delinquency is non violent and while thefts are more common than any kind of assault, they are, relatively rare. violence when it does occur is a response to apparent insults or rejection by specific people, not a random outpouring of senseless aggression.

David Matza

David Matza (1964) argued that, rather than being committed to delinquency, young people drifted between conventional and unconventional behaviour. The initial socialization did introduce an understanding of social expectations and a sense of guilt if those expectations were not met, but that individuals developed techniques of neutralization to avoid feeling guilty. To some extent, society also helped to neutralize the guilt by blaming the parents for failing properly to supervise their children. Matza also argued that the search for excitement was classless. It was simply that working class youth had fewer opportunities for legitimate activities. Nevertheless, deviancy can be fun for everyone. There is a certain excitement in exercising free will and breaking rules knowing that there is little chance of being caught. This implies a degree of rational choice within structural constraints. The offenders are individuals who feel powerless. They are tired of being pushed around and simply feel like defying the system. If they are caught and come before a court, they appear victimized among their peer group and gain status.

P. Cohen

Phil Cohen (1972) studied the youth of East London in the early 1970s. He examined the immediate and the wider context to determine how two different youth subcultures reacted to the changes occurring in their community. He suggested that the Mod reaction was to the new ideology of affluence. They wanted to show that they had money and knew how to spend it. In contrast, skinheads looked back to the more traditional working class community. Each generation tries to find employment or adapts to unemployment. But the 1920s had very different economic circumstances to later decades. Cohen argued that youth develop a cultural style as a means of coping with their particular circumstances and of resisting the dominant values of society. This casts working class youth as the standard bearers of class struggle. There is little in real terms that youth can do to change society, but resistance offers subjective satisfaction which can be shown through style: the clothes, haircuts, music and language of the different youth cultures. Cohen argued that these styles are not meaningless, but are deeply layered in meaning. This is an application of Marxist Subcultural Theory which synthesised the structuralism of Marxism with the Labelling Theory. The approach matched that of the Centre for Contemporary Cultural Studies at Birmingham University. This approach places emphasis on the contents of youth culture and on the differences produced by class background. The assumption is that a capitalist society attempts to achieve hegemony by using the cultural values of society for their own benefit. The domination of the adults is enforced through the system of mortgages, credit cards, and family commitments, and they are seduced into accepting the relative security of capitalism. But the youth are relatively free of long term commitment or responsibility for a family and, with many unemployed, the youth are the weakest point in the structure of hegemony.

Control Theories

In criminology, Social Control Theory as represented in the work of Travis Hirschi fits into the Positivist School, Neo-Classical School, and, later, Right Realism. It proposes that exploiting the process of socialization and social learning builds self-control and reduces the inclination to indulge in behaviour recognized as antisocial. It was derived from Functionalist theories of crime and Ivan Nye (1958) proposed that there are four types of control:

- Direct: by which punishment is threatened or applied for wrongful behaviour, and compliance is rewarded by parents, family, and authority figures.
- Internal: by which a youth refrains from delinquency through the conscience or superego.
- Indirect: by identification with those who influence behaviour, say because his or her delinquent act might cause pain and disappointment to parents and others with whom he or she has close relationships.
- Control through needs satisfaction, i.e. if all an individual's needs are met, there is no point in criminal activity.

Discussion

Social Control Theory proposes that people's relationships, commitments, values, norms, and beliefs encourage them not to break the law. Thus, if moral codes are internalized and individuals are tied into, and have a stake in their wider community, they will voluntarily limit their propensity to commit deviant acts. The theory seeks to understand the ways in which it is possible to reduce the likelihood of criminality developing in individuals. It does not consider motivational issues, simply stating that human beings may choose to engage in a wide range of activities, unless the range is limited by the processes of socialization and social learning. This derives from a Hobbesian view of human nature as represented in Leviathan, i.e. that all choices are constrained by implicit social contracts, agreements and arrangements among people. Thus, morality is created in the construction of social order, assigning costs and consequences to certain choices and defining some as evil, immoral and/or illegal.

Albert J. Reiss

The earliest form of the theory (or at least the earliest recorded) was proposed by Reiss (1951: 196) who defined delinquency as, "...behaviour consequent to the failure of personal and social controls." Personal control was defined as, "...the ability of the individual to refrain from meeting needs in ways which conflict with the norms and rules of the community" while social control was, "...the ability of social groups or institutions to make norms or rules effective." Reiss' version did not specify the sources of such "abilities" nor the specific control mechanisms leading to conformity, but he did assert that the failure of primary groups such as the family to provide reinforcement for non-delinquent roles and values was crucial to the explanation of delinquency.

Jackson Toby

Toby (1957), argued that "the uncommitted adolescent is a candidate for gang socialization." acknowledging "gang socialization" as part of the causal, motivational, dynamic leading to delinquency, but introduced the concept of "stakes in conformity" to explain "candidacy" for such learning experiences. He believed that all could be tempted into delinquency, but most refused because they considered that they had too much to lose. But the young who had few stakes or investments in conformity were more likely to be drawn into gang activity. The notion of "stakes in conformity" fits very well with concepts invoked in later versions of social control theory.

F. Ivan Nye

Nye (1958) not only elaborated a social control theory of delinquency, but specified ways to "operationalize" (measure) control mechanisms and related them to self-reports of delinquent behaviour. He formulated the theory having formally interviewed 780 young people in Washington State, but the sample was criticized because it contained no-one from an urban environment and those selected might be those more willing to describe their families unfavorably. Some were concerned that criminal activity was only mentioned in two of the questions so the extrapolations to crime in general were considered unsafe. Like Reiss, he focused on the family as a source of control. Moreover, Nye specified different types of control:

- direct control = punishments and rewards
- indirect control = affectionate identification with non-criminals; and
- internal control = conscience or sense of guilt.

Youth may be directly controlled through constraints imposed by parents, limiting the opportunity for delinquency, as well as through parental rewards and punishments. However, they may be constrained when free from direct control by their anticipation of parental disapproval (indirect control), or through the development of a conscience, an internal constraint on behaviour. The focus on the family as a source of control was in marked contrast to the emphasis on economic circumstances as a source of criminogenic motivation at the time. Although he acknowledged motivational forces by stating that, "...some delinquent behaviour results from a combination of positive learning and weak and ineffective social control" (1958: 4), he adopted a control-theory position when he proposed that, "..most delinquent behaviour is the result of insufficient social control..."

Walter Reckless

Reckless (1961) developed Containment Theory by focusing on a youth's self-conception or self-image of being a good person as an insulator against peer pressure to engage in delinquency.

- inner containment = positive sense of self;
- outer containment = supervision and discipline.

This inner containment through self-images is developed within the family and is essentially formed by about the age of twelve. Outer containment was a reflection of strong social relationships with teachers and other sources of conventional socialization within the neighbourhood. The basic proposition is there are "pushes" and "pulls" that will produce delinquent behaviour unless they are counteracted by containment. The motivations to deviate as pushes are:

- discontent with living conditions and family conflicts;
- aggressiveness and hostility, perhaps due to biological factors; and
- frustration and boredom, say arising from membership of a minority group or through lack of opportunities to advance in school or find employment;

and the pulls are:

- delinquent peers, and
- delinquent subcultures.

David Matza

An analysis of 'neutralization' was developed by Sykes and Matza (1957) who believed that there was little difference between delinquents and non-delinquents, with delinquents engaging in non-delinquent behaviour most of the time. They also asserted that most delinquents eventually opt out of the delinquent lifestyle as they grow older, suggesting that there is a basic code of morality in place but that the young are able to deviate by using techniques of neutralization, i.e. they can temporarily suspend the applicability of norms by developing attitudes "favorable to deviant behaviour". The five common techniques were:

- denial of responsibility (I couldn't help myself)
- denial of injury (nobody got hurt)
- denial of victim (they had it coming)
- condemnation of the condemners (what right do they have to criticize me?)
- appeal to higher loyalties (I did it for someone else).

Later Matza (1964) developed his theory of "drift" which proposed that people used neutralization to drift in and out of conventional behaviour, taking a temporary break from moral restraints. Matza based his "drift" theory upon four observations which were:

- Delinquents express guilt over their criminal acts
- Delinquents often respect law-abiding individuals
- A line is drawn between those they can victimize and those they can not
- Delinquents are not immune to the demands of conforming

Although Drift Theory has not been widely supported by empirical tests, it remains a key idea in criminology despite not answering why some conform and others don't.

Travis Hirschi

Hirschi adopted Toby's concept of an investment in conventionality or "stake in conformity". He stressed the rationality in the decision whether to engage in crime and argued that a person was less likely to choose crime if they had strong social bonds.

The General Theory of Crime

Self-control Theory of Crime

The Self-control theory of crime, often referred to as the General Theory of Crime, is a criminological theory about the lack of individual self-control as the main factor behind criminal behaviour.

The theory was originally developed by criminologists Travis Hirschi and Michael Gottfredson, but has since been subject to a great deal of theoretical debate and a large and growing empirical literature.

Theory and Background

Springing from interest in bonding theory, Hirschi—in cooperation with Gottfredson—has developed the "General Theory of Crime" or *self-control theory* from 1990 onwards. Based on the empirical observation of the strong, consistent connection between criminal behaviour and age, Hirschi and Gottfredson theorized the single most important factor behind crime is individual lack of self-control. Individual self-control improves with age as a result of many factors: changing biology through hormonal development, socialization and increasing opportunity costs of losing control. In addition, criminal acts are often markedly non-controlled; they are both opportunistic and short-sighted.

Criticisms and Defence

Akers (1991) argued that a major weakness of this new theory was that Gottfredson and Hirschi did not define self-control and the tendency toward criminal behaviour separately. By not deliberately operationalising self-control traits and criminal behaviour or criminal acts individually, it suggests that the concepts of low self-control and propensity for criminal behaviour are one and the same. Hirschi and Gottfredson (1993) rebutted Akers argument by suggesting it was actually an indication of the consistency of the General Theory. That is, the theory is internally consistent by conceptualizing crime and deriving from that a concept of the offender's traits.

Empirical Support

The research community remains divided on whether the General Theory of Crime is sustainable but there is emerging confirmation of some of its predictions. A number of empirical studies - including meta-analysis - have confirmed that individual self-control is in fact one of the strongest predictors of crime, when compared to a range of factors at various levels of analysis.

Hirschi has since moved away from his bonding theory, and in cooperation with Gottfredson, developed a General Theory or "Self-Control Theory" in 1990. Akers (1991) argued that a major weakness of this new theory was that Gottfredson and Hirschi did not define self-control and the tendency toward criminal behaviour separately. By not deliberately operationalized self-control traits and criminal behaviour or criminal acts individually, it suggests that the concepts of low self-control and propensity for criminal behaviour are the same. Hirschi and Gottfredson (1993) rebutted Akers argument by suggesting it was actually an indication of the consistency of General Theory. That is, the theory is internally consistent by conceptualizing crime and deriving from that a concept of the offender's traits. The research community remains divided on whether the General Theory is sustainable but there is emerging confirmation of some of its predictions.

Jack P. Gibbs

Gibbs (1989) has redefined social control and applied it to develop a control theory of homicide. Any attempt to get an individual to do or refrain from doing something can be considered an attempt at control. To qualify as 'social' control, such attempts must involve three parties. One or more individuals intends to manipulate the behaviour of another by or through a third party.

Gibbs' third party can be an actual person or a reference to "society", "expectations" or "norms". For example, if one party attempts to influence another by threatening to refer the matter to a third party assumed to have authority, this is referential social control. If one party attempts to control another by punishing a third (e.g. general deterrence), it is a form of vicarious social control. The presence of the third party distinguishes social control from mere external behavioural control, simple interpersonal responses, or issuing orders for someone to do something. This definition clearly distinguishes social control from mere "reactions to deviance" and from deviant behaviour itself.

Gibbs argues that "Homicide can be described either as control or as resulting from control failure" (1989: 35), and proposes that the homicide rate is a function not just of the sheer volume of disputes, but also of the frequency of recourse to a third party for peaceful dispute settlement. When one person fails to control the actions of another through the third party, murder represents another violent attempt at direct control.

People resort to self-help when forms of social control are unavailable or fail. Gibbs is critical of Hirschi's Social Control Theory because it merely assumes that social relationships, personal investments and beliefs that discourage delinquency are social controls (which is one reason why Hirschi's theory is often referred to as a Social Bond Theory).

Critique

Much of the early research is based on self-reporting studies which can be problematic because there may be different motives for disclosing information and, in any event, questions may be interpreted differently. Nevertheless, many of the conclusions are intuitively convincing, e.g. that individuals will not engage in crime if they think that this will sacrifice the affection or respect of significant others, or cause them to lose employment or their autonomy if they face imprisonment. Davies (1994 and 2004) reports that, in the late-nineteenth century Britain, crime rates fell dramatically, as did drug and alcohol abuse, and illegitimacy became less common. All these indexes of deviance were fairly steady between World War I and 1955. After 1955 they all rose to create a U-curve of deviance, over the period from 1847 to 1997. He attributes the initial shift to adoption of a culture in which the assumptions of Protestant Christianity were taken for granted. Few people believed strongly, but everyone believed a little in a moral code of helping others that was rooted in all religions. The same social norms for the defence of the person and property that informed the law before 1955 remain the policy norms. That more people are uncontrollable and may offend against those norms in social interactions cannot be explained by simply counting how many people practice the golden rule.

Shame Society

A shame society is one in which the primary device for gaining control over children and maintaining control over adults is the inculcation of shame and the complementary threat of ostracism. A shame society is to be distinguished from a guilt society in which control is maintained by creating and continually reinforcing the feeling of guilt (and the expectation of punishment now or in the hereafter) for certain condemned behaviours.

Japan

The society of traditional Japan was long held to be a good example of one in which shame is the primary agent of social control. The first book to cogently explain the workings of the Japanese society for the Western reader was *The*

Chrysanthemum and the Sword. This book was produced under less than ideal circumstances since it was written during the early years of World War II in an attempt to understand the people who had become such a powerful enemy of the West. Under the conditions of war it was impossible to do field research in Japan.

Nevertheless, depending on the study of members of that culture who were available for interview and study in the West, namely war prisoners at detention centers, as well as literary and other such records pertaining to cultural features, American anthropologist and folklorist Ruth Benedict drew what some regard as a clear picture of the basic workings of Japanese society.

Her study has been challenged and is not relied upon by anthropologists of Japan today.

The high rate of suicide in Japan may be linked to this societal structure, as well as in South Korea, where there is a similar shame society.

Western Society

Contemporary Western society uses shame as one modality of control, but its primary dependence rests on guilt, and, when that does not work, on the criminal justice system.

Paul Hiebert characterizes the shame society as follows:

Shame is a reaction to other people's criticism, an acute personal chagrin at our failure to live up to our obligations and the expectations others have of us. In true shame oriented cultures, every person has a place and a duty in the society. One maintains self-respect, not by choosing what is good rather than what is evil, but by choosing what is expected of one.

Personal desires are sunk in the collective expectation. Those who fail will often turn their aggression against themselves instead of using violence against others.

By punishing themselves they maintain their self-respect before others, for shame cannot be relieved, as guilt can be, by confession and atonement. Shame is removed and honor restored only when a person does what the society expects of him or her in the situation, including committing suicide if necessary.

Romani

To the Roma, though living as local minorities in mostly Christian or Islamic societies, the concept of *lajav* ("shame") is important, while the concept of *bezax* ("sin") does not have such significance. This concept probably stemmed from millennia of living on the edges of other civilizations.

Guilt Society

A guilt society is one in which the primary method of social control is the inculcation of feelings of guilt for behaviours that the society defines as undesirable. As such it is opposed to a shame society. It involves creating the expectation of punishment now (when the behaviour fails to be kept secret) and/or in the hereafter.

A prominent feature of guilt societies is the provision of sanctioned releases from guilt for certain behaviours either before the fact, as when one condemns sexuality but permits it conditionally in the context of marriage, or after the fact. There is a clear opportunity in such cases for authority figures to derive power, monetary and/or other advantages, etc. by manipulating the conditions of guilt and the forgiveness of guilt.

Paul Hiebert characterizes the guilt society as follows:

Guilt is a feeling that arises when we violate the absolute standards of morality within us, when we violate our conscience. A person may suffer from guilt although no one else knows of his or her misdeed; this feeling of guilt is relieved by confessing the misdeed and making restitution. True guilt cultures rely on an internalized conviction of sin as the enforcer of good behaviour, not, as shame cultures do, on external sanctions. Guilt cultures emphasize punishment and forgiveness as ways of restoring the moral order; shame cultures stress self-denial and humility as ways of restoring the social order.

8

Radical Criminology

One of the first things to note and/or understand is that "Marxism", as a theoretical perspective, involves a number of different variants (or "ways of seeing" the social world). In this respect, although we often tend to talk about Marxism as if there were only one kind (just as we tend to talk about other sociological perspectives - such as Functionalism - as if it only involved one basic set of ideas), it is evident that Marxism, as a school of thought, has been interpreted in a number of different ways by various writers.

However, just as it's important to realise that any sociological perspective will involve writers who may interpret the social world in small, but important ways, it's also important not to go too far in the other direction and see the work of any writer as being "complete unto itself" (that is, to treat the work of individual sociologists almost as "perspectives" in their own right.

Writers who call themselves Marxists do have a number of things in common and, whilst it's important not to over-estimate this "Communality of ideas", it's also important to recognise that what they share is a broad set of basic assumptions about both the nature of the social world and how to study that world. Having noted the above, a brief discussion of the basic theoretical tradition that has informed much Radical Criminology will be useful for a number of reasons:

1. Firstly, because it will help you to recognise a couple of basic variations in Marxist thought.

2. Secondly, the next Study Pack in this series concentrates on the work of Marxist Conflict theorists who have criticised Radical Criminology from another Marxist perspective ("New Left Realism"). It will, therefore, be instructive to look-at and understand the theoretical traditions that each draws upon in order to understand both the differences in interpretation involved and, most importantly, the basis of the "New Left Realist" rejection of Radical Criminology on theoretical - as opposed to ideological - grounds.
3. Finally, by understanding some of the theoretical assumptions of Radical Criminology it should make it easier for you to carry-out an evaluation of this particular brand of Marxist Conflict theory.

The basic idea to understand in this respect is that "Instrumental Marxists" argue that the operation of all social institutions (for example, work, family, education, legal systems and so forth) and specific agencies of social control (the police, mass media and the like) can be linked - either directly or indirectly - to the needs, purposes and basic interests of a Capitalist "ruling class".

In this respect, all institutions in our society are seen to "function" in a more-or-less seamless way to promote the interests of a ruling class.

Whilst it's important to note that Instrumental Marxists do not use the concept of "function" in the same way as Functionalist sociologists, the idea that social institutions somehow function in the interests of a ruling class (rather than "society as a whole") has been criticised - as we shall see in a moment - by other Marxists. In some ways, therefore, the way in which social institutions are organised and operate can be seen as a kind of "giant conspiracy" that exists to ensure that the members of a ruling class always "come out on top" whenever conflict occurs in society. Whilst the Instrumental Marxist position is a bit more sophisticated than this, the idea of a "hidden, unstated, conspiracy" is quite useful as a way of sensitising you to the basic theoretical impetus of the perspective (just as long as you don't go overboard with it and start arguing that everything that happens in our society is the result of some "secret conspiracy/agreement" between members of the ruling class to keep their powerful, privileged, positions...).

The basis of the idea that institutions in society somehow exist to "serve the interests of a ruling class" can be seen in two main things:

1. Firstly, the idea of a "dominant ideology" (to which all other "ways of seeing and interpreting" the social world are subservient) which allows a ruling class to insinuate its ideas and interests into the consciousness of people through such things as the socialisation process, peoples "experiences" in society (education, work and so forth) and the like.

   This "dominant ideology" represents a kind of "theoretical justification" not just of the Capitalist system (that it is superior to all others forms of economic organisation), but also of such things as inequality, poverty, unemployment, personal wealth and so forth.
2. Secondly, the interlocking relationships between the members of various elite groups in society. For example, an economic elite may have direct links with a political elite through the common membership of schools ("the old school tie"), clubs and so forth. In this respect, two ideas are stressed:
   a. That, on a personal level, members of a ruling class share a similar social background. In this respect, they will have been socialised to understand their privileged, powerful, position (and so understand their common basic interest in the maintenance of their privileged position).
   b. That, on an institutional level, politicians, for example, frequently act as directors of companies. High ranking civil servants may also join the boards of major corporations (after they "retire" perhaps) as "advisers", just as senior military figures may act as "advisers" to government...

In the above respect, it is not difficult to find examples of the way in which influential members of economic and political institutions are inter-locked (even a cursory glance through a "business directory" will furnish you with examples). As an exercise, try looking through something like "Kelly's Business Directory" in the library to see if you can identify examples of such things as:

Individuals who hold multiple directorships.

Prominent politicians who are directors of major companies.

An obvious recent example in the above respect is that of Nigel Lawson who resigned from his job as both a Member of Parliament and Chancellor of the Exchequer to take -up a position as "adviser" to Barclays Bank. In fact, if you look at the background interests of almost any Conservative MP, you are likely to find that they are personally involved as directors of many different major companies. It should, of course, be noted that - in the interests of objectivity, value-freedom and the all-round undesirability of being sued for libel - there is nothing "improper" in this arrangement. Clearly, no MP would be recruited by a company simply to buy influence or, heaven-forbid that you should think any such thing, encourage the government to introduce legislation favourable to sectional business interests. In addition, the fact that many businesses/individuals contribute vast sums of money to the Conservative Party should in no way be construed as a sordid attempt to buy privileges or preferential treatment (and certainly not a Knighthood or Peerage). In many ways, the theoretical position outlined up is similar to Functionalist forms of theoretical analysis, the main differences being that:

a. Society is seen to "function" in terms of the general interests of a ruling class rather than "everyone".
b. The potential for class conflict (and other forms of conflict of course) is always present - a ruling class has to continually act to reproduce its domination of other classes in society.

As I've noted above, this form of Marxism has been criticised "internally" by other Marxists and it would be useful to draw your attention to a number of these criticisms concerning the general theoretical background to Radical Criminology.

Firstly, it tends to be argued that, in many ways, "Instrumental Marxism" is similar theoretically, to Functionalist forms of analysis (hence the somewhat disparaging dismissal of Radical Criminology as "Left Functionalism"), the main differences being:

a. That society "functions" in terms of the general interests of a ruling class rather than "society as a whole".
b. The potential for conflict is always present (but is continually negated/neutralised by the power of a ruling class).

Criminology is an advanced, theoretical field of study. It can be defined as the study of crime, the causes of crime (etiology), the meaning of crime in terms of law, and community reaction to crime. Not too long ago, criminology separated from its mother discipline, sociology, and although there are some historical continuities, it has since developed habits and methods of thinking about crime and criminal behaviour that are uniquely its own.

Crime is not something that just happens because people are "bad" or "evil" (as most "common-sense" explanations of crime tend to ultimately suggest). Crime - at least in Capitalist societies - is related to inequalities of power, authority, economic ownership, wealth and so forth. In this respect, it is necessary to locate individual behaviour in a cultural context that encourages or discourages certain forms of thinking and behaviour. For example, in a society that generally encourages racist or sexist ideas, these forms of deviance will be fairly common.

Some theories in criminology believe that criminality is a function of individual socialization, how individuals have been influenced by their experiences or relationships with family relationships, peer groups, teachers, church, authority figures, and other agents of socialization.

These are called learning theories, and specifically social learning theories, because criminology never really embraced the psychological determinism inherent in most learning psychologies. They are also less concerned for the content of what is learned (like cultural deviance theories), and more concerned with explaining the social process by which anyone, regardless of race, class, or gender, would have the potential to become a criminal. Social Learning, Control, and Labelling theories are all examples of social process theories.

Anarchy against the Discipline

Method in Criminology: A Philosophical Primer is a deceptively innocuous title for a wonderfully outrageous enterprise: a thoroughgoing epistemic attack which launches on both the day-to-day operations of criminology and the philosophical foundations on which these operations rest. In this brief but engaging book, carefully and ruthlessly (1972) dismantles the basic assumptions which under gird scientific criminology. In so doing, he exposes not only their internal illogic, but their external utility for the bureaucratic control of both crime and criminology, and for the structural maintenance of inequitable social relations. In place of the dangerous fraud which is scientific criminology, then, proposes an anarchic criminology — a criminology which embraces alternative methods and epistemologies, encourages imaginative solutions to social and criminal problems, and in the process continually undermines encrusted hierarchies of certainty, truth, and power.

Having demonstrated the futility of causal analysis for criminology, generously offers those who would pursue a scientific criminology a variety of less stringent options — probability, prediction, falsification — and then proceeds to undermine these possibilities as well. Drawing heavily on (1975) brilliant attack on science and scientific method, and on philosophers of science like (1970), (1968), and (1989), dismisses probability and prediction due to their reliance on wholly unreliable methods of induction and inductive reasoning. He likewise exposes the falsity of a falsification method which fails to understand that theories and the facts by which they are allegedly falsified in reality interpenetrate and intermingle. Finally, he considers the least stringent of options — that certain methods are, if not scientifically sound, at least the most plausible means for pursuing criminological goals. Again, though, he finds that fundamental epistemic uncertainty destroys any hierarchy of plausibility.

Significantly, demonstrates that this consideration of criminology's underlying principles constitutes much more than an exercise in abstract philosophy. First, he shows that mainstream criminology is carefully guarded by various gatekeepers of scientific authority and methodological purity: journal and book editors and reviewers, curriculum designers, granting agencies, and others.

In demanding that criminological work meet the standards of science, and excluding that work which does not, these authorities shape the discipline around narrow (and, as argues, unfounded) definitions of scholarship (1993; 1991; 1984). Beyond this, the framing of criminology as objective science contributes to the functional rationality of the modern criminal justice system, and is in turn "especially conducive to the maintenance of inequitable distributions of power" ().

As persuasively argues, the authority of allegedly objective knowledge, the sheen of scientific method and quantification, both construct new realms of legal domination and social control and at the same time distance those in control from responsibility for their actions.

Against a criminology which is both unjustifiably narrow in its scope and overtly harmful in its consequences, therefore, suggests an anarchic criminology characterized by openness, creativity, and inclusion. In place of the stale straightjacket of (pseudo)scientific criminology, anarchic criminology promotes the widest possible range of theories and methods, values marginal and even "unreasonable" knowledge, and revitalizes the "criminological imagination" (1984).

In place of the false objectivity of contemporary criminology, anarchic criminology employs a sort of "reflexive hermeneutics" () which encourages both interpretive knowledge and critical awareness. In place of a criminology which is all too useful for inequitable social and legal control, anarchic criminology takes shape in humble conversation with those outside the domains of criminology and criminal justice.

This notion of an open, anarchic criminology sheds light on a variety of ongoing discussions within and beyond contemporary criminology. To begin with, it provides a useful framework for making sense of the various alternative criminologies which have emerged in recent years. The Russian anarchist infamous injunction — that "the passion for destruction is a creative passion, too" (1974) — here reflects the notion that the destruction of paradigmatic hegemony in criminology in fact opens up intellectual space for the creation of various alternative criminologies.

If the deconstruction of theoretical certainty and methodological privilege by and those who have gone before him has created a sort of negative space, an epistemic void, it is a void that has been quickly filled by a healthy tangle of fresh perspectives. In this sense, the plethora of criminologies which have blossomed in recent times — peacemaking, news making, feminist, narrative, cultural, anarchist — constitutes perhaps a crisis of criminological certainty, but more so a measure of disciplinary life.

Finally, anarchic criminology as sketched by and others clearly informs, and is informed by, those orientations grouped under headings like "postmodernism" and "cultural studies." notes that "perhaps the most refreshing anarchic developments in criminology will be sifted from the work of postmodern criminologists" (), and indeed anarchic and postmodern criminologies have much in common.

The epistemic assault on various forms of legal and intellectual authority; the decentering of both centralized power and the certainty which accompanies it; the rejection of metanarratives which position themselves as true and universal accounts of social or criminal life — these are the projects of postmodern and anarchic criminologies alike. And as these projects open up the constricted intellectual space of scientific criminology, they at the same time lead criminology into new domains of research and analysis. in this sense argues that "criminological inquiry is more than a question of logic. Questions of aesthetics and morality are just as important" (). Like others (1995), he thus recognizes the importance of aesthetic and stylistic processes in constituting both criminology and criminal action, and attempts to reclaim this "cultural trash" from the dustbin of scientific, rationalist criminology.

He might also have more thoroughly rooted his anarchic criminology not only in prior anarchist work within criminology, but in the long history of anarchist thought. Though brevity may be the soul of wit, a hundred page book might well be expanded to include more thorough exploration, and a few more pages. In addition, the book, though simply and understandably written, would have benefited in places from a good round of editing. Utilizing conventional language in new or intentionally inappropriate ways certainly carries anarchic potential; simply writing "and so forth" or "etc." into sentences seems more sloppy than seditious.

These, though, are minor criticisms of an exciting and courageous contribution to criminological thinking. *Method in Criminology* transcends its own limitations in inventing a far-reaching critique of contemporary criminology, and imagining a humane and flexible alternative to it. And in this spirit of anarchist imagination, (1995) offer a closing note as to means and ends, process and product. concludes that, given anarchic criminology's promotion of "freedom of thought and creativity" (), an anarchic criminology benefits criminology as a whole, despite the fact that it may never be fully accomplished. (1995) agree, but go a step further to argue that anarchic criminology is beneficial precisely *because* it can never be fully realized. By its own logic, anarchic criminology serves best, it seems, as an unfinished and uncertain project, an emerging sensibility floating around and "against criminology" (1988), a critique which folds back on itself so as to undermine not only mainstream criminological rigidity but its own encrustation as well. And in this sense, we arrive at an anarchic criminology only as we continue to stumble toward it.

Deviance and Social Control (Radical Criminology in Britain)

"Deviance" is a wide-ranging term used by sociologists to refer to behaviour that varies, in some way, from a social norm. In this respect, it is evident that the concept of deviance refers to some form of "rule-breaking" behaviour.

In relation to deviance, therefore, the concept relates to all forms of rule-breaking (whether this involves such things as murder, theft or arson - the breaking of formal social rules - or such things as wearing inappropriate clothing for a given social situation, failing to produce homework at school or being cheeky to a parent, teacher and so forth - more-or-less the breaking of relatively informal social rules).

As should be apparent, criminal behaviour is a form of deviance (one that is defined as the breaking of legal rules) and, whilst we will be concentrating upon this area of deviance, it needs to be remembered that it is only one aspect - albeit a very significant one - in relation to the concept of deviant behaviour in any society.

As a general rule, therefore, we can say that there is a distinction between crime and deviance in terms of:

"All crime is, by definition, deviant behaviour, but not all forms of deviance are criminal".

Generally, the study of "crime" tends to be seen as the preserve of the criminologist, whereas sociologists tend to focus their attention and interest upon the wider social implications of all forms of rule-breaking (and, of course, rule creating) behaviour in any given society. However, as we shall see, this does include the analysis of crime and criminal behaviour considered as forms of deviance.

Radical Criminology and the Deviant Reaction

The idea of a new, radical, form of criminology - one based upon concepts such as class, power and ideology developed by Marxists in their analysis of Capitalist society - developed initially in Britain and the United States in the early 1970's.

The prime movers behind the development of Radical Criminology in Britain were Paul Taylor, Ian Walton and Jock Young and the first statement of their intent to formulate a "new theory of deviance" came in the book "The New Criminology", 1973 (which, not surprisingly, is why Radical Criminology is sometimes referred-to as the "New Criminology" or even "Critical Criminology" following the publication of an anthology of the same name in 1975).

Radical criminology originated in Britain in the early 1970's, mainly through the work of ("The New Criminology", 1973; "Critical Criminology", 1975

Radical criminology attempted to combine various Marxist concepts (social structure, economic exploitation, alienation and so forth) with a number of Interactionist concepts (social reaction, primary and secondary deviation and so forth) in a "new" theory of crime and deviance. In this respect, Radical criminology attempted to combine a Marxist theory of power with a form of labelling theory.

In order to understand both criminal and non-criminal behaviour, Radical criminologists argued that we have to understand the social framework within which laws are created and applied by and to various groups in society.

"Laws" are not "neutral" expressions of social relationships; on the contrary, they are created and applied in capitalist societies for two main reasons:

a. To protect certain property rights (laws governing theft, contract rights, etc.).
b. To maintain a form of social order that is conducive to the continued economic exploitation of the working class by the ruling class (various "public order" offences - violence, picketing, political activity and so forth).

Deviants are not seen to be "passive victims" of a labelling process, since it involves a level of choice on the part of the deviant (primary deviance). However, in terms of secondary deviation, the social reaction is conditioned by the ability of powerful groups to proscribe ("make unlawful") and prosecute various forms of deviance.

A "fully social" theory of deviance involves consideration of the following:

a. The wider origins of a deviant act.
b. The immediate origins of a deviant act.
c. The act itself.
d. The immediate origins of a social reaction.
e. The wider origins of a deviant reaction.
f. The outcome of the social reaction to a deviant's further actions.
g. The nature of the deviant process as a whole.

A major weakness in the Radical criminology perspective appears to be that although they illustrate the way it is possible to arrive at a "social theory of deviance" no attempt was ever made to put this theory into practice. Radical criminologists have been accused of "romanticizing criminals" as being somehow in the revolutionary vanguard of the fight against Capitalism (mainly because criminals are seen to disrupt and threaten the accumulation of capital/profit). Traditional Marxism warns against this type of view (as does Functionalism for that matter), since there appears to be more evidence to support the view that criminals are simply involved in exploiting others through criminal means.

Radical criminology is a branch of Marxism that is termed "instrumental Marxism" because it focuses upon empirical demonstrations of the way in which a ruling class is held together by common class backgrounds, experiences and values.

9

Feminist Criminology

Feminist criminology today is primarily concerned with the victimization of women. Other issues, such as female delinquency, prostitution and gender inequality in the law and criminal justice system are also receiving attention.Feminism seeks the elimination of all forms of gender inequality. The goal is not to push men out but to pull women in.

Feminism is a set of theories about women's oppression and a set of strategies to change it.

Remember that gender is not a natural fact (sex is) but a complex social, historical and cultural product. It is related to, but not simply derived from, biological sex difference and reproductive capacities.

Liberal Feminism Freda Adler and Rita Simon

This is the most widely recognized feminist theory in North America. It emerged in the 1960's.

Liberal feminists contend that women are discriminated against on the basis of their sex, so that they are denied access to the same political, financial, career and personal opportunities as men. This can be eliminated by removing all obstacles to women's access to education, paid employment and political activity, by enabling women to participate equally with men in the public sphere and by enacting legal change.

The problem for gender inequality can be solved by clearing the way for women's rapid integration into what has been the world of men.

Adler and Simon challenged sexist assertions made by Lombrosian crimonologists. They argue that sociological factors, not physiology, best explain women's criminality.

There is a strong relationship between women's emancipation and the increase in female crime rates. As women become more liberated and become more involved in full time jobs, they are more likely to engage in the types of crime that men commit.

But this lacks empirical support. Most of the crimes committed by women were not related to improved labour market opportunities. Even now women primarily commit petty property crimes, such as shoplifting, bad checks, and welfare fraud, which are offences caused by an increasing feminization of poverty. Women's crimes tend to follow their traditional roles as shoppers, consumers, and health care providers within the family.

They commit primarily feminine offences, they write bad checks and take items useful for them as homemakers and for feminine appearances. Female violent crime rates are significantly lower than male rates. But societal reactions to their behaviours have become more punitive, e.g., the public is more likely to report violent females, the police are more likely to arrest them. Women who challenge the traditional patriarchal gender role structure are viewed as unruly women worthy of punishment.

Marxist Feminism Julia And Herman Schwendinger

Marxist theory argues that the economic formation of a society is the primary determinant of other social relations, such as gender relations. Marxist feminism emerged in the late 1960's in response to the masculine bias in the Marxist social theory. Rather as simply ignoring women as did traditional Marxist theory, Marxist feminism agreed with liberal feminism that women are dominated by men and are prevented from full participation in all aspects of society. As Marxists, they believe that ultimately the key explanatory factor is the nature of the economy. The gender division of labour is viewed as the product of the class division of labour. Because women are seen as being primarily dominated by capital and secondarily by men, the main strategy for change is the transformation from a capitalist to a democratic socialist society.

Rape is not common in all societies. Capitalist societies have the highest rape rates because they produce unequal gender relations that foster violence. The exploitative modes of production that have culminated in the formation of class societies have either produced or intensified sexual inequality and violence.

Radical Feminism

Radical Feminism has dominated feminist perspectives on woman abuse and it was the first radical perspective to criticize the assertions of liberal feminism as simplistic. Radical feminists see male power and privilege as the root cause of all social relations, inequality and crime. The most important relations in any society are found in patriarchy (masculine control of the labour power and sexuality of women). All other relations such as class are secondary and derive from male female relations.

The main causes of gender inequality are (i) the needs of men to control women's sexuality and reproductive potential, and (ii) patriarchy.

Their work has focused on female victims/survivors of male violence. Radical feminist theory contends that men physically, sexually and psychologically victimize women mainly because they need to desire to control them.

Socialist Feminism Piers Beirne And James Messerschmidt

It is informed by both Marxist and radical feminism. Class and gender relations are viewed as equally important. To understand class we must recognize how it is structured by gender, conversely to understand gender requires an examination of how it is structured by class. In sum, socialist feminists argue that we are influenced by both gender and class relations.

Crime is mainly seen as the product of patriarchal capitalism.

A Feminist Perspective on Women and Crime

Criminology refers to any kind of study concerned with crime and criminal justice. It is a term used to include a multitude of topics and approaches. Feminist perspectives, over the past thirty years have not only put some new topics under the criminological cover, they have challenged the theories, concepts, methods and assumptions of most of the people already involved in the study of crime. Criminology, has for most feminist writers and researchers been a constraining rather than a constructive and creative influence. Theories of criminality have been developed from male subjects and validated on male subjects. Whilst there is nothing wrong with this, the problem is that these theories have been extended generally to include all criminals, defendants and prisoners. It was assumed that the theories would apply to women; most do not appear to do so.

Usually feminism is included in chapters about 'Gender and Crime' and woman as offenders are more likely to be discussed within the boundaries of sexual and petty offences such as prostitution and shop lifting. Voigt et al, in their recent book called *Criminology and Justice,* make particular mention of the inadequacies of criminology texts suggesting that 'criminology is nothing more than specialised theories of male delinquency and crime' (1994: 238-249). In other words, the facts about crime tend to be based on the sex of the offender and not the crime itself. This 'sexism' in criminology is more in keeping with Gelsthorpe's critique of 'accumulated wisdom' about female offenders. She proposes that women are discriminated against in areas such as crime because of their sex and this sexism influences the sentencing, punishment and incarceration of women. She accuses many police, welfare institutions and judges among others as assuming 'sweeping generalisations' about crime as something *men* are expected to do, because they are men'. Women are not expected to be criminals and if they are, they may be described as '*mad* not *bad* '.

The perception that women may be *mad* because they 'dared to go against their natural biological givens such as 'passivity' and a 'weakness of compliance' ' appears to originate from the view that women who conform as pure, obedient daughters, wives and mothers benefit society and men (Feinman, 1994: 16). Women became 'doubly damned' that is, they are seen as weak and in need of protection while being judged as having 'uncontrollable sexuality' (prostitutes and delinquent girls) (Bottoms, 1996: 1). Results from studies conducted by Gelsthorpe showed how sexual promiscuity amongst girls resulted in them being institutionalised and treated for 'abnormal' behaviour. On the other hand male's sexual permissiveness was encouraged and thought to be 'natural' to the male persona (1989: 34). According to Cain, these equity studies were 'androcentric' as 'women and girls appeared to exist as Other'. Men were used as the 'yardsticks' against which actions and treatment were measured (1990: 2).

Such androcentric studies urged many feminist writers to develop theories that engaged in negative and/or reactive projects and/or criticised social, theoretical, and political relations, thereby challenging theories that currently existed. Critique and construct were important creative alternatives for the production of feminist, not simply anti-sexist theory, and without them according to Grosz, problems of the past, especially patriarchal assumptions, could have been repeated (1990: 59). According to Spelman, feminist theory has not changed all that much and has neglected to include the 'problem of difference'. She suggests that 'feminists have extrapolated the condition of the most privileged type of woman - the white, middle-class, heterosexual - to all women' and the 'conflation of women in feminist theory has not produced a melting pot of different ages, colours and classes' (1988: 4). She also suggests that white feminist criminologists, although objecting to the 'stereotypical representations of female offenders', have had little to say about indigenous women or those from developing countries. To fail to see differences in racial groups is to 'reinstate the white woman's assumption that the problem is always first one of gender, never one of difference'. This apparent absence of race and other factors such as employment are mentioned in the following discussion.

Could women's emancipation account for the apparent increases in crime?

If not, what has?

The word 'feminism' today remains entrenched in some people's minds as the 'cause of most of societies problems'. Chesney-Lind suggests that 'the invention of the liberated woman' has forced women to bear the brunt of the hostility towards the women's movement (1980: 15). Prominent feminist theorists such as Freda Adler (1975) and her 'Sisters in Crime' seems to have done little to alleviate these negative assumptions. Real problems within the criminal justice system appear to have been obscured and such deflection may have provided those opposed to the women's movement with scientific evidence of the 'dark side of liberation' as is discussed below.

Freda Adler believed that the arrival of the Second Wave of Feminism during the 1970s consequently coincided with a 'dramatic' upsurge in women's criminal activity. She claimed while 'women have demanded equal opportunity in the fields of legitimate endeavours, a similar number of determined women have forced their way into the world of major crime such as white collar crime, murder and robbery'. That women criminals today represent a 'new breed' can be demonstrated, according to Adler, by evidence of the changing nature of female involvement in a wide variety of crimes. The emergence of this 'new female criminal' engaged in predatory crimes of violence and corporate fraud has broken into a man's world. For example, female white-collar crime has increased since the 'liberation' of women. Adler suggests that as women are 'climbing up the corporate business ladder', they are making use of their 'vocational liberation' to pursue careers in white-collar crime.

Adler's theory has invited much criticism from other feminist writers such as Brown. She describes it as an 'embarrassment to feminism' and argues instead that feminism has made female crime more visible through increased reporting, policing and sentencing of female offenders. She mentions that the degree of sentencing (more severe penalties) would be a more acceptable index of increases in offences among women rather than statistical measures as adopted by Adler (1986: 374). Carol Smart argues that Adler's theory is based on 'statistical illusions caused by a smallness of the base' (1979: 53). Carlen argues that Adler's 'new female criminal' is cast as the 'biological female' who is essentially masculine. The 'new female' criminal turns out to be the 'old maladjusted masculinist female' of traditional criminology, rejecting her proper feminine role (1983: 376-377) such as institutionalising rather than incarcerating women who commit 'male' offences such as robbery. In other words, Adler's 'sisters in crime' appears to work within the frameworks of traditional criminology rather than a feminist one. Her perspective also seems to exclude factors such as race, ethnicity, age and class. Many feminist writers see these factors as very important. For example, Jane Chapman's (1980) studies of the connection between labour force participation and female crime revealed an increase in criminal activity during times of economic hardship. The smallest increases in arrests coincided with periods of the greatest increase in economic activity with the most common offence being that of shop lifting. These findings would seem to support a theory of a relationship between employment and crime (economic perspective) rather than that offered by the 'women's liberation thesis'. When times are good, the offending woman appears to stabilise rather than escalate. An absence rather than availability of employment opportunities (liberation thesis) would seem a more plausible explanation for increases in female crime. Naffine believes the criminal woman's motive appears more rational and straight forward than manifesting her gender-role concerns or seeking to compete with the criminal male (1987: 99).

Giordano and Cerkovich conducted studies in 1979 involving women between the ages of 17 and 29. Their findings suggested that the 'more liberated' the response to questions, the less delinquent participants were. For example, they found that women who believed women should enter the workforce and a woman's role was not necessarily that of housewife and mother, were the least delinquent (1979: 477). James and Thornton revealed from studies involving women prisoners that those incarcerated were primarily from impoverished and uneducated backgrounds. When asked why they offended, responses did not appear to be 'liberation' motivated (1980: 240). In other words, contrary to Adler's theory of emancipation, feminism appeared to be a positive force for conformity when there was opportunity to offend.

10

Crime Victims

Crime has an Impact on Everyone – Especially the Victim

Victims of crime and their significant others (family and friends) go through a difficult adjustment period following a crime. Whether they have been physically hurt or had their house broken into, chances are the crime will have an impact.

The trauma that people experience after being victimized is not a sign of weakness.

It is a stress reaction to the loss of safety and security brought about by the crime.

If you or someone close to you has been the victim of a crime, you many find that you are experiencing some or all of the reactions listed below:

Feeling:

- Extremely fearful!
- Angry, resentful/revengeful and easily agitated
- Anxious - on edge, easily startled and suspicious of everyone
- Violated and vulnerable
- Embarrassed about some of the details of the event
- Guilty – about your actions or reactions
- Alone – disconnected and different from others
- Scattered – unable to focus on work or daily activities.

Wondering:

- Why Me?
- What If...
- If Only...

Having:

- Sleepless nights, nightmares, headaches, changes in appetite
- Recurring thoughts about the event
- Difficulty concentrating on work/school.

Traumatic memories are stored in the form of vivid sensations and images that may be fragmented and without context. When something happens in the present that reminds you of the crime, it may "trigger" the same emotional/physical reactions you had when it first happened.

Although these thoughts and feelings are most upsetting, it is important to remember that they are normal reactions to trauma and/or victimization. These reactions can last for several hours, days, weeks, months or even years depending on the individual and the circumstances that they are faced with.

Talk about it!

Talking with others about your experience and about your feelings can keep them from having harmful long-term effects on you. Sometimes a good listener is the best therapy a victim can have. However, there are times when family and friend do not know what to say or how to help. This is when you need to reach out and talk to someone who understands trauma. It's O.K. to need help!

Some Other Helpful Hints!

Learn about trauma. Not everyone understands trauma or what it feels like. Seek support from those who do understand and can help you get connected with others who can help.

Realize that your efforts to avoid the unwanted feelings and reactions will not make them go away! As painful as it is, it is better to work through the experience.

Remember to keep the blame where the blame belongs which is with the offender.

Don't be too hard on yourself when judging your actions or reactions – you reacted to the crime in the way that made the most sense to you at the time.

Allow yourself time to grieve your losses; set boundaries, pace yourself, diminish the intensity of your life.

- Take care of your physical needs; get enough sleep, eat properly, exercise (if you can)
- Avoid alcohol, caffeine, sugar, and sleeping pills
- Avoid isolation; spend time with people you care about
- Listen to music, read, write in a journal, take a nap.

In criminology and criminal law, a victim of a crime is an identifiable person who has been harmed individually and directly by the perpetrator, rather than merely the society as a whole. However, this may not always be the case, as with victims of white collar crime, who may not be clearly identifiable or directly linked to the crime. Victims of white collar crime are often denied their status as victims by the social construction of the concept (Croall, 2001). Not all criminologists accept the concept of victimization or victimology. It also remains a controversial topic within women's studies.

The Supreme Court of the United States first recognized the rights of crime victims to make a victim impact statement in the sentencing phase of a criminal trial in the case of *Payne v. Tennessee* 501 U.S. 808 (1991).

A victim impact panel is a form of community-based or restorative justice in which the crime victims (or relatives and friends of deceased crime victims) meet with the defendant after conviction to tell the convict about how the criminal activity affected them, in the hope of rehabilitation or deterrence.

Consequences of Crimes

Emotional distress as the result of crime is a recurring theme for all victims of crime. The most common problem, affecting three quarters of victims, were psychological problems, including: fear, anxiety, nervousness, self-blame, anger, shame, and difficulty sleeping. These problems often result in the development of chronic PTSD (post-traumatic stress disorder). Post crime distress is also linked to pre-existing emotional problems and sociodemographic variables. This has known to become a leading case of the elderly to be more adversely affected.

Victims may experience the following psychological reactions:

- Increase in the belief of personal vulnerability.
- The perception of the world as meaningless and incomprehensible.
- The view of themselves in a negative light.

The experience of victimization may result in an increasing fear of the victim of the crime, and the spread of fear in the community.

Victim Proneness

One of the most controversial sub-topics within the broader topic is victim proneness. The concept of victim proneness is a "highly moralistic way of assigning guilt" to the *victim of a crime*, also known as victim blaming. One theory, the *environmental theory*, posits that the location and context of the crime gets the victim of the crime and the perpetrator of that crime together..

There have been some studies recently to quantify the real existence of victim-proneness. Contrary to the urban legend that more women are repeat victims, and thus more victim-prone than men, actually men in their prime (24 to 34 year old males) are more likely to be victims of repeated crimes. While each study used different methodology, their results must be taken seriously and further studies are warranted.

The study of victimology may also include the "culture of victimhood," wherein the victim of a crime revels in his status, proclaiming that self-created victimhood throughout a community by winning the sympathy of professionals and peers.

In the case of juvenile offenders, the study results also show that people are more likely to be victimized as a result of a serious offense by someone they know; the most frequent crimes committed by adolescents towards someone they know were sexual assault, common assault, and homicide. Adolescents victimizing people they did not know generally committed common assault, forcible confinement, armed robbery, and robbery

Examples

One particularly well known example of a class at increased risk to varying forms of attacks is the prostitute. These people have been known anecdotally to have an abnormally high incidence of violent crime, and such crimes go frequently unresolved. Victimological studies of the matter might investigate current societal mores (expectations, roles, social status), legal status of prostitutes, typical working/living conditions, statistical analysis of the actual increased risk and secondary risk factors, and the economic activity of a prostitute.

Another example of increased risk is in a situation that the victim actively precipitates or initiates the crime scene, for example, by starting a fight or baiting another individual.

Victim Facilitation

Victim facilitation, another controversial sub-topic, but a more accepted theory than victim blaming, finds its roots in the writings of criminologists Marvin Wolfgang. The choice to use victim facilitation as opposed to "victim blaming" or some other term is that victim facilitation is not blaming the victim, but rather the interactions of the victim that make he/she vulnerable to a crime.

While victim facilitation relates to "victim blaming" the idea behind victim facilitation is to study the elements that make a victim more accessible or vulnerable to an attack. In an article that summarizes the major movements in victimology internationally, Schneider expresses victim facilitation as a model that ultimately describes only the misinterpretation of victim behaviour of the offender. It is based upon the theory of a symbolic interaction and does not alleviate the offender of his/her exclusive responsibility.

In Eric Hickey's *Serial Murderers and their Vicitms,* a major analysis of 329 serial killers in America is conducted. As part of Hickey's analysis, he categorized victims as high, low, or mixed regarding the victim's facilitation of the murder. Categorization was based upon lifestyle risk (example, amount of time spent interacting with strangers), type of employment, and their location at the time of the killing (example, bar, home or place of business). Hickey found that 13-15% of victims had high facilitation, 60-64% of victims had low facilitation and 23-25% of victims had a combination of high and low facilitation. Hickey also noted that among serial killer victims after 1975, one in five victims placed themselves at risk either by hitchhiking, working as a prostitute or involving themselves in situations in which they often came into contact with strangers.

There is importance in studying and understanding victim facilitation as well as continuing to research it as a sub-topic of victimization. For instance, a study of victim facilitation increases public awareness, leads to more research on victim-offender relationship, and advances theoretical etiologies of violent crime. One of the ultimate purposes of this type of knowledge is to inform the public and increase awareness so less people become victims. Another goal of studying victim facilitation, as stated by Godwin, is to aid in investigations. Godwin discusses the theory of victim social networks as a concept in which one looks at the areas of highest risk for victimization from a serial killer. This can be connected to victim facilitation because the victim social networks are the locations in which the victim is most vulnerable to the serial killer. Using this process, investigators can create a profile of places where the serial killer and victim both frequent.

Studies

The study of victims is multidisciplinary. It does not just cover victims of crime, but also victims of (traffic) accidents, natural disasters, war crimes and abuse of power. The professionals involved in victimology may be scientists, practitioners and policy makers. Studying victims can be done from the perspective of the individual victim, a third person, or from an epidemiological point of view.

Victimization Rate in United States

The National Crime Victimization Survey (NCVS) is a tool to measure the existence of actual, rather than reported crimes—the victimization rate. The National Crime Victimization Survey is the United States': "primary source of information on crime victimization. Each year, data are obtained from a nationally represented sample of 77,200 households comprising nearly 134,000 persons on the frequency, characteristics and consequences of criminal victimization in the United States. This survey enables the (government) to estimate the likelihood of victimization by rape, sexual assault, robbery, assault, theft, household burglary, and motor vehicle theft for the population as a whole as well as for segments of the population such as women, the elderly, members of various racial groups, city dwellers, or other groups." According to the Bureau of Justice Statistics (BJS), the NCVS reveals that, from 1994 to 2005, violent crime rates have declined, reaching the lowest levels ever recorded. Property crimes continue to decline.

International Crime Victims Survey

Many countries have such victimization surveys. They give a much better account for the volume crimes but are less accurate for crimes that occur with a (relative) low frequency such as homicide, or victimless 'crimes' such as drug (ab)use. Attempts to use the data from these national surveys for international comparison have failed. Differences in definitions of crime and other methodological differences are too big for proper comparison.

A dedicated survey for international comparison: A group of European criminologists started an international victimization study with the sole purpose to generate international comparative crime and victimization data. The project is now known as the International Crime Victims Survey (ICVS). After the first round in 1989, the surveys were repeated in 1992, 1996, and 2000 and 2004/2005.

Society as Crime Victim

There is one strain of thought that society itself is the victim of many crimes, especially such homicide felonies as murder and manslaughter. This sentiment has been espoused by many lawyers, judges, and academics. Some district attorneys feel they represent all of society, while some feel they are the lawyer for the crime victim. Say there was a serious crime, a murder. You read about it in the news. You are definitely not a victim, but it has affected your life in various ways. Maybe you will be more cautious, less trusting, and show a colder shoulder to strangers. Your attitude affects everyone you come across in your daily life, and it has repercussions on all of them. There you have it. All of them are part of society and this shall spread.

As contradictory as it may seem, the victim and his/her closed ones also may blame society. Where was the police? Where was help and help was most needed? Where was the good samaritan? Where was anyone? Please! Please? Please! Finally, where was God?

Penal Couple

The *penal couple* is defined as the relationship between perpetrator and victim of a crime. A sociologist invented the term in 1963. The term is now accepted by many sociologists. The concept is, essentially, that "when a crime takes place, it has two partners, one the offender and second the victim, who is providing opportunity to the criminal in committing the crime." The victim, in this view, is "a participant in the penal couple and should bear some 'functional responsibility' for the crime." The very idea is strongly rejected by some other victimologists as blaming the victim.

Rights of Victims

In 1985, the UN General Assembly adopted the Declaration on the Basic Principles of Justice for Victims of Crime and Abuse of Power. Also, the International Victimology Institute Tilburg (INTERVICT) and the World Society of Victimology developed a UN Convention for Victims of Crime and Abuse of Power.

White-collar Crime

Within the field of criminology, white-collar crime has been defined by Edwin Sutherland as "a crime committed by a person of respectability and high social status in the course of his occupation" (1939). Sutherland was a proponent of Symbolic Interactionism, and believed that criminal behaviour was learned from interpersonal interaction with others. White-collar crime, therefore, overlaps with corporate crime because the opportunity for fraud, bribery, insider trading, embezzlement, computer crime, copyright infringement, money laundering, identity theft, and forgery is more available to white-collar employees.

Historical Background

The term white-collar crime only dates back to 1939. Professor Edwin Hardin Sutherland was the first to coin the term, and hypothesize white-collar criminals attributed different characteristics and motives than typical street criminals. Mr. Sutherland originally presented his theory in an address to the American Sociological Society in attempt to study two fields, crime and high society, which had no previous empirical correlation. He defined his idea as "crime committed by a person of respectability and high social status in the course of his occupation" (Sutherland, 1939). Many denote the invention of Sutherland's idiom to the explosion of U.S business in the years following the Great Depression. Sutherland noted that in his time, "less than two percent of the persons committed to prisons in a year belong to the upper-class." His goal was to prove a relation between money, social status, and likelihood of going to jail for a white-collar crime, compared to more visible, typical crimes. Although the percentage is a bit higher today, numbers still show a large majority of those in jail are poor, "blue-collar" criminals, despite efforts to crack down on corporate crime.

Other fiscal laws were passed in the years prior to Sutherland's studies including antitrust laws in the 1920's, and social welfare laws in the 1930's. After the Depression, people went to great lengths to rebuild their financial security, and it is theorized this led many hard workers, who felt they were underpaid, to take advantage of their positions.

Much of Sutherland's work was to separate and define the differences in blue collar street crimes, such as arson, burglary, theft, assault, rape and vandalism, which are often blamed on psychological, associational, and structural factors. Instead, white-collar criminals are opportunists, who over time learn they can take advantage of their circumstances to accumulate financial gain. They are educated, intelligent, affluent, confident individuals, who were qualified enough to get a job which allows them the unmonitored access to often large sums of money. Many also use their intelligence to con their victims into believing and trusting in their credentials. Many do not start out as criminals, and in many cases never see themselves as such.

Definitional Issues

Modern criminology generally rejects a limitation of the term by reference, rather classifies the type of crime and the topic:

- By the type of offense, e.g. property crime, economic crime, and other corporate crimes like environmental and health and safety law violations. Some crime is only possible because of the identity of the offender, e.g. transnational money laundering requires the participation of senior officers employed in banks. But the Federal Bureau of Investigation has adopted the narrow approach, defining white-collar crime as "those illegal acts which are characterized by deceit, concealment, or violation of trust and which are not dependent upon the application or threat of physical force or violence" (1989, 3). This approach is relatively pervasive in the United States, the record-keeping does not adequately collect data on the socioeconomic status of offenders which, in turn, makes research and policy evaluation problematic. While the true extent and cost of white-collar crime are unknown, it is estimated to cost the United States somewhere between $300-$660 billion annually, according to the FBI.
- By the type of offender, e.g. by social class or high socioeconomic status, the occupation of positions of trust or profession, or academic qualification, researching the motivations for criminal behaviour, e.g. greed or fear of loss of face if economic difficulties become obvious. Shover and Wright (2000) point to the essential neutrality of a crime as enacted in a statute. It almost inevitably describes conduct in the abstract, not by reference to the character of the persons performing it.

Thus, the only way that one crime differs from another is in the backgrounds and characteristics of its perpetrators. Most if not all white-collar offenders are distinguished by lives of privilege, much of it with origins in class inequality.

- By organizational culture rather than the offender or offense which overlaps with organized crime. Appelbaum and Chambliss (1997, 117) offer a twofold definition:
  - Occupational crime which occurs when crimes are committed to promote personal interests, say, by altering records and overcharging, or by the cheating of clients by professionals.
  - Organizational or corporate crime which occurs when corporate executives commit criminal acts to benefit their company by overcharging or price fixing, false advertising, etc.

Relationship to other Types of Crime

Blue-collar Crime

The types of crime committed are a function of what is available to the potential offender. Thus, those employed in relatively unskilled environments and living in inner-city areas have fewer "situations" to exploit than those who work in "situations" where large financial transactions occur and live in areas where there is relative prosperity.

Blue-collar crime tends to be more obvious and thus attracts more active police attention (e.g. for crimes such as vandalism or shoplifting, where physical property is involved). In contrast, white-collar employees can incorporate legitimate and criminal behaviour, thus making themselves less obvious when committing the crime.

Therefore, blue-collar crime will more often use physical force, whereas in the corporate world, the identification of a victim is less obvious and the issue of reporting is complicated by a culture of commercial confidentiality to protect shareholder value. It is estimated that a great deal of white-collar crime is undetected or, if detected, it is not reported.

State-corporate Crime

The negotiation of agreements between a state and a corporation will be at a relatively senior level on both sides, this is almost exclusively a white-collar "situation" which offers the opportunity for crime. White-collar crime has become a priority of law enforcement.

Fraud

In the broadest sense, a fraud is an intentional deception made for personal gain or to damage another individual; the related adjective is fraudulent. The specific legal definition varies by legal jurisdiction. Fraud is a crime, and also a civil law violation. Defrauding people or entities of money or valuables is a common purpose of fraud, but there have also been fraudulent "discoveries", e.g. in science, to gain prestige rather than immediate monetary gain.

A hoax also involves deception, but without the intention of gain, or of damaging or depriving the victim; the intention is often humorous.

Types of Fraudulent Acts

Fraud can be committed through many media, including mail, wire, phone, and the Internet (computer crime and Internet fraud). The international dimensions of the web and ease with which users can hide their location, the difficulty of checking identity and legitimacy online, and the simplicity with which crackers can divert browsers to dishonest sites and steal credit card details have all contributed to the very rapid growth of Internet fraud.

Types of criminal fraud include:

- bait and switch
- bankruptcy fraud
- benefit fraud, committing fraud to get government benefits
- counterfeiting of currency, documents or valuable goods
- charlatanism
- confidence tricks such as the 419 fraud and Spanish Prisoner

- creation of false companies or "long firms"
- embezzlement, taking money which one has been entrusted with on behalf of another party
- false advertising
- false billing
- false insurance claims
- forgery of documents or signatures,
- fraud upon the court
- health fraud, for example selling of products known not to be effective, such as quack medicines,
- identity theft
- investment frauds, such as Ponzi schemes and Pyramid schemes
- Moving scam
- religious fraud
- marriage fraud to obtain immigration rights without entitlement
- rigged gambling games such as the shell game
- securities frauds such as pump and dump
- tax fraud, not reporting revenue or illegally avoiding taxes. In some countries, tax fraud is also prosecuted under false billing or tax forgery.

Elements of Fraud

Common law fraud has nine elements:

1. a representation of an existing fact;
2. its materiality;
3. its falsity;
4. the speaker's knowledge of its falsity;
5. the speaker's intent that it shall be acted upon by the plaintiff;
6. plaintiff's ignorance of its falsity;
7. plaintiff's reliance on the truth of the representation;
8. plaintiff's right to rely upon it; and
9. consequent damages suffered by plaintiff.

Most jurisdictions in the United States require that each element be pled with particularity and be proved with clear, cogent, and convincing evidence (very probable evidence) to establish a claim of fraud. The measure of damages in fraud cases is to be computed by the "benefit of bargain" rule, which is the difference between the value of the property had it been as represented, and its actual value. Special damages may be allowed if shown proximately caused by defendant's fraud and the damage amounts are proved with specificity.

National Fraud Authority

The National Fraud Authority (NFA) is the government agency co-ordinating the counter-fraud response in the UK. The NFA works with a wide range of partners with the aim of making fraud more difficult to commit in the UK. The NFA was established following the government's 2006 Fraud Review. It concluded that fraud is a significantly under-reported crime, and while various agencies and organisations were attempting to tackle the issue, greater cooperation was needed to achieve a real impact in the public sector. The scale of the problem pointed to the need for a small but high-powered body to bring together the numerous counter-fraud initiatives that existed, which is when the NFA was formed.

The NFA works to tackle frauds across the spectrum, but also works on fraud types and fraud issues that are a notable problem. These include identity fraud, mortgage fraud, accommodation addresses, mass marketing fraud and fraud affecting small and medium sized businesses. The NFA also produces the Annual Fraud Indicator, which estimates the cost of fraud. The current estimate puts the cost of fraud to the UK at £30 billion a year, which equates to £621 a year for every adult in England and Wales. Working with the charity, Victim Support, the NFA has also done some significant work with victims, to ensure they receive the support they deserve if they have been a victim of the crime. The NFA also runs Action Fraud - the UK's National Fraud Reporting Centre.

Action Fraud

Action Fraud is the UK's national fraud reporting service, run by the National Fraud Authority. Action Fraud is the place to go to get information and advice about fraud, as well as to report fraud. UK citizens can report fraud online or by calling 0300 123 2040. When a fraud is reported to Action Fraud, victims are given a crime reference number and their case is passed on to the National Fraud Intelligence Bureau (NFIB), which is run by the City of London's police service.

The Action Fraud website also has an A-Z of fraud describing different types of fraud, and offers prevention advice.

Notable Fraudsters

- Frank Abagnale Jr., US impostor who wrote bad checks and falsely represented himself as a qualified member of professions such as airline pilot, doctor, and attorney. The film *Catch Me If You Can* is based on his life.
- Eddie Antar, founder of Crazy Eddie, who has about $1 billion worth of judgments against him stemming from fraudulent accounting practices at that company.
- Cassie Chadwick, who pretended to be Andrew Carnegie's illegitimate daughter to get loans.
- Salim Damji is a convicted fraud artist who defrauded millions of dollars in an affinity fraud. The money came mostly from relatives and members of the closely-knit Ismaili community. His $75 million scam was among the largest in Canadian history
- Charles Dawson, an amateur British archeologist who claimed to have found the Piltdown man.
- Marc Dreier, Managing founder of Attorney firm Dreir LLP. Prosecutors allege that from 2004 through December 2008, He sold approximately $700 million worth of fictitious promissory notes.
- Richard Eaton, an English businessman who was business partners with mobster Paul Vario and Jimmy Burke and was involved in the Lufthansa heist. An associate of the Lucchese crime family
- Bernard Ebbers, founder of WorldCom, which inflated its asset statements by about $11 billion.
- Ramón Báez Figueroa, banker from the Dominican Republic and former President of Banco

Intercontinental. Sentenced on October 21, 2007 to ten years in prison for a US $2.2 billion fraud case that drove the Caribbean nation into an economic crisis in 2003.

- Martin Frankel is a former U.S. financier, convicted in 2002 of insurance fraud worth $208 million, racketeering and money laundering.
- Samuel Israel III, former hedge fund manager that ran the former fraudulent Bayou Hedge Fund Group. He faked suicide.
- Ashok Jadejahas been accused of cheating people from across India of scores of rupees on the pretext of having divine blessings.
- Konrad Kujau, German fraudster and forger responsible for the "Hitler Diaries".
- Kenneth Lay, the American businessman who built energy company Enron. He was one of the highest paid CEOs in America until he was ousted as Chairman and was convicted of fraud and conspiracy, although as a result of his death, his conviction was vacated.
- Nick Leeson, English trader whose unsupervised speculative trading caused the collapse of Barings Bank.
- James Paul Lewis, Jr., ran one of the biggest ($311 million) and longest running Ponzi Schemes (20 years) in US history.
- Gregor MacGregor, Scottish conman who tried to attract investment and settlers for the non-existent country of Poyais.
- Bernard Madoff, creator of a $65 billion Ponzi scheme - the largest investor fraud ever attributed to a single individual.
- Colleen McCabe, British headmistress who stole £½ million from her school.
- Gaston Means, a professional conman during U.S. President Warren G. Harding's administration.
- Matt the Knife, American born con artist, card cheat and pickpocket who, from the ages of approximately 14

through 21, bilked dozens of casinos, corporations and at least one Mafia crime family out of untold sums.

- Barry Minkow and the *ZZZZ Best* scam.
- Michael Monus, founder of Phar-Mor, which ultimately cost its investors more than $1 billion.
- F. Bam Morrison, who conned the town of Wetumka, Oklahoma by promoting a circus that never came.
- Lou Pearlman, former boy-band manager indicted by a federal grand jury in Orlando on charges that he schemed to bilk banks out of more than $100 million.
- Frederick Emerson Peters, US impersonator who wrote bad checks.
- Thomas Petters is an American masquerading as a business man who turned out to be a con man and was the former CEO and chairman of Petters Group Worldwide. Petters resigned his position as CEO on September 29, 2008, amid mounting criminal investigations. He later was convicted for turning Petters Group Worldwide into a $3.65 billion Ponzi scheme and was sentenced to 50 years in federal prison.
- Charles Ponzi and the Ponzi scheme.
- Alves Reis, who forged documents to print 100,000,000 PTE in official escudo banknotes (adjusted for inflation, it would be worth about US$150 million today).
- Christopher Rocancourt, a Rockefeller impersonator who defrauded Hollywood celebrities.
- Scott W. Rothstein, a disbarred lawyer from Ft. Lauderdale, Florida, who perpetrated a Ponzi scheme which defrauded investors of over $1 billion.
- Michael Sabo, best known as a check, stocks and bonds forger. He became notorious in the 1960s throughout the 1990s as a "Great Impostor" over 100 aliases, and earned millions from such.
- John Spano, a struggling businessman who faked massive success in an attempt to buy out the New York Islanders of the NHL.
- John Stonehouse, the last Postmaster-General of the UK and MP who faked his death to marry his mistress.

- Kevin Trudeau, US writer and billiards promoter, convicted of fraud and larceny in 1991, known for a series of late-night infomercials and his series of books about "Natural Cures "They" Don't Want You to Know About".
- Richard Whitney, who stole from the New York Stock Exchange Gratuity Fund in the 1930s.
- Robert Douglas Hartmann, an American con man & felon implicated in a real estate mortgage investment Ponzi scheme which defrauded both private lenders & banks in excess of $34 million.

The Role of Victims in Criminal Investigations and Prosecutions

Throughout the criminal justice system, prosecutors have wide discretion to exercise their authority in determining what crimes should be prosecuted. This discretion has historic support through both constitutional separation of powers doctrines and public policy. This discretion is based on a variety of factors, including the severity of the crime, the extent of the evidence, prosecutorial resources and other facts involved in the specific case. Victim cooperation and participation in the investigation and prosecution of crime often is a key element in this analysis. Historically, in the effective administration of the criminal justice system, the role of the victim in criminal prosecutions has been critical. Victim testimony often is the most important element of a successful prosecution. Moreover, a victim's cooperation in an investigation and prosecution often results in a prosecutor's exercise of discretion in favour of criminal prosecution. This participation is therefore both critical and desirable. Accordingly, public policy, as embodied in statutes and extensive case law, is designed to encourage and support the role of victims in the prosecution of crime. Within this basic framework, actions that limit the victim's role in the criminal process in a significant way will make the criminal process less effective. Moreover, the broad discretion afforded to prosecutors in the criminal process allows prosecutors to make use of victim information and resources in whatever way the prosecutor deems appropriate.

As white collar crimes have become a more significant component of the law enforcement agenda, the insurance industry has played a leading role in assisting prosecutors in the investigation and prosecution of insurance fraud, involving health care providers, lawyers, bogus claimants and a vast array of participants in the endless schemes to defraud insurance companies and their customers. Throughout the country, insurers routinely cooperate with law enforcement officials that are investigating insurance fraud, providing information, specialized expertise and technical and administrative support for these complicated investigations. Cooperation can involve investigations prior to referrals to law enforcement, assistance with ongoing law enforcement investigations and the provision of expertise or financial assistance in the investigation of this complex crime. The recent federal health insurance fraud statute even requires cooperation between private insurers and law enforcement officials on fraud investigations.

Prosecutors have broad discretion to capitalize on this cooperation and expertise as they feel appropriate. In fact, any requirement that prosecutors distance themselves from victims - typically the most effective sources of information about crime - cannot be supported by constitutional or public policy considerations. The fact that some victim cooperation and assistance may make it easier for a prosecutor to exercise his or her responsibilities should be considered a positive factor in the administration of the criminal justice system.

Nonetheless, despite this historic cooperative relationship between victims and prosecutors and the effectiveness of this cooperation in the prosecution of crime, the California Supreme Court recently sent a message that may cause some inappropriate and unnecessary effects on the prosecution of insurance fraud and perhaps other white collar crimes as well. In *People v. Eubanks, 927 F.2d 310 (Cal. 1996)*, the Court held that payment by a victim of investigative expenses incurred by the prosecutor's office in the course of a lawful criminal investigation may disqualify the prosecutor from pursuing a criminal case. This message runs counter to decades of court and legislature-sanctioned cooperation between victims of crime and prosecutors, which has proven to be critical to the effective prosecution of white collar crime. While this decision is exceedingly narrow in its holding, significant restrictions on the ability of victims to cooperate and assist in the investigation and prosecution of crime at the prosecutor's discretion are contrary to history, law and policy, and should be rejected by other courts around the country. This memorandum describes the history and policy supporting the involvement of victims in criminal investigations, focusing on the insurance industry's historic and consistent support for these principles. This cooperation intersects with a prosecutor's broad discretion in evaluating what cases should be investigated and prosecuted. These bedrock principles demonstrate why prosecutors should continue to rely on victim assistance as they feel appropriate, and why any further limitations on this cooperation should be rejected.

Prosecutorial Discretion

In the criminal justice system, the prosecutor bears responsibility for determining what crimes will be prosecuted. The "legal system has traditionally accorded wide discretion to criminal prosecutors in the enforcement process." *Marshall v. Jerrico, Inc., 446 U.S. 238, 248 (1980)*. The Government retains "broad discretion" as to whom to prosecute. *United States v. Goodwin, 457 U.S. 368, 380, n. 11 (1982)*. "[S]o long as the prosecutor has probable cause to believe that the accused committed an offense defined by statute, the decision whether or not to prosecute and what charge to file or bring before a grand jury, generally rests entirely in his discretion." Bordenkircher v. Hayes, 434 U.S. 357, 364 (1978).

The basis for this discretion rests on the nature of the prosecutorial function. This broad discretion rests largely on the recognition that the decision to prosecute is particularly ill-suited to judicial review. Such factors as the strength of the case, the prosecution's general deterrence value, the Government's enforcement priorities, and the case's relationship to the Government's overall enforcement plan are not readily susceptible to the kind of analysis the courts are competent to undertake. Judicial supervision in this area, moreover, entails systemic costs of particular concern. Examining the basis of prosecution delays the criminal proceeding, threatens to chill law enforcement by subjecting the prosecutor's motives and decisionmaking to outside inquiry, and may undermine prosecutorial effectiveness by revealing the Government's enforcement policy. All these are substantial concerns that make the courts properly hesitant to examine the decision whether to prosecute. Wayte v. United States, 470 U.S. 598, 607-08 (1985).

While this discretion is broad, it is not "'unfettered.' Selectivity in the enforcement of criminal laws is... subject to constitutional constraints." *United States v. Batchelder, 442 U.S. 114, 125 (1979)* (footnote omitted). In particular, the decision to prosecute may not be "deliberately based upon an unjustifiable standard such as race, religion, or other arbitrary classification," *Bordenkircher, 434 U.S. at 364* (citation omitted), including the exercise of protected statutory and constitutional rights. *Goodwin, 457 U.S. at 372; Wayte, 470 U.S. at 607.* Beyond these constitutional limitations, there is an "extreme deference the courts must give to prosecutorial charging decisions" and a trial judge "must accord a presumption of constitutionality to prosecutorial decisions, and approach the inquiry with appropriate respect for the judgments exercised by officers of a coordinate branch of government." *United States v. Redondo-Lemos, 27 F.3d 439, 444 (9th Cir. 1994).*

Within these boundaries, the Supreme Court's various pronouncements on these issues uniformly have recognized that courts normally must defer to prosecutorial decisions as to whom to prosecute. The reasons for judicial deference are well known. Prosecutorial charging decisions are rarely simple. In addition to assessing the strength and importance of a case, prosecutors also must consider other tangible and intangible factors, such as government enforcement priorities. Finally, they also must decide how best to allocate the scarce resources of a criminal justice system that simply cannot accommodate the litigation of every serious criminal charge. Because these decisions "are not readily susceptible to the kind of analysis the courts are competent to undertake," the Supreme Court has been "properly hesitant to examine the decision whether to prosecute." Within this long-standing set of principles, prosecutors exercise their substantial discretion, and courts are loathe to interfere with prosecutors' judgments. This latitude often plays out in the context of a defendant's efforts to challenge a prosecutor's (or more broadly an entire prosecutor's office) participation in a particular criminal prosecution. The standard for prosecutorial disqualification is quite high, and efforts to disqualify prosecutors should not be allowed to interfere with the broad discretion afforded to prosecutors in the criminal process. It is clear that disqualification of a criminal prosecutor "is a drastic measure which courts should hesitate to impose except when absolutely necessary." *In the Matter of Grand Jury Subpoena,* 873 F.2d 170, 176 (7th Cir. 1989) (quoting Freeman v. Chicago Musical Instrument Co., 689 *F.2d 715, 721 (7th Cir. 1982)).* Also, the relevant question for prosecutors is not the same as it is for the judicial functions. Prosecutors need not be entirely "neutral and detached," as judges are expected to be, as "[i]n an adversary system, [prosecutors] are necessarily permitted to be zealous in their enforcement of the law." *Marshall, 446 U.S. at 248.*

Of course, a prosecutor need not be disinterested on the issue whether a prospective defendant has committed the crime with which he is charged. If honestly convinced of the defendant's guilt, the prosecutor is free, indeed obligated, to be deeply interested in urging that view by any fair means. True disinterest on the issue of such a defendant's guilt is the domain of the judge and the jury not the prosecutor. Wright v. United States, 732 F.2d 1048, 1056 (2d Cir. 1984) (citations omitted). To enforce a prosecutor's ability to exercise discretion, most courts require that any perceived conflict of interest be "actual." To succeed on a claim of conflict of interest, therefore, a defendant must "point to specific instances in the record to suggest an actual conflict or impairment of his or her own interests...." *State v. Webb, 790 P.2d 65, 75 (Utah Ct. App. 1990).* Defendants cannot claim error based on the mere appearance or hypothetical existence of conflict. Disqualification is not required "whenever there exists a possible appearance problem. 'The courts, as a general rule, should remove a public prosecutor only to protect a defendant from actual prejudice arising from a demonstrated conflict of interest or a substantial risk of an abuse of confidence... and the appearance of impropriety, standing alone, might not be grounds for disqualification. The objector should demonstrate actual prejudice or so substantial a risk thereof as could not be ignored.'" *People v. Herr, 635 N.Y.S.2d 159, 160 (1995)* (citations omitted).

These disqualifications are tied to direct and personal issues, not broad assertions of general favoritism or other unsupported assertions about a lack of neutrality. A more broad claim of general prejudice by a prosecutor, or even generalized personal involvement, should be insufficient.

Indeed, "prosecutorial disqualification can be divided into two major categories. The first is where the prosecutor has had some attorney-client relationship with the parties involved whereby he obtained privileged information that may be adverse to the defendant's interest in regard to the pending criminal charges. A second category is where the prosecutor has some direct personal interest arising from animosity, a financial interest, kinship, or close friendship such that his objectivity and impartiality are called into question." *Nicholas v. Sammons, 363 S.E.2d 517 (W.* Va. 1987) (syllabus point 1); State v. James R., 422 S.E.2d 521, 522 (W.Va. 1992) (syllabus point 1) (same).

The primary basis for "conflict of interest" disqualifications of criminal prosecutors therefore is distinctly personal, a financial or personal motive that distorts a prosecutor's ability to make reasonable judgments. See, e.g., *Shaw v. Garrison, 467 F.2d 113 (5th Cir. 1972)* (where prosecutor had a "significant financial interest in the continued prosecution" because of a book contract, prosecution brought for harassment purposes could be enjoined); *Lewis v. Superior Court, 62 Cal. Rptr. 2d 331 (Ct. App. 1997)* (where prosecutor's office was direct victim of crime, prosecutor was potentially implicated in crime and prosecutor had been involved in efforts to repair political and financial damage from crime, prosecutor could be disqualified); *State v. Bell, 370 P.2d 508 (Idaho 1962)* (special prosecutor should be appointed where prosecutor was close personal friend of defendant); *City of Maple Heights v. Redi Car Wash, 554 N.E.2d 929 (Ohio Ct. App. 1988)* (individual prosecutor disqualified where there was deep personal animosity between prosecutor and defendant, and prosecutor had filed a personal libel suit against defendant); *Parkerson v. Norris, 529 So.2d 1392 (La. Ct. App. 1988)* (prosecutor could not participate because he was the victim of the crime being investigated). None of these categories remotely encompasses obtaining the cooperation or support of the victim of crime. These similar concepts of bias and neutrality have been analysed extensively in the context of "private prosecutors." Many states allow private citizens to act as public prosecutors, with the consent of local law enforcement. In jurisdictions where private prosecutors are allowed, so long as the private prosecutor is not "in control" of the prosecution, courts have approved of their use. In these cases, private prosecutors are allowed to proceed unless they have a distinctly personal interest in the case that makes this participation improper. In these cases, it is not the perception of a potential taint that is relevant, but a direct and personal conflict between a private responsibility to a client and the public obligations imposed on a prosecutor that provides the only significant limitation.

For example, in a situation where a prosecutor's office was insufficiently staffed, it was appropriate for the victims to provide financial support for retention of a private prosecutor, and this prosecutor was allowed to proceed with the case as long as the "control" rested with the public prosecutor. See *Woods v. Linahan, 648 F.2d 973 (5th Cir. 1981)* (where prosecution staff was "inundated" with cases and needed help, sheriff's office could solicit victim's family and friends to hire a private attorney to assist in the investigation, interview witnesses, and even file motions, so long as private attorney remained under ultimate control of the District Attorney).

The only significant limitation in this area has involved situations where the "private prosecutor" also represented the victim in a separate civil action. In those cases, combining the prosecutor's function with the private litigant's obligations created inconsistent responsibilities and this "dual representation" has generally been held to violate a defendant's due process rights. In the typical situation where the victim provides assistance to an investigation, there is no combination of the prosecutor function with private obligations. Instead, the public prosecutor is obligated to fulfil his or her responsibilities to the State, which may include seeking information from victims, but there is no abandonment of control or responsibility.

The victims cannot dictate how the prosecutor's office exercises its responsibilities. Further, the prosecutor bears the responsibility for all decisionmaking in the area where he or she has discretion - whether to charge, what charges to bring and how the case should be prosecuted.

The Role of Victims in the Criminal Process

These principles mandate that prosecutors have broad discretion in determining what cases will be prosecuted, and that the primary (and often exclusive) basis for challenging a prosecutor's decision to prosecute or participation in a prosecution involves personal bias in the prosecution, based on personal financial interest or other self-interested motives.

Within this exercise of discretion, prosecutors often rely on crime victims as crucial sources of information and may choose to make use of victim information and resources in making prosecutorial decisions. Indeed, while prosecutors represent the government, not the crime victims per se, prosecutors are encouraged and often required to consider the victim's interests as well. Any efforts to require a wall of separation between prosecutors and victims should be rejected, as counterproductive and unnecessary for any public policy or constitutional reason. In all kinds of cases, ranging from the most serious to the "smallest," law enforcement relies on cooperation from the public. In a typical assault case, a victim must first contact the police to report the crime, relay the details of the incident, often participate in perpetrator identification (through police line-ups), testify at trial and, if the defendant is convicted, make a victim impact statement at sentencing. Costs involved in this process are ordinarily incurred by the victim, even though the benefit of the victim's participation accrues to the State.

Cooperation from an assault victim usually only entails small costs that do not appear to directly benefit law enforcement officials or relieve them of any budget burdens. However, consider the cooperation store owners give to police in routine shoplifting cases. Shoplifters are caught almost exclusively by private security officers working for the victimized retailer. The private security officers must observe the crime, investigate it if necessary, apprehend and detain the suspect, report it to the local law enforcement authority, and then testify at the defendant's trial. All of these costs are directly underwritten by the victimized corporation. If this cooperation was not allowed between these crime victims and law enforcement, shoplifters could either steal with impunity, or law enforcement would be forced to shift resources away from higher-priority areas to combat shoplifting. Either of these scenarios clearly undermines sound public policy. Embezzlement cases present another typical example. Embezzlement victims are best situated to know their own finances, and know what expenditures should raise "red flags" and which are legitimate. Thus, it is logical, expedient and cost-effective for them to pay for accountings and investigations into possible embezzlement, and then cooperate with law enforcement authorities, if circumstances warrant that. Under this system, corporations can meet their confidentiality needs in the preliminary stages of an investigation. Also, law enforcement is not forced into a complex field they have little experience with, an arrangement that virtually guarantees a mutually beneficial relationship for both the victim and law enforcement.

Victim participation therefore is critical to an effective law enforcement process. The law enforcement system often depends on the voluntary participation of crime victims in order to investigate and prosecute criminals successfully. The willingness of victims to come forward is vital to the successful prosecution of criminals. Without this assistance in reporting crime, more crime effectively will go unpunished, as the criminal justice system is "absolutely dependent" on victim cooperation. *Karen L. Kennard, The Victim's Veto: A* Way to Increase Victim Impact on Criminal Case Dispositions, 77 Cal. L. Rev. 417, 425 n.42 (1989) (quoting President's Task Force on Victims of Crime, Final Report V (Dec. 1982)). And while this cooperation is desirable, the Supreme Court also has stated that victim concerns must be considered in the criminal process.

[I]n the administration of criminal justice, courts may not ignore the concerns of victims. Apart from all other factors, such a course would hardly encourage victims to report violations to the proper authorities; this is especially so when the crime is one calling for public testimony about a humiliating and degrading experience such as was involved here. Precisely what weight should be given to the ordeal of reliving such an experience for the third time need not be decided now; but that factor is not to be ignored by the courts. Morris v. Slappy, 461 U.S. 1, 14-15 (1983).

Therefore, prosecutors are required to consider the victim's rights and interests, and are not in any way required to keep the victim at arm's length in investigating and prosecuting victimrelated crimes.

The role of victims today is very different than in our earlier history. The crime victim once had a more prominent part in directing the progress of the criminal justice system. Today, participation in the contemporary criminal process imposes numerous burdens on victims; many feel victimized not only by the crime, but by the process as well, so that they increasingly fail to assist law enforcement agencies, to the detriment of the public at large. As one scholar has stressed:

> [t]he criminal justice system's current response to the interests of beleaguered crime victims is no better than timely, and possibly very late. A sense of alienation with the criminal justice system has reached such heights that many pieces of literature now discuss the problem in terms descriptive of a crisis. Surveys of crime victims reveal intense displeasure with the criminal justice system. Victims often do not report to the police the crimes that have been committed against them, prompting [one commentator] to blame the "decline of faith" in the criminal justice system for this corrosive effect: "Victims report few crimes to the authorities because they do not expect them to be responsive."

Cardenas, The Crime Victim in the Prosecutorial Process, 9 Harv. L.J. & Pub. Pol'y 357, 357-58 (1986) (citations and footnotes omitted).

So while this role has changed over time, public policy across the country consistently and strongly encourages private actions to support public law enforcement efforts. Moreover, the encouragement of victim participation in the criminal process is also reflected in the public policy across the country which places significant burdens on tort actions against those who assist in the prosecution of crime. "[P]ublic policy has developed an immunity to protect those who act in a reasonable manner in bringing to justice those they believe are criminals. That immunity cannot be broken down upon a mere allegation of negligence or even gross negligence." No cause of action can arise for any such alleged negligence because "to allow an action in negligence against a citizen who makes an honest mistake in reporting to the police would stifle citizen cooperation." Claims against those who provide information about suspected crime have "never been regarded with any favour by the courts, and [are] hedged with restrictions which make [them] very difficult to maintain." *W. Keeton, Prosser and Keeton on Torts § 119 at 876 (5th Ed. 1984)*. "This disfavor of [these] actions represents a value choice based on public policy considerations. Sound public policy and the aims of justice require the uncovering of crime and the prosecution of criminals." *Williams v. Ryder/P.I.E. Nationwide, Inc., 786 F.2d 854, 857 (8th Cir. 1986)* (citation omitted). Generally, these actions are disfavored because "[t]hey have an undesirable tendency to unduly discourage citizens from seeking redress in the courts," *Chittenden Trust Co. v. Marshall, 146 Vt. 543, 507 A.2d 965, 969-70 (1986)*, and because they tend to discourage prosecution of crime. *Kimbley v. City of Green River, 663 P.2d 871, 882 (Wyo. 1983)*. As one court noted, "[t]here is almost universal agreement that sound public policy dictates that the law should encourage the uncovering and prosecution of crime. Any 'policy that discourages citizens from reporting crime or aiding in prosecution would be undesirable and detrimental to society in general.'" *Sanders v. Daniel Int'l Corp., 682 S.W.2d 803, 806 (Mo. 1984)* (citation omitted).

Following the desirability of victim cooperation and the public policy protection and support for active victim participation in the criminal process, the insurance industry has been particularly focused on assisting law enforcement with criminal investigations. Insurance fraud is an enormous financial problem across the United States. According to the Coalition Against Insurance Fraud, insurance claims fraud amounted to $85.3 billion in 1995, resulting in a cost of more than $1,030 to each American family in the form of higher insurance premiums, taxes and the increase in the cost of goods and services affected by this fraud. Organizations like the Coalition, the National Insurance Crime Bureau and the National Health Care Anti-Fraud Association exist primarily to assist law enforcement in the detection, investigation and prosecution of insurance-related crimes and to encourage cooperation between fraud victims and law enforcement.

This private sector participation is crucial to the effective prosecution of these crimes. In addition to the staggering amounts at issue, the nature of insurance fraud demonstrates why cooperation between public and private entities is so critical. For example, most of the nation's total health care bill - 56% - is paid with private-sector dollars (37% by insurers and 19% by consumer outof- pocket payments). Second, experience clearly shows that the health care provider who is defrauding Medicare, Medicaid, CHAMPUS or other government programs in all likelihood is also defrauding private payers - and vice-versa. According to the Department of Justice, "[p]erpetrators of health care fraud rarely infiltrate just one health care system or limit their fraud solely to public health care programs. Fraudulent schemes often cut across health care systems."

Next, although insurers and the government may be the immediate targets of health care fraud, the general public is the ultimate victim of insurance fraud - as consumers and patients who pay health insurance premiums, co-payments and deductibles; as employers who purchase health coverage for their employees; and as taxpayers, where we are doubly victimized when public payment programs are defrauded.

With these financial implications, insurance fraud represents an area where there is a unique public/private victimization at the hands of corrupt health care providers and other insurance fraud perpetrators. In addition, unlike many criminal areas, the private sector plays an active and aggressive role in fighting fraud. Insurers have active anti-fraud programs and work extensively with a wide range of public law enforcement officials to ferret out fraud. Accordingly, private payers are an important line of defence in the fight against fraud.

The Health Insurance Portability and Accountability Act of 1996 (HIPAA) takes this practice of cooperation one step further, by requiring that private insurers and law enforcement officials cooperate in the investigation and prosecution of health care fraud. In organizing its anti-fraud activities, federal law enforcement officials must "consult with, and arrange for the sharing of data with representatives of health plans" in their efforts to fight fraud. As a supplement to this legislative mandate, the Department of Justice and the Department of Health and Human Services recently issued guidelines mandating the sharing of a wide range of investigative information between public law enforcement and private payers. Accordingly, the practice and mandate in insurance fraud efforts is to encourage and even require broader cooperation between crime victims and law enforcement.

Victim Participation in Law Enforcement Investigations

Within this context, victim participation is an important part of the criminal process, resulting in enhanced enforcement of the criminal laws and a more effective use of prosecutorial resources. This cooperation is routine, useful and effective.

One recent case demonstrates how effective this cooperation can be. In *Int'l Bus. Machs. Corp. v. Brown, 857 F. Supp. 1384 (N.D. Cal. 1994)*, IBM brought suit against individual and corporate defendants accused of defrauding the company. Suspicious of some of its employees, IBM had cooperated with local police in a successful sting operation. At the time of the civil suit, a criminal prosecution arising from the sting was ongoing. The civil defendants sought a stay in the civil proceedings pending the outcome of the criminal trial, arguing that by participating in the sting, IBM and the police engaged in misconduct. *Id. at 1387.*

The court characterized the defendant's argument as suggesting "that there is something inherently outrageous in the fact that plaintiff, having discovered circumstances [indicating] it was being defrauded, first complained to the LAPD, triggering a criminal investigation, and then proceeded to bring a civil suit, which resulted in sharing information between LAPD and plaintiff." The court, on the other hand, found nothing at all "inherently outrageous" in the arrangement.

Id. at 1388. Because the defendants could not make showings of prosecutorial misconduct or impropriety, their request for a stay was rejected.

In fact, the court went out of its way to highlight the problems corporations have in obtaining justice from the criminal system. *Id.* It noted that "often it is difficult and virtually impossible for large corporate victims to secure prosecution of crimes committed against them," and that prosecutors and police were unlikely to have sufficient resources to rectify that problem. Id. However, the court did not think that businesses were hamstrung to fix this problem. "Large corporate victims... have resources, if they choose, to help law enforcement agencies pursue and apprehend the criminals who victimize them." *Id.* The court felt this was especially appropriate in the fraud context, where "very large expenditures of funds and resources are often necessary before a bona fide suspicion can be affirmed." *Id. at 1389*. Where a private investigation unearthed criminal fraud, the court held that the government was not barred from using that information as a basis for prosecution just because it had not paid for it. *Id.* "If the ultimate result of such private investigation is that criminals can be brought to justice with a minimum diversion of public resources, the interests of society are irrefutably served." *Id.* The logic of Brown is irrefutable. There are no constitutional or statutory provisions that require prosecutors to fight crime with one hand tied behind their back - by avoiding contact or cooperation from those with perhaps the most information about a suspected crime and the most ability to advance an effective criminal investigation.

Morder and Robberies

Murder, as defined in common law countries, is the unlawful killing of another human being with "malice aforethought", and generally this state of mind distinguishes murder from other forms of unlawful homicide (such as manslaughter). As the loss of a human being inflicts enormous grief upon the individuals close to the victim, as well as the fact that the commission of a murder is highly detrimental to the good order within society, most societies both present and in antiquity have considered it a most serious crime worthy of the harshest of punishment. In the US, a person convicted of murder is typically given a life sentence or even the death penalty for such an act. A person who commits murder is called a *murderer* ; the term *murderess*, meaning a woman who murders, has largely fallen into disuse.

Legal Analysis of Murder

William Blackstone (citing Edward Coke), in his *Commentaries on the Laws of England* set out the common law definition of murder as

"when a person, of sound memory and discretion, unlawfully killeth any reasonable creature in being and under the king's peace, with malice aforethought, either express or implied. "

The elements of common law murder are:

1. the killing
2. of a human being
3. by another human being
4. with malice aforethought.

The killing—At common law life ended with cardiopulmonary arrest —the total and permanent cessation of blood circulation and respiration. With advances in medical technology courts have adopted irreversible cessation of all brain function as marking the end of life. of a human being—This element presents the issue of when life begins. At common law a fetus was not a human being. Life began when the fetus passed through the birth canal and took its first breath by another human being—at early common law suicide was considered murder. The requirement that the person killed be someone other than the perpetrator excluded suicide from the definition of murder with malice aforethought—originally "malice aforethought" carried its everyday meaning—a deliberate and premeditated killing of another motivated by ill will. Murder necessarily required that an appreciable time pass between the formation and execution of the intent to kill. The courts broadened the scope of murder by eliminating the requirement of actual premeditation and deliberation as well as true malice. All that was required for malice aforethought to exist is that the perpetrator act with one of the four states of mind that constitutes "malice". The four states of mind recognized as constituting "malice" are:

i. Intent to kill,
ii. Intent to inflict grievous bodily harm short of death,
iii. Reckless indifference to an unjustifiably high risk to human life (sometimes described as an "abandoned and malignant heart"), or
iv. Intent to commit a dangerous felony (the "felony-murder" doctrine).

Under state of mind (i), intent to kill, the *deadly weapon rule* applies. Thus, if the defendant intentionally uses a deadly weapon or instrument against the victim, such use authorizes a permissive inference of intent to kill. An example of a deadly weapon or instrument is a gun, a knife, or even a car when intentionally used to strike the victim.

Under state of mind (iii), an "abandoned and malignant heart", the killing must result from defendant's conduct involving a reckless indifference to human life and a conscious disregard of an unreasonable risk of death or serious bodily injury. An example of this is a 2007 law in California where an individual could be convicted of third-degree murder if he or she kills another person while operating a motor vehicle while being under the influence of alcohol, drugs, or controlled substances.

Under state of mind (iv), the felony-murder doctrine, the felony committed must be an inherently dangerous felony, such as burglary, arson, rape, robbery or kidnapping. Importantly, the underlying felony *cannot* be a lesser included offense such as assault, otherwise all criminal homicides would be murder as all are felonies.

Many jurisdictions divide murder by degrees. The most common divisions are between first and second degree murder. Generally second degree murder is common law murder with first degree being an aggravated form. The aggravating factors that distinguish first degree murder from second degree are first degree murder requires a specific intent to kill and premeditation and deliberation. In addition murder committed by acts such as strangulation, poisoning, or lying in wait are treated as first degree murder.

Origins

Murder in Religion

One of the oldest known prohibitions against murder appears in the Sumerian Code of Ur-Nammu written sometime between 2100 and 2050 BC. The code states, "If a man commits a murder, that man must be killed."

In Abrahamic religions, the prohibition against murder is one of the Ten Commandments given by God to Moses in (Exodus: 20v13) and (Deuteronomy 5v17). The Vulgate and subsequent early English translations of the Bible used the term *secretly killeth his neighbour* or *smiteth his neighbour secretly* rather than *murder* for the Latin *clam percusserit proximum.*

Later editions such as Young's Literal Translation and the World English Bible have translated the Latin *occides* simply as *murder* rather than the alternatives of *kill*, *assassinate*, *fall upon* or *slay*. Christian churches have some doctrinal differences about what forms of homicide are prohibited biblically, though all agree murder is.

In Islam according to the Qur'an, one of the greatest sins is to kill a human being who has committed no fault. "For that cause We decreed for the Children of Israel that whosoever killeth a human being for other than manslaughter or corruption in the earth, it shall be as if he had killed all mankind, and whoso saveth the life of one, it shall be as if he had saved the life of all mankind." "Those who invoke not, with Allah, any other god, nor slay such life as Allah has made sacred except for just cause, nor commit fornication; - and any that does this (not only) meets punishment. "

The term 'Assassin' derives from Hashshashin, a militant Ismaili Shi-ite sect, active from the eighth to the fourteenth centuries. This mystic secret society killed members of the Abbasid, Fatimid, Seljuq and Crusader elite for political and religious reasons. The Thuggee cult that plagued India was devoted to Kali, the goddess of death and destruction. According to the *Guinness Book of Records* the Thuggee cult was responsible for approximately 2 million deaths. According to Ross Hassig, author of *Aztec Warfare*, "between 10,000 and 80,400 persons" were sacrificed in the 1487 re-consecration of the Great Pyramid of Tenochtitlan.

Legal Definition

As with most legal terms, the precise definition of murder varies between jurisdictions and is usually codified in some form of legislation.

At Common Law

According to Blackstone, English common law identified murder as a *public wrong*. At common law, murder is considered to be *malum in se*, that is an act which is evil within itself. An act such as murder is wrong/evil by its very nature. And it is the very nature of the act which does not require any specific detailing or definition in the law to consider murder a crime.

Some jurisdictions still take a common law view of murder. In such jurisdictions, precedent case law or previous decisions of the courts of law defines what is considered murder. However, it tends to be rare and the majority of jurisdictions have some statutory prohibition against murder.

Exclusions

- Unlawful killings without malice or intent are considered manslaughter.
- Justified or accidental killings are considered homicides. Depending on the circumstances, these may or may not be considered criminal offences.
- Suicide is not considered murder in most societies. Assisting a suicide, however, may be considered murder in some circumstances.
- Capital punishment ordered by a legitimate court of law as the result of a conviction in a criminal trial with due process for a serious crime.
- Killing of enemy combatants by lawful combatants in accordance with lawful orders in war, although illicit

killings within a war may constitute murder or homicidal war crimes.

- The administration of lethal drugs by a doctor to a terminally ill patient, if the intention is solely to alleviate pain, is seen in many jurisdictions as a special case
- In some cases, killing a person who is attempting to kill another can be classified as self-defence and thus, not murder.

Self-defence

Acting in self-defence or in defence of another person is generally accepted as legal justification for killing a person in situations that would otherwise have been murder. However, a self-defence killing might be considered manslaughter if the killer established control of the situation before the killing took place. In the case of self-defence it is called a "justifiable homicide".

Victim

All jurisdictions require that the victim be a natural person; that is a human being who was still alive at the time of being murdered. In other words, under the law, one cannot murder a cadaver, a corporation, a non-human animal, or any other non-human organism.

California's murder statute, Penal Code Section 187, was interpreted by the Supreme Court of California in 1994 as not requiring *any* proof of the viability of the fetus as a prerequisite to a murder conviction. This holding has two peculiar implications.

The first is that a defendant in California can be convicted for murdering a fetus which the mother herself could legally abort under the framework established in *Roe v. Wade* (1973). However, only the woman's right to abort and thereby kill the fetus before the third trimester is constitutionally protected by *Roe v. Wade* (1973) and therefore although this nullifies the effect of any federal or state legislation criminalizing abortion of a fetus before that point, it does not apply to other persons who kill the fetus. The even stranger part of this holding, as pointed out by Justice Stanley Mosk in dissent, is that a nonviable fetus may be so small, and thus not externally visible, that a defendant can be convicted of intentionally murdering a person he did not even know existed.

Mitigating Circumstances

Some countries allow conditions that "affect the balance of the mind" to be regarded as mitigating circumstances. This means that a person may be found guilty of "manslaughter" on the basis of "diminished responsibility" rather than murder, if it can be proved that the killer was suffering from a condition that affected their judgment at the time. Depression, post-traumatic stress disorder and medication side-effects are examples of conditions that may be taken into account when assessing responsibility.

Insanity

Mental disorder may apply to a wide range of disorders including psychosis caused by schizophrenia and dementia, and excuse the person from the need to undergo the stress of a trial as to liability. In some jurisdictions, following the pre-trial hearing to determine the extent of the disorder, the defence of "not guilty by reason of insanity" may be used to get a not guilty verdict. This defence has two elements:

1. That the defendant had a serious mental illness, disease, or defect.
2. That the defendant's mental condition, at the time of the killing, rendered the perpetrator unable to determine right from wrong, or that what he or she was doing was wrong.

Under New York law, for example:

Mental disease or defect. In any prosecution for an offense, it is an affirmative defence that when the defendant engaged in the proscribed conduct, he lacked criminal responsibility by reason of mental disease or defect.

Such lack of criminal responsibility means that at the time of such conduct, as a result of mental disease or defect, he lacked substantial capacity to know or appreciate either: 1. The nature and consequences of such conduct; or 2. That such conduct was wrong.

Under the French Penal Code:

Article 122-1

- A person is not criminally liable who, when the act was committed, was suffering from a psychological or neuropsychological disorder which destroyed his discernment or his ability to control his actions.
- A person who, at the time he acted, was suffering from a psychological or neuropsychological disorder which reduced his discernment or impeded his ability to control his actions, remains punishable; however, the court shall take this into account when it decides the penalty and determines its regime.

Those who successfully argue a defence based on a mental disorder are usually referred to mandatory clinical treatment until they are certified safe to be released back into the community, rather than prison.

Post-partum Depression

Some countries, such as Canada, Italy, Norway, Sweden, the United Kingdom, New Zealand and Australia, allow postpartum depression (also known as post-natal depression) as a defence against murder of a child by a mother, provided that a child is less than two years old (this may be the specific offense of infanticide rather than murder and include the effects of lactation and other aspects of post-natal care).

In 2009, Texas state representative Jessica Farrar proposed similar rules for her home state.

Unintentional

For a killing to be considered murder, there normally needs to be an element of intent. For this argument to be successful the killer generally needs to demonstrate that they took precautions not to kill and that the death could not have been anticipated or was unavoidable, whatever action they took. As a general rule, manslaughter constitutes reckless killing, while criminally negligent homicide is a grossly negligent killing.

Diminished Capacity

In those jurisdictions using the Uniform Penal Code, such

as California, diminished capacity may be a defence. For example, Dan White used this defence to obtain a manslaughter conviction, instead of murder, in the assassination of Mayor George Moscone and Supervisor Harvey Milk.

Aggravating Circumstances

Murder with specified aggravating circumstances is often punished more harshly. Depending on the jurisdiction, such circumstances may include:

- Premeditation
- Poisoning
- Murder of a police officer, judge, fireman or witness to a crime
- Where the victim was a pregnant woman
- Committed for pay or other reward
- Exceptional brutality or cruelty.

In the United States these aggravated murders are referred to as First Degree murders.

Year-and-a-day Rule

In some common law jurisdictions, a defendant accused of murder is not guilty if the victim survives for longer than one year and one day after the attack. This reflects the likelihood that if the victim dies, other factors will have contributed to the cause of death, breaking the chain of causation. Subject to any statute of limitations, the accused could still be charged with an offence representing the seriousness of the initial assault.

With advances in modern medicine, most countries have abandoned a fixed time period and test causation on the facts of the case.

In the UK, due to medical advancements, the "year-and-a-day-rule" is no longer in use. However, if death occurs three years or more after the original attack then prosecution can take place only with the Attorney-General's approval.

In the United States, many jurisdictions have abolished the rule as well. Abolition of the rule has been accomplished by enactment of statutory criminal codes, which had the effect of displacing the common-law definitions of crimes and corresponding defenses. In 2001, the Supreme Court of the United States held that retroactive application of a state supreme court decision abolishing the year-and-a-day rule did not violate the Ex Post Facto Clause of Article I of the United States Constitution.

In Philadelphia, Pennsylvania, a 74-year-old man, William Barnes, was acquitted of murder charges on May 24, 2010. He was on trial for murder for the death of Philadelphia police officer Walter Barkley. Barnes shot Barkley on November 27, 1966, and served 16 years in prison for attempted murder. Barkley died on August 19, 2007, allegedly from complications of the wounds suffered nearly 41 years earlier.

Epidemiology

An estimated 520,000 people were murdered in 2000 around the globe. Two-fifths of them were young people between the ages of 10 and 29 who were killed by other young people.

Murder rates vary greatly among countries and societies around the world. In the Western world, murder rates in most countries have declined significantly during the 20th century and are now between 1-4 cases per 100,000 people per year. Murder rates in Japan, Ireland and Iceland are among the lowest in the world, around 0.5; the rate of the United States is among the highest of developed countries, around 5.5 in 2004, with rates in larger cities sometimes over 40 per 100,000. 666,160 people have been killed in the United States between 1960 and 1996.

Within the Western world, nearly 90% of all murders are committed by males, with males also being the victims of 74.6% of murders (according the United States Department of Justice). There is a sharp peak in the age distribution of murderers between the ages of 17 and 30. People become less likely to commit a murder as they age. Incidents of children and adolescents committing murders are also extremely rare.

The following absolute murder counts per-country are not comparable because they are not adjusted by each country's total population. Nonetheless, they are included here for reference. There are an estimated 55,000 murders in Brazil every year, about 30,000 murders committed annually in the early 2000s (down to 17000 in 2009) in Russia, approximately 16,000 murders in Colombia in 2009 (the murder rate was 36 per 100,000 people, in 2005 murders went down to 15,000), approximately 20,000 murders each year in South Africa, approximately 17,000 murders in the United States, approximately 15,000 murders in Mexico, approximately 16,000 murders in Venezuela, approximately 6,000 murders in El Salvador, approximately 1,600 murders in Jamaica, approximately 1,000 murders in France, approximately 580 murders per year in Canada, and approximately 200 murders in Chile. The murder rate in Port Moresby, Papua New Guinea is 23 times that of London. 32,719 murder cases were registered across India in 2007. Pakistan reported 9,631 murders.

Murder is the leading cause of death for African American males aged 15 to 34. In 2006, FBI's Supplementary Homicide Report indicated that most of the 14,990 murder victims were Black (7421). In the year 2007 non-negligent homicides, there were 3,221 black victims and 3,587 white victims. While 2,905 of the black victims were killed by a black offender, 2,918 of the white victims were killed by white offenders. There were 566 white victims of black offenders and 245 black victims of white offenders. It should be noted that the "white" category in the Uniform Crime Reports (UCR) includes non-black Hispanics. In London in 2006, 75% of the victims of gun crime and 79% of the suspects were "from the African/Caribbean community." More than 500,000 people have been killed by firearms in Brazil between 1979 and 2003.

Murder demographics are affected by the improvement of trauma care, leading to reduced lethality of violent assaults—thus the murder rate may not necessarily indicate the overall level of social violence.

Development of murder rates over time in different countries is often used by both supporters and opponents of capital punishment and gun control. Using properly filtered data, it is possible to make the case for or against either of these issues. For example, one could look at murder rates in the United States from 1950 to 2000, and notice that those rates went up sharply shortly after a moratorium on death sentences was effectively imposed in the late 1960s. This fact has been used to argue that capital punishment serves as a deterrent and, as such, it is morally justified. Capital punishment opponents frequently counter that the United States has much higher murder rates than Canada and most European Union countries, although all those countries have abolished the death penalty. Overall, the global pattern is too complex, and on average, the influence of both these factors may not be significant and could be more social, economic, and cultural.

The fraction of murders solved has decreased in the United States, from 90% in 1960 to 61% in 2007. Solved murder rates in major U.S. cities varied in 2007 from 36% in Boston, Massachusetts to 76% in San Jose, California. Major factors affecting the arrest rate include witness cooperation and the number of people assigned to investigate the case.

History

According to scholar Pieter Spierenburg murder rates per 100,000 in Europe have fallen over the centuries, from 35 per 100,000 in medieval times, to 20 in 1500 AD, 5 in 1700, to below two per 100,000 "where it has held steady, with minor fluctuations, for the past century." In the United States, murders rates have been higher and have fluctuated. They rose during the nineteenth century, dropped in the years following World War II, before rising again. The rate reached eleven per 100,000 in 1991 before falling to five per 100,000 in present times.

In Corsica, vendetta was a social code that required Corsicans to kill anyone who wronged the family honor. It has been estimated that between 1683 and 1715, nearly 30,000 out of 120,000 Corsicans lost their lives to vendetta, and between 1821 and 1852, no less than 4,300 murders were perpetrated in Corsica.

In India according to the Indian Penal Code, 1860 murder is defined as follows:

Murder.—Except in the cases hereinafter excepted, culpable homicide is murder, if the act by which the death is caused is done with the intention of causing death, or- 167 2ndly.-If it is done with the intention of causing such bodily injury as the offender knows to be likely to cause the death of the person to whom the harm is caused. or- 3rdly.-If it is done with the intention of causing bodily injury to any person and the bodily injury intended to be inflicted is sufficient in the ordinary course of nature to cause death, or- 4thly.-If the person committing the act knows that it is so imminently dangerous that it must, in all probability, cause death, or such bodily injury as is likely to cause death, and commits such act without any excuse for incurring the risk of causing death or such injury as aforesaid.

On the other hand, culpable homicide is defined as;

... by causing death of person other than person whose death was intended.—If a person, by doing anything which he intends or knows to be likely to cause death, commits culpable homicide by causing the death of any person, whose death he neither intends nor knows himself to be likely to cause, the culpable homicide committed by the offender is of the description of which it would have been if he had caused the death of the person whose death he intended or knew himself to he likely to cause. —*Indian Penal Code, 1860*

Robbery

Robbery is the crime of taking or attempting to take something of value by force or threat of force and/or by putting the victim in fear. At common law, robbery is defined as taking the property of another, with the intent to permanently deprive the person of that property, by means of force or fear. Precise definitions of the offence may vary between jurisdictions. Robbery differs from simple theft in its use of violence and intimidation.

The word "rob" came via French from Late Latin words (e.g. *deraubare*) of Germanic origin, from Common Germanic *raub* — "theft"

Among the types of robbery are piracy, armed robbery involving use of a weapon, and aggravated robbery involving use of a deadly weapon or something that appears to be a deadly weapon. Highway robbery or "mugging" takes place outside and in a public place such as a sidewalk, street, or parking lot. Carjacking is the act of stealing a car from a victim by force. Extortion is the threat to do something illegal, or the offer to not do something illegal, in the event that goods are not given, primarily using words instead of actions.

Criminal slang for robbery includes "blagging" (armed robbery, usually of a bank) or "stick-up" (derived from the verbal threat enforcement addressed to the authorities to raise their armed hands in the air), and "steaming" (organized robbery on underground train systems).

English Law

Under section 8(1) of the Theft Act 1968, robbery is an indictable only offence which occurs if the defendant

steals, and immediately before or at the time of doing so, and in order to do so, he uses force on any person or puts or seeks to put any person in fear of being then and there subjected to force.

Steals

This requires evidence to prove a theft as set out in s.1(1) Theft Act, 1968. In R v Robinson (1977), the defendant threatened the victim with a knife in order to recover money which he was actually owed. His conviction for robbery was quashed on the basis that Robinson had an honest, although unreasonable, belief (under Section 2(1)(a) of the Act) in his legal right to the money.

In R v Hale (1979), the application of force and the stealing took place in different locations, and it was not possible to establish the timing; it was held that the appropriation necessary to prove theft was a continuing act, and the jury could correctly convict of robbery; this approach was followed in R v Lockley (1995) when the force was applied to a shopkeeper after property had been taken. It was argued that the theft should be regarded as complete by this time, and R v Gomez (1993), should apply; the court disagreed, preferring to follow R v Hale.

Actual or Threatened Force against a Person

Threat or use of force must be immediate in the presence of the victim. Force used after the completion of *theft* may not elevate theft to robbery. It was held in R v Dawson and James (1978) that "force" is an ordinary English word and its meaning should be left to the jury. This approach was confirmed in R v Clouden (1987) and Corcoran v Anderton (1980), both handbag-snatching cases.

Threat

The victim must be placed in apprehension or fear that force would be used immediately before or at the time of the taking of the property. A threat is not immediate if the wrongdoer threatens to use force of violence some future time.

Robbery occurs if an aggressor forcibly snatched a mobile phone or if he used a knife to make an implied threat of violence to the holder and then took the phone. The person being threatened does not need to be the owner of the property. It is not necessary that the victim was actually frightened, but the defendant must have put or sought to put the victim or some other person in fear of immediate force.

The force or threat may be directed against a third party, for example a customer in a jeweller's shop. (Smith v Desmond [1965] HL) Theft accompanied by a threat to damage property will not constitute robbery, but may disclose an offence of blackmail.

Dishonestly dealing with property stolen during a robbery will constitute an offence of handling.

Assault with Intent to Rob

If a robbery is foiled before it can be completed, an alternative offence under section 8(2) of the 1968 Act is assault; any act which intentionally or recklessly causes another to fear the immediate and unlawful use of force, with an intent to rob, will suffice.

Jurisdiction and Sentence

The definition applies only to England and Wales, by Section 36 of the Theft act 1968.

The maximum sentence is life imprisonment. Robbery and assault with intent to rob are also subject to the mandatory sentencing regime under the Criminal Justice Act 2003. On the 25 July 2006 the Sentencing Guidelines Council published Definitive Guideline on Robbery.

Following *R v Mitchell* (2005) All ER (D) 74, the sentencing guidelines provided in *Attorney General's References (Nos 4 and 7 of 2002)* (2002) EWCA Crim 127 no longer apply to street robbery involving the use of guns for which more severe deterrent sentences will almost invariably be required. In November 2005, the Sentencing Guidelines Council issued new draft guidelines concerning robbery.

United States

In the United States robbery is generally treated as an aggravated form of common law larceny. The elements of robbery are:

1. a trespassory
2. taking and
3. carrying away
4. of the personal property
5. of another
6. with the intent to steal
7. from the person or presence of the victim
8. by force or threat of force.

The first six elements are the same as common law larceny. It is the last two elements that aggravate the crime to common law robbery.

From the person or presence of the victim - robbery requires that the property be taken directly from the person of the victim or from his presence. Note that this is different from larceny which simply requires that property be taken from the victim's possession, actual or constructive. Property is "on the victim's person" if the victim is actually holding the property, or the property is contained within clothing the vicitim is wearing or is attached to victim's body such as a watch or earrings. Property is in a person's presence when it is within the area of his immediate control. The property has to be close enough to the victim's person that the victim could have prevented its taking if she had not been placed in fear or intimidation.

By force or threat of force - the use of force or threat of force is the defining element of robbery. For there to be robbery there must be "force or fear" in perpetrating the theft. Questions concerning the degree of force necessary for robbery have been the subject of much litigation. Merely snatching the property from the victim's person is not sufficient force unless the victim resists or one of the items is attached or carried in such a way that a significant amount of force must be used to free the item from the victim's person.

For robbery the victim must be placed in "fear" of immediate harm by threat or intimidation. The threat need not be directed at the victim personally. Threats to third parties are sufficient. The threat must be one of present rather than future personal harm. Fear does not mean "fright". It means apprehension - an awareness of the danger of immediate bodily harm.

11

Children as Victims

Current concerns about family violence focus on the women who are usually the victims and the men who are usually the assailants. But children are also part of families where violence is happening. Their lives, too, are being affected. Yet we know surprisingly little about their involvement.

A New Zealand study conducted by the National Collective of Independent Women's Refuges (1991) suggested that, for women receiving help from refuges, 90% of their children had witnessed violence and 50% of the children had also been physically abused. Overseas research (Jaffe, 1990; 1992) also confirms that children are often involved directly and indirectly in family violence and that this is likely to have damaging consequences for them both immediately and in the longer term.

Data recorded by the Hamilton Abuse Intervention Pilot Project (Haipp) offered an opportunity to explore further the involvement of children in incidents of family violence in New Zealand. The procedure in Hamilton is for all incidents reported to the police in that Police District to be also reported to Haipp. When an arrest has been made, the Refuge Crisisline is also contacted by the police. Refuge advocates then visit the victim and a victims' "Advocate Form" is completed and collected by Haipp. The form covers details of the incident, the assailant and the victim, including whether or not children were present, witnessed the violence and were abused themselves. One important use of the information is to make it available to the court advocate. In addition some information is routinely computerised although other information, including that on children, is only recorded in the written files.

From the written files we were able to create a computer database of 528 records of police incidents collected by Haipp between July 1991 and April 1994. This included all police incidents which involved a physical assault involving family or people in a close relationship and on which Haipp Advocate Forms had been collected.

From the database it was possible to determine whether or not the victims of family violence had children in their care who were present and who were caught up in the violence; the type of violence that the children witnessed and experienced; and how the children reacted at the time. This paper presents these results, discusses the possible longer term effects of the violence on these children and suggests options for us as a society to protect the children more effectively.

Questions can be raised about the representativeness of the incidents recorded in the database. Haipp Advocate forms were only present for 46% of the police incidents reported to Haipp. The absence of a Haipp Advocate Form could come about because: the woman had left the scene before the advocate arrived; the incident was not notified to the Crisisline at the time and only came to Haipp's attention when the assailant appeared in court, the form was not filled out because information was telephoned directly to the court advocate; the victim did not wish to speak to the advocate; the incident may have been in a remote area outside that in which the advocates were able to operate.

In addition, we did not record details unless it was clear that a physical assault or a serious threat had been made. It is not possible to put numbers on the various reasons and hence it is not possible to establish the representativeness of the data. On the other hand, there is little reason to suppose that the reasons that led to victims not being interviewed were related to the nature of the involvement of children, and in this sense the data is likely to be indicative of what might be expected in a more randomly selected sample of police incidents of family violence in New Zealand.

The Assailants, the Victims, and the Children in the Victims' Care

There was little descriptive data on the assailants. Ethnicity was recorded for 23% and employment for 4%. We have not, therefore, reported any breakdown on these factors because there must be doubt about the reliability of the details. However, all but four of the assailants were male, all but one was over the age of 17, their average age was 31 years and 76% were aged between 20 and 39 years. Furthermore, approximately half (53%) had been convicted previously of an offence involving violence.

The average age of the victims was fairly similar to that of the assailants - 29 years; and 72% were aged between 20 and 39 years. However, twice as many of the victims were under the age of 20 compared with the assailants - 12% of victims but only 6% of assailants - and 3% of the victims were under the age of 17. At least 84% of the victims were female; we do not know the sex of the remaining 16%.

The victim sample was made up of Maori or Pakeha in equal percentages (each group made up 48% of the victim population whose ethnicity was known). This indicates that the victims in this sample are 3 to 4 times as likely to be Maori as would be expected from the 1991 census data on the ethnicity of the population of Hamilton city. However, it is important not to assume from this data that family violence is more likely in Maori families - overseas research suggests that there are considerable differences in the likelihood that the police will become involved in family violence in different groups in the population.

An analysis of the 528 recorded incidents showed that at least 62% of the victims had children under the age of 17 in their care. Those with children had, on average, two each.

How Often do Children Witness the Violence?

Analysis of the data clearly established that children were frequently present when family violence occurred. In 58% of all the incidents on which there was information, children were present in the house at the time.

Because many incidents involved victims who had children in their care, these children were very likely to have been present when the incident occurred. The data show that children were present for 79% of the cases in which victims had children in their care.

Even when victims did not have children in their care, there were children present in the house during 21% of the incidents. These were most likely to be the siblings of a young victim, the assailant's children or the children of other relatives of the assailant or the victim.

When children were present, they were very likely to witness the violence; 73% did so. Other children who were not actually in the same room would often have heard the screams, the thuds and the shouting that must surely have accompanied the assaults:

He kicked & punched her body, grabbed her by the hair and dragged her around the room. He threatened to harm her family and the baby. She was held down to the ground while he slapped and punched her face. He came to the house and broke down the door and threatened the woman. She was punched and kicked. He threatened to hit her with a piece of four by two. He threatened to take the baby.

Some of the comments confirmed that the children did indeed hear what happened even when they did not watch it:

The child, aged 7 years, woke twice and was very frightened. The children heard what happened and the things he was saying about them. The children were in and out of the room. The daughter went to help her mother but he told the kids to get out. The children were in the back room. The 12 year old heard the noise and rang the police.

Afterwards, the children who did not actually see what had happened, would have seen the injuries: *When the victim's cousin, a child, saw the injuries he was afraid and went home.*

In some cases very young babies were in the room. It is not possible to judge the extent to which they would have been affected, but in several examples they were in a crib in the same room as the victim, or in the victim's arms, while the assault was occurring.

What the Children Saw or Heard

Most of the violence that occurred when children were present did not involve objects or weapons - the violence came directly from hands, fists, feet, heads, teeth and bodies (84%). However, 10% of the incidents did involve objects which were used to hit or to throw at the victim. Sometimes the objects seemed like natural weapons: bottles, belts, the hoses of vacuum cleaners and so on. But often they were everyday household articles which were handy at the time: eggs, a plastic vegetable rack, plates, and even a stuffed toy. A minority of the assaults involved weapons: knives or an axe were used, usually to threaten rather than to cut, by 4%, and the use of a gun was threatened in 1% of cases.

The degree of violence was by no means trivial. Table 1 below sets out a classification of the different types of assaults in cases where children witnessed the attack.

Table 1. Table 1: Types of assaults witnessed by children: percentages (N=188)

Percentage(%)	*Types of Assault*
1	Sexual attack
10	Hitting or throwing things at
13	Kicking
27	General attack
34	Punching
7	Pushing and shoving
5	Slapping
5	Threats

Threats were the least obviously injurious but these threats were almost always very drastic: usually a threat to kill or to damage severely. Sometimes they were made or backed up by the display of objects, knives or guns. Slapping or pushing and shoving were the most prominent methods in a number of the incidents to which police were called; in some of these cases there were no visible injuries but in others the women were severely bruised and hurt by being knocked to the ground or against the furniture. Punching was the most frequent method of assault and the results in many of these cases were moderately serious. The next most frequent category was that of general attack, which usually included a range of methods such as pushing, knocking over, dragging along the ground, slamming the victim against a wall or other object, threatening, jumping on the victim and punching or slapping; in many of these cases the injuries were quite severe. Kicking, sometimes accompanied by punching and other forms of attack, often led to severe injuries, especially when the assailant wore steel-capped boots. Only 10% of the victims were hit with objects or had objects thrown at them, in contrast to the 85% who were attacked with hands, feet, heads and bodies. And finally there were a small number of cases which included a sexual assault.

The very brief categorisation above of the assaults gives some indication of their severity; but even more vivid are the full accounts which sometimes ran to several pages. We summarised the accounts in order to fit them into one and a half lines on our computer. Below are some of these summaries. The cases that have been selected are neither the mildest nor the most severe but rather those that are typical:

He hit her with the steel table leg over the body and punched her in the face and head. Pushing her with his hand around her throat, he kept on punching her. She was fist punched, backhanded, pushed against the wall and he attempted to strangle her. Knocked on the floor, kicked in the head, pushed over. Then he pulled a knife and threatened to kill her. He slapped her several times, twisted her arm, pushed her against the cupboards and threatened to break her arm. Picked her up and threw her at the wall and the fridge eight times. Hit her with a cupboard and threatened her with a gun. He threw a chair at her, smashed her into a wall. Then he threw vacuum cleaner pieces at her. Kicked her in the back, punched her face, threw her against a wall and attempted to strangle her. Dragged her around the house by the hair, banged her head on the floor, punched her in the face, grabbed her head and slammed it against the towel rail.

These were traumatic scenes for children to be watching. And in the days following the violence, the children in the victim's care would have seen the impact on their caregiver of the injuries that had been sustained.

Table 2. Table 2: Types of injuries sustained by the victims and the part of the body injured: percentages (N=476)

Percentage	*Type of Injury*
3	Fracture
3	Cut requiring stitches
1	Teeth broken or knocked out
0.5	Rendered unconscious
7	Black eyes
61	Bruises, laceration, redness, swelling etc.
26	No visible injuries

Table 3. Part of body injured (N= 345 visibly injured victims)

Percentage	*Body parts*
80	Head (or head and other parts)
10	Body (or body and limbs)
10	Limbs only

The above table shows that a quarter of the victims reported no visible injuries, but 61% reported being left with visible marks in the form of cuts, bruises, lacerations, swelling and redness. The remainder reported more serious injuries, in the form of black eyes (7%), or damaged teeth, stitches and/or fractures (another 7%). It is noticeable that most of the reported injuries (80%) were to the head, neck and face, so that they would have been very visible. Only 20% of the visible injuries were confined to the body and limbs. The pattern of injuries reported was the same regardless of whether or not children were present or watching.

The reality behind the statistics presented in the above table was detailed on the files:

She had a dislocated jaw, lumps on the head, a broken cartilage on her ear, bruised arms and sore ribs. Two black eyes and a cut above the eye. Bruises on her face and stitches in her head. A black eye, a split lip, a bruised body and lumps on the head. Bruising and teethmarks on her face. A swollen face and red marks around her neck. Damaged wrist, lacerations, swollen hand and twisted neck.

For some of the children, this would not have been the first time they had seen family violence. The records show that for 16% of the assailants there had been a previous violent incident reported to Haipp.

Comments recorded on the Haipp Advocate Form sometimes referred to other incidents:

The children have witnessed me being hit before and they have been affected by the emotional and mental abuse. My daughter has witnessed other assaults.

Sometimes these previous incidents had involved a child rather than an adult as the victim:

The baby was hospitalised before with brain injuries from an assault.

Who was violent to whom in the presence of children.

Most of the children on whom there was information watched an incident in which either the victim or the assailant was their mother or father or in which both of their parents were involved (93%). Another three percent watched a brother or sister being assaulted. The remaining four percent had different relationship to the victim or assailant; for instance: grandchildren, nephew, neighbour, and so on.

In the cases where the children watched one or the other of their parents attacking or being attacked, the relationship between the pair is described in Table 3.

The table shows how close the relationship was between the assailant and the victim. In 63% of the incidents, the children were present during an assault involving both their caregivers. In 17% of cases there had been a close live-in relationship between the assailant and victim previously. Another 11% of the children, although not watching both their caregivers, were watching a couple who were involved in a non live-in romantic relationship. Together these relationships accounted for 90% of the incidents.

In the remaining 10% of the incidents the children who were present watched their fathers attack their siblings, their siblings attack their mothers or one of their parents attacking or being attacked by another relative or friend.

Table 4. Table 3: Relationship between victim and assailant in cases where the victim and/or assailant's child or children was present: percentages (N=250)

Percentage	*Relationship*
27	Married
36	Partners
63	Total in a current live-in relationship
4	Previously married
13	Previously partnered
17	Total in a live-in relationship previously
8	Boyfriend/girlfriend
3	Previously boyfriend/girlfriend
11	Total previous or current non live-in relationship
1	Father attacking his child
2	Son attacking his mother
4	A relative attacking another
3	Other relationships

What Happened to the Children who Watched

Unfortunately the files do not tell us much about the reactions of the children; but the brief comments that were made provided some insight into what probably happened in most of the cases.

The first thing to note is that there was not a single record which suggested that the child witnesses endorsed, joined in or applauded the violence. Where comments were made on the emotional reactions of the children, distress and fear were almost universally recorded:

Children very upset and crying. Children yelling; crying for the assailant to stop; 9 year old boy yelling leave my mum alone; 3 year old calling out "Mum! Dad! Mum! Dad!" The 2 year old was very distressed; screaming and crying. When the daughter found her mother [lying unconscious] she was afraid and tried to waken her mother.

In 15% of the cases when children were present, the children were recorded as having actively attempted to prevent what was happening. Some (6%) tried to get help:

The 14 year old was told to get out of house last night and ran to the neighbours for help. The 7 year old was screaming for her father to stop and the 14 year old ran away to get help. The 5 year old called the police and described the assault to them.

Some (10%) tried actively to intervene to protect the victim or to prevent further harm:

The 14 year old tried to intervene, crying, and the 18 year old also tried to stop what was happening. The 5 year old was crying and yelling for him to leave mum alone. This child had also been assaulted previously by the assailant. The 7 year old jumped on the assailant's back telling him to stop and then ran next door and called the police. The small child was crying and punching the assailant's back saying: "Leave Mummy alone". The children were all crying and their mother was scared for her daughter because the daughter tried to help her.

And some of those who tried to intervene, or even just cried out, were also abused either verbally or physically:

The child screamed and was hit by the assailant. The 2 oldest children tried to intervene and were shouted at and threatened. He threatened the 5 year old with the death of his mother. The children were scared and ran outside. The son [14 years] tried to intervene but was also whacked and pushed. The victim's son [the assailant] picked up a hockey stick and hit his brother on the shoulder when the younger boy tried to intervene. When the son intervened the assailant took him to the washhouse and gave him a hiding. A brother of the 14 year old victim got punched when he tried to intervene.

Sometimes the children seem to have been hurt almost accidentally or as a side product of the attack on another victim:

The chair missed the mother and hit the baby. The baby who was in the mother's arms got hit instead sometimes. The 6 year old boy was screaming and saying: "Don't hurt my mummy". The baby was screaming and so the assailant pushed a toy panda down on the baby. The assailant threw a wooden cot at the baby and knocked the 14 year old to the ground.

The injuries for these children who became caught up in the violence were sometimes life threatening:

The baby was pulled from the mother, dropped on the floor and punched. It was later hospitalised with a fractured skull.

In another case, the threat to a child seemed potentially very dangerous:

He had a rope around the 2 year old's neck connected to the ceiling while he punched the mother around the head and body [he has sole custody of the children].

Altogether, in 16% of the incidents on which there were records of children being present, the children too became victims of the physical violence. In a few cases (3%), the principal object of the violence was a child. The descriptions below outline some of the attacks that were made on children:

Hit with a belt for an hour; massive bruising to the bodies of the children. Hit 12 year old child in the face with a tent pole; broken cheekbone, chipped teeth, stitched face and cut mouth. 14 year old - punched around head and body; bruised head and leg, redness and soreness. 5 year old was hit around the leg with the jug cord, punched in the face and threatened to harm; there were welts on the legs and a bruised cheek.

In at least 30 cases (6% of those where children were present) a pregnant woman was the victim. In 5 of these cases the assault seemed directed, at least in part, toward the unborn child. For example:

She was hit with the fist in the body and stomach. He punched her head, kicked her abdomen, bit her hand and hit her on the head with a handbag. He put her in a headlock and squeezed her stomach. He grabbed her, punched her face and legs, delivered body slaps to her stomach, shoved her and threatened to kill her babies and her; she sustained facial swelling, bruising, a lump on the head and bruised legs and stomach.

And in one case the file noted that the pregnant victim had already miscarried once after a previous beating. A later incident involving the same people was noted in the Haipp files and this time, although the second pregnancy should have resulted in a birth by that date, no children were recorded as being in the care of the woman.

What Happened Afterwards

The violence is only the first part of the incident. Police attended all these scenes, so that the children were likely to have also watched their parents, whether victims or assailants, being interviewed by the police. In 93% of cases the assailants were arrested and taken into police custody. Most of them were later sentenced in court: 14% were given a sentence of imprisonment, 48% received community sentences or monetary penalties and another 24% were given suspended sentences. In addition to these penalties, involvement in a Haipp programme was a condition of their sentence for 62%.

The victims went to the doctor to have their injuries attended in 30% of cases. And in 10% of cases women went to a refuge. All these events are likely to have affected the children in a variety of ways and in different degrees.

Conclusions

Family violence is usually seen as occurring between men and women in intimate relationships. The reality is in many cases more complex. The data recorded on the Haipp files paints a vivid picture of the extent to which children are intimately involved with family violence The two principals involved in the incidents were often parents who were caring for children (in at least 62% of incidents in the sample the victim was a parent of children under 17). Children were present in the house while the violence was occurring in 87% of the incidents in which their parent was the victim. They usually witnessed the violence, or at least heard it. The beatings often occurred to the punctuation of screams and cries from frightened children. Sometimes the children became directly involved in the incident by trying to intervene (10%) or by seeking help (6%). And, in nearly one in 5 incidents, the children were themselves the targets either principally or as well: unborn children were attacked as they lay in their mothers womb, babies were punched by mistake or thrown from their mother's arms, children were belted and punched and threats were made to take them away or to hurt them.

As well as this direct involvement, the children are likely to be affected by what they see and hear. Over and above the immediate fear of being in a violent situation, there are a number of other elements that may create conflict for the children. First, the children are watching at least one of their parents act violently or being the target of violence. When both caregivers are involved there must be a conflict between the child's loyalty to the assailant and to the victim. Second, regardless of loyalties, the children are faced with the practical question of what should they do about the violence. Third, the child is seeing violence portrayed as part of a close sexual relationship between adults. These experiences are likely to have a powerful effect on the child's developing understanding of intimate adult life and the role of violence in human relationships. Nor can one feel much more sanguine about the impact on the children who witnessed the other assaults.

What will be the future of children whose vivid early memories of close human relationships enshrine violence and victimisation? Overseas research (Jaffe et al, 1992 reviews much of this work) increasingly suggests that children who have witnessed family violence demonstrate adjustment difficulties in a number of areas including health problems, cognitive deficits, adolescent hostility and aggression and difficulties in adult relationships with the opposite sex. Research also suggests that these are the children who are likely to grow up to fight and bully their peers, to beat their wives and to commit violent crimes; or, especially if they are female, who are likely to acquiesce in victimisation and accept violence from their friends and partners.

The data described in this paper come from records of incidents that came to police attention because of a primary focus on men's violence towards women. The fact that there were so many cases where the violence towards children during these incidents remained in the background, raises the question of how much more violence towards children goes unrecorded. Certainly it seems reasonable to assume from this data that, despite the growing awareness of the need to call the police when men hit women, there is not the same recognition of the need to call the police when children are the victims. To beat or belt a child, or even to punch them, is still seen by many as a legitimate part of parenting. A recent study from this

Office showed that 2% of a random sample of over 300 current parents said that they had given their child "a really severe thrashing" and 11% reported that they had "hit with a strap, stick or something similar". Such behaviour is likely to continue to be seen as acceptable parenting rather than violence towards children so long as it is supported by the fact that Section 59 of the Crimes Act 1961 exempts from a charge of assault parents who use "reasonable force" towards their children.

Not only is there too little information in New Zealand on the incidence and prevalence of family violence that involves children, but we also know too little of the impact that family violence has on children who are caught up in it. Locally the only research on the effects on children of involvement in family violence comes from a recent thesis by Tanya Pocock (1994), which compares children in refuges with children who are not.

Although research is needed, the information that is already available clearly establishes that a problem exists. It is time to include children in policies about family violence.

If New Zealand is to assert the importance of laying charges when women are assaulted, the police should equally be required to lay charges when children have been assaulted. Here, the problem may be in part one of awareness. Routine inquiries by police who attend incidents of family violence about whether or not any children have also suffered from the violence may lead to better protection of children; especially if the police are also required to act on any case where there is evidence of violence towards children.

Domestic Protection orders are currently available only to those in a spousal relationship (although a woman's children may also be named on protection orders). Restraining orders are available under the Children, Young Persons and Their Families Act 1989 to protect children but they are not readily available on the first occasion an incident of violence involving a child is reported. Alterations to the Domestic Protection Act which are currently being considered could protect children in families where violence has occurred or been threatened and orders to protect children could be made available on an ex parte basis in the same way as they are available to an adult partner (Office of the Commissioner for Children, 1994). Further, the police should be included as a party able to make application for orders for the protection of a child where there are grounds to believe that the child may be in danger.

At present, custody orders can be made without those conducting inquiries being required to ascertain whether or not there has been a history of violence in the relationship between the adults and the children involved - these practices should be reviewed. Recently Justice Sir Ronald Davison (1994) has proposed that a primary concern in all dealings with situations where family violence has occurred should be - are the children safe? He specifically proposes that a parent who has used violence against a spouse should not be granted custody or unsupervised access until they can show that the child will be safe with them. Other North American jurisdictions are currently considering or have developed codes that include a concern for the potential physical danger to children (Hart, 1992). Such proposals deserve consideration in relation to Family Court proceedings and in relation to all other inquiries about the placement of children.

It's nearly unthinkable, but every year thousands of children become victims of crime—whether it's through kidnappings, violent attacks, or sexual abuse.

It is necessary to reach children with messages about crime, violence, and drug prevention. We may like to think that children don't yet need to know about these topics, but many kids are exposed to crime, violence, and drugs at home, in their neighbourhoods, and in the news media.

Law enforcement officers, teachers, and other adults can play an important role in protecting children and helping them to gain the skills they need to make positive decisions for the rest of their lives.

Many law enforcement officers and other adults work with children to teach them how to protect themselves and keep themselves safe. Often, they will visit schools, scout meetings, and community events to talk with children about these topics. McGruff can help you reach children with fun and educational messages – he's a proven communicator to children of all ages.

Victims of Violence by Lovers

During one media reprieve from infamy, O.J. Simpson said, "Assume that I killed her. It was only because I loved her so much." This chilling concession isn't uncommon. Most violent crimes are "love crimes", motivated by an intimate relationship that has dissolved into the inflamed passions of jealousy and anger. We all would, if we could, but can't, expunge the ill consequences that can flow from the failures of the highest and noblest passion of all, love for another. Yet, no one suggests that these crimes warrant a more severe punishment, simply because they were motivated by lost love. They may actually evoke pity and a lesser penalty. That is the humane face of deliberative justice, which is quite distinct from the critically different element of established intent.

English common law has long recognized intent as a valid mitigating factor in crime. That's why we have clear distinctions between pre-meditated and passionate murders, manslaughter, and accidents. Though not always clearly demonstrable, intent always counts. The fundamental objective of all laws is (or ought to be) just deserts. Justice cannot be accomplished if there was no intent to cause injury. One factor in establishing intent is discovering motive. Showing a reason why the accused may have intended the crime can be circumstantial evidence of intent. Clear intent will bear on the severity of the accusation and the punishment. But, intent is not the crime and neither is motive. In various degrees and kinds, it is the act -and only the act - of inflicting injury that constitutes the crime, not the actor's mental inclination. Mitigating this principle of punishing bad acts can only damage justice.

The second most common motive for crime is hate. Frequently, it is as much self-hate as it is hatred of the intended victim. Like love, hate is just another human emotion that can overcome our better judgement. Hatred is not always an evil emotion. Because we hate crime, we punish the perpetrator. We hate the totalitarian despot who murders innocent subjects. Hatred can be justified by the extremes of evil. We can even hate the hatred that is unjust and erroneous. It is this later kind of hatred that has brought us "hate crimes". Is it contemptible to hate those who act violently on the basisof irrational prejudice and fear? Of course not. We ought to roundly condemn and correct those whose motives are either impure or perverted. That, however, is a process of persuasion and rational council, not the province of justice. Though their motives may be pernicious and damnable, it is only when they act on them that we can invoke the rule of law. Any other course brings us to the verge of "thought crimes".

Perhaps there are those who can honestly say that they harbor no prejudice toward anyone and never entertain irrational fears. The self-righteous among them will proceed quickly to claim that the also know what everyone else ought to think. The fools among them will proceed quickly to propose constraints and punishment on those who harbor any ill-conceived notions about the world or reality. And they are fools, not because their intent is bad, but because their penal acts would violate the fundamental principles of justice and civil discourse. For the ideals they love, they would exacerbate and entrench the hatred they fear.

Battling ill-founded hatred and fear is a task granted to every human. We ought to contribute in every way possible to improving communication, knowledge, and tolerance among those with different skin colours and different superegos. Rational discussion and civil debate is the only tool available to accomplish that end. Passing laws that impose criminal penalties on ill-will is little more than self-delusion. Free speech is nothing without free thought. Free thought requires trial and error before there can be learning. Executing every criminal, burning every book, banning every idea that fails to conform will not advance civilization. Expanding sanctions for crimes motivated by hatred will not advance justice.

When it comes to crime, there is one motive more horrendous than either love or hate. It is beyond thoughtless, crude or inhumane. The motive is: no motive at all. There are humans (if they can be called that) who get their pleasure from giving others pain. They have no hate or love for themselves or their victims. They have no respect for human, or any other variation, of life. They kill, maim, and destroy, not for profit or comfort, but purely for their own pleasure. They are the monsters of fiction and history. If there were any motive worthy of the most severe punishment, it would be no motive at all. We want to understand motives in order to combat the root causes of crime. That's a worthy goal for education and persuasion, but adding incremental punishments of some motives over others accomplishes nothing. The fundamental principle of civilization, which must be exposed to our children and imposed on criminals, is that initiating force is never an acceptable solution to any problem. Hate or love as your will inclines, but only resort to violence in self-defence. Hate crime, hate the criminal if you must, but always love and cherish justice.

Hate Crime

Hate crimes (also known as bias-motivated crimes) occur when a perpetrator targets a victim because of his or her perceived membership in a certain social group, usually defined by racial group, religion, sexual orientation, disability, class, ethnicity, nationality, age, gender, gender identity, or political affiliation.

"Hate crime" generally refers to criminal acts which are seen to have been motivated by bias against one or more of the types above, or of their derivatives. Incidents may involve physical assault, damage to property, bullying, harassment, verbal abuse or insults, or offensive graffiti or letters (hate mail).

History

Examples from the past include Roman persecution of Christians, the Ottoman genocide of Armenians, and various Nazi pogroms, starting out as locally-sanctioned anti-Jewish activity in the early years of Nazi occupations and eventually reaching its apex in the Final Solution for the Jews.

More recently, ethnic conflicts in Bosnia and Herzegovina and genocide in Rwanda have been described as mass-based hate crimes, but the term "hate crime" did not really begin to be used until after World War II and the end of most major government-sanctioned racial cleansing projects that had been linked with official fascism. The term "hate crime" is now used more often than in the past mainly because the groups that used to have official endorsement under fascist-linked regimes have now broken up into smaller grouplets that are still committed to the underlying racist and xenophobic ideas, but whose only real outlet for those ideas is individual actions rather than administratively-approved ones. Thus, "hate crime" as that term is most often used today is largely seen as, and dealt with, in a law enforcement capacity by police in individual areas, rather than on a larger scale with intergovernmental and/or armed forces involvement.

Concern about hate crimes has become increasingly prominent among policymakers in many nations and at all levels of government in recent years. There have been many examples throughout modern-day Europe by groups who harass and threaten many different racial groups.

In the United States, racial and religious biases have inspired most hate crimes. As Europeans began to colonize the New World in the 16th and 17th centuries, Native Americans increasingly became the targets of bias-motivated intimidation and violence.

During the past two centuries, some of the more typical examples of hate crimes in the U.S. include lynchings of African Americans, cross burnings to drive black families from predominantly white neighbourhoods, assaults on white people traveling in predominantly black neighbourhoods, assaults on lesbian, gay, bisexual and transgender people, the painting of swastikas on Jewish synagogues and xenophobic responses to a variety of minority ethnic groups.

Examples like the murder of Channon Christian and Christopher Newsom and the Wichita Massacre tend not to be classified as "hate crimes" by U.S. investigative officials, but they have meanwhile been blasted as "hate crimes against whites by blacks" by right-wing commentators such as David Horowitz (a right-wing author and academic) and Michelle Malkin (a commentator for the Fox News channel and a prolific conservative author).

The district attorneys in both these cases have specifically stated that while these incidents were indeed horrible, and had tremendous impacts on the communities affected by them, neither displayed evidence of being black-on-white racism, either upon initial or more in-depth review.

Hate Crime Victims

In the United States, racist anti-black bias is the most frequently reported hate crime motivation. African-Americans constitute the second-largest minority group with Hispanics being the first largest. Of the nearly 8,000 hate crimes reported to the FBI in 1995, the most frequently reported motivation was bias against blacks, almost 3,000, other frequently reported bias motivations were anti-white, Jewish, Gay, Muslim, Asian, Native American, and Hispanic.

Psychological Effects

From a psychological standpoint, hate crimes may have extreme consequences. A manual issued by the Attorney-General of the Province of Ontario in Canada lists the following consequences:

- *effects on people* – psychological and affective disturbances; repercussion on the victim's identity and self-esteem; both reinforced by the degree of violence of a hate crime, usually stronger than that of a common one.
- *effect on the targeted group* – generalized terror in the group to which the victim belongs, inspiring feelings of vulnerability over the other members, who could be the next victims.
- *effect on other vulnerable groups* – ominous effects over minoritarian groups or over groups that identify themselves with the targeted one, especially when the referred hate is based on an ideology or doctrine that preaches simultaneously against several groups. Hate Crime is reported to the FBI

Hate Crime Laws

Hate crime laws generally fall into one of several categories: (1) laws defining specific bias-motivated acts as distinct crimes; (2) criminal penalty-enhancement laws; (3) laws creating a distinct civil cause of action for hate crimes; and (4) laws requiring administrative agencies to collect hate crime statistics. Sometimes (as in Bosnia and Herzegovina), the laws focus on war crimes, genocide, and crimes against humanity with the prohibition against discriminatory action limited to public officials.

Eurasia

Andorra

Discriminatory acts constituting harassment or infringement of a person's dignity on the basis of origin, citizenship, race, religion, or sex. Courts have cited bias-based motivation in delivering sentences, but there is no explicit penalty enhancement provision in the Criminal Code. The government does not track hate crime statistics, although they are relatively rare.

Armenia

Armenia has a penalty-enhancement statute for crimes with ethnic, racial, or religious motives.

Austria

Austria has a penalty-enhancement statute for crimes with racist or xenophobic motivation.

Azerbaijan

Azerbaijan has a penalty-enhancement statute for crimes motivated by racial, national, or religious hatred. Murder and infliction of serious bodily injury motivated by racial, religious, national, or ethnic intolerance are distinct crimes.

Belarus

Belarus has a penalty-enhancement statute for crimes motivated by racial, national, and religious hatred and discord.

Belgium

Belgium's Act of 25 February 2003 (""aimed at combating discrimination and modifying the Act of 15 February 1993 which establishes the Centre for Equal Opportunities and the Fight against Racism"") establishes a penalty-enhancement for crimes involving discrimination on the basis of sex, supposed race, color, descent, national or ethnic origin, sexual orientation, civil status, birth, fortune, age, religious or philosophical beliefs, current or future state of health and handicap or physical features. The Act also "provides for a civil remedy to address discrimination." The Act, along with the Act of 20 January 2003 ("on strengthening legislation against racism""), requires the Centre to collect and publish statistical data on racism and discriminatory crimes.

Bosnia and Herzegovina

The Criminal Code of Bosnia and Herzegovina (enacted 2003) "contains provisions prohibiting discrimination by public officials on grounds, inter alia, of race, skin colour, national or ethnic background, religion and language and prohibiting the restriction by public officials of the language rights of the citizens in their relations with the authorities."

Bulgaria

Bulgarian criminal law prohibits certain crimes motivated by racism and xenophobia, but a 1999 report by the European Commission against Racism and Intolerance found that it does not appear that those provisions "have ever resulted in convictions before the courts in Bulgaria."

Croatia

Croatian law allows for consideration of any extenuating or aggravating circumstances in sentencing, but no explicit provision is made for bias-based motivations.

Czech Republic

"The Czech Criminal Code defines racist motivation as a specific aggravating circumstance that judges are required to take into account in sentencing, as well as defining specific racist acts as crimes. Section 196 punishes "'violence against a group of inhabitants and against individuals on the basis of race, nationality, political conviction or religion.""

Denmark

Although Danish law does not include explicit hate crime provisions, "section 80(1) of the Criminal Code instructs courts to take into account the gravity of the offence and the offender's motive when meting out penalty, and therefore to attach importance to the racist motive of crimes in determining sentence." In recent years judges have used this provision to increase sentences on the basis of racist motives.

Since 1992, the Danish Civil Security Service (PET) has released statistics on crimes with apparent racist motivation.

Finland

Finnish Criminal Code 515/2003 (enacted January 31, 2003) makes "committing a crime against a person, because of his national, racial, ethnical or equivalent group" an aggravating circumstance in sentencing. In addition, ethnic agitation is criminalized and carries a fine or a prison sentence of not more than two years.

The prosecution need not prove that an actual danger to an ethnic group is caused but only that malicious message is emissioned. A more aggravated hate crime, warmongering (Finnish: *sotaan yllyttäminen*), carries a prison sentence of one to ten years. However, in case of warmongering, the prosecution must prove an overt act that evidently increases the risk that Finland is involved in a war or becomes a target for a military operation. The act in question may consist of

1. illegal violence directed against foreign country or her citizens,
2. systematic dissemination of false information on Finnish foreign policy or defence
3. public influence on the public opinion towards a pro-war viewpoint or
4. public suggestion that a foreign country or Finland should engage in an aggressive act.

France

In 2003, France enacted penalty-enhancement hate crime laws for crimes motivated by bias against the victim's actual or perceived ethnicity, nation, race, religion, or sexual orientation. The penalties for murder were raised from 30 years (for non-hate crimes) to life imprisonment (for hate crimes), and the penalties for violent attacks leading to permanent disability were raised from 10 years (for non-hate crimes) to 15 years (for hate crimes).

Georgia

"There is no general provision in Georgian law for racist motivation to be considered an aggravating circumstance in prosecutions of ordinary offences. Certain crimes involving racist motivation are, however, defined as specific offences in the Georgian Criminal Code of 1999, including murder motivated by racial, religious, national or ethnic intolerance; infliction of serious injuries motivated by racial, religious, national or ethnic intolerance; and torture motivated by racial, religious, national or ethnic intolerance. ECRI reported no knowledge of cases in which this law has been enforced. There is no systematic monitoring or data collection on discrimination in Georgia."

Germany

Modern-day Germany has very tough anti-Nazi laws, and BfV monitors the neo-Nazi groups that choose to defy these laws and take actions in accordance with the ideas of Nazism. German law specifically states that any group of this type is closely watched and that any attempt on their part to grow to a point where they could have influence in the German government will be stopped.

The German administrative structure is very wary of any group, fascist or not, that vies for absolute power. That being said, the German Criminal Code does not specifically acknowledge any direct penalty in connection with hate or bias more generally.

In the German legal framework motivation is not taken into account while identifying the element of the offence. However, within the sentencing procedure the judge can define certain principles for determining punishment. In section 46 of the German Criminal Code it is stated that "the motives and aims of the perpetrator; the state of mind reflected in the act and the wilfulness involved in its commission." can be taken into consideration when determining the punishment. In the past hate and bias was regarded here.

The only section in the German Criminal Code where hate and/or bias could be taken into consideration directly in case of a violent hate crime is 211 (Murder). The qualification for murder (imprisonment for life) instead of manslaughter (imprisonment not less than five years) is stated in paragraph 2 of section 211: "A murderer is, whoever kills a human being out of murderous lust, to satisfy his sexual desires, from greed or otherwise base motives, treacherously or cruelly or with means dangerous to the public or in order to make another crime possible or cover it up." In the past judges confirmed racial hate and xenophobia as being "otherwise base motives" that enhances a manslaughter to murder.

Besides that the German Criminal Code holds sections against hate speech. Sections 86, 86a were introduced to defend against the ideas of National Socialism. The underlying principle is that propaganda material from forbidden organizations and parties (to which the NSDAP but also modern hate groups belong) can affect the public peace and safety as well as the Free Democratic Basic Order of Germany and therefore may lead to violence.

Section 130 states: "(1) Whoever, in a manner that is capable of disturbing the public peace: 1. incites hatred against segments of the population or calls for violent or arbitrary measures against them; or 2. assaults the human dignity of others by insulting, maliciously maligning, or defaming segments of the population, shall be punished with imprisonment from three months to five years. (...) (3) Whoever publicly or in a meeting approves of, denies or renders harmless an act committed under the rule of National Socialism of the type indicated in Section 220a subsection (1), in a manner capable of disturbing the public peace shall be punished with imprisonment for not more than five years or a fine."

Again the public peace and safety is protected and not the bodily integrity of an individual. Especially paragraph 3 shows a huge difference between Germany and (for example) the U.S. in defining the freedom of speech.

In this case the so called "Auschwitz lie" – denying, approving or rendering harmless the Holocaust – is considered to disrespect the suffering of all victims. The legally protected interest of the human dignity (in Germany section 1 of the Grundgesetz (constitution)) limits the legally protected interest of freedom of speech (section 5 of the German Grundgesetz). In the U.S. this would be vice versa.

Greece

Article Law 927/1979 "Section 1,1 penalises incitement to discrimination, hatred or violence towards individuals or groups because of their racial, national or religious origin, through public written or oral expressions; Section 1,2 prohibits the establishment of, and membership in, organisations which organise propaganda and activities aimed at racial discrimination; Section 2 punishes public expression of offensive ideas; Section 3 penalises the act of refusing, in the exercise of one's occupation, to sell a commodity or to supply a service on racial grounds." Public prosecutors may press charges even if the victim does not file a complaint. However, as of 2003, no convictions had been attained under the law.

Hungary

Violent action, cruelty, and coercion by threat made on the basis of the victim's actual or perceived national, ethnic, or religious status are punishable under article 174/B of the Hungarian Criminal Code.

Iceland

Section 233 of the Icelandic Penal Code states "Anyone who in a ridiculing, slanderous, insulting, threatening or any other manner publicly assaults a person or a group of people on the basis of their nationality, skin colour, race, religion or sexual orientation, shall be fined or jailed for up to 2 years." (The word "assault" in this context does not refer to physical violence, only to expressions of hatred.)

Iran

The Iranian constitution, article 14 states: "In accordance with the sacred verse 'God does not forbid you to deal kindly and justly with those who have not fought against you because of your religion and who have not expelled you from your homes' [60:8], the government of the Islamic Republic of Iran and all Muslims are duty-bound to treat non-Muslims in conformity with ethical norms and the principles of Islamic justice and equity, and to respect their human rights. This principle applies to all who refrain from engaging in conspiracy or activity against Islam and the Islamic Republic of Iran."

Sexual orientation is not recognized as a protected class within the state: homosexuality is punishable by death, and executions under this provision are common.

Ireland

"The Prohibition of Incitement to Hatred Act 1989" makes it an offense to incite hatred against any group of persons on account of their race, color, nationality, religion, sexual orientation, ethnic or national origins, or membership of the Traveller community, an indigenous minority group."

Ireland does not systematically collect hate crime data.

Italy

Italian criminal law, at Section 3 of Law No. 205/1993, contains a penalty-enhancement provision for all crimes motived by racial, ethnic, national, or religious bias.

Kazakhstan

In Kazakhstan, there are constitutional provisions prohibiting propaganda promoting racial or ethnic superiority.

Kyrgyzstan

In Kyrgyzstan, "the Constitution of the State party prohibits any kind of discrimination on grounds of origin, sex, race, nationality, language, faith, political or religious convictions or any other personal or social trait or circumstance, and that the prohibition against racial discrimination is also included in other legislation, such as the Civil, Penal and Labour Codes."

Article 299 of the Criminal Code defines incitement to national, racist, or religious hatred as a specific offense. This article has been used in political trials of suspected members of the banned organization Hizb-ut-Tahrir.

Scotland

In Scottish Common law the courts can take any aggravating factor into account when sentencing someone found guilty of an offence. There is specific legislation dealing with the offences of incitement of racial hatred, racially-aggravated harassment and offences aggravated by religious prejudice. A Scottish Executive working party examined the issue of hate crime and ways of combating crime motivated by social prejudice, reporting in 2004. Its main recommendations were not implemented, but in their manifestos for the Scottish Parliament election, 2007 several political parties included commitments to legislate in this area, including the Scottish National Party who now form the Scottish Government. The Offences (Aggravation by Prejudice) (Scotland) Bill was introduced on 19 May 2008 by Patrick Harvie MSP, having been prepared with support from the Scottish Government, and passed unanimously by the parliament on 3 June 2009.

Spain

Article 22(4) of the Spanish Penal Code includes a penalty-enhancement provision for crimes motivated by bias against the victim's ideology, beliefs, religion, ethnicity, race, nationality, gender, sexual orientation, illness, or disability.

Sweden

Article 29 of the Swedish Penal Code includes a penalty-enhancement provision for crimes motivated by bias against the victim's race, color, nationality, ethnicity, sexual orientation, religion, or "other circumstance" of the victim.

United Kingdom

For England, Wales, and Scotland, the Crime and Disorder Act 1998 makes hateful behaviour towards a victim based on the victim's membership (or presumed membership) in a racial group or a religious group an aggravation in sentencing for specified crimes. For Northern Ireland, Public Order (Northern Ireland) Order 1987 (S.I. 1987/463 (N.I. 7)) serves the same purpose. A "racial group" is a group of persons defined by reference to race, colour, nationality (including citizenship) or ethnic or national origins. A "religious group" is a group of persons defined by reference to religious belief or lack of religious belief. The specified crimes are assault, criminal damage, offences under the Public Order Act 1986, and offences under the Protection from Harassment Act 1997.

The Criminal Justice Act 2003 compels a court to consider whether a crime which is not specified by the Crime and Disorder Act 1998 is racially or religiously aggravated. The Act compels a court also to consider whether the following circumstances were pertinent to the crime:

(a) that, at the time of committing the offence, or immediately before or after doing so, the offender demonstrated towards the victim of the offence hostility based on—

(i) the sexual orientation (or presumed sexual orientation) of the victim, or

(ii) a disability (or presumed disability) of the victim, or

(b) that the offence is motivated (wholly or partly)—

(i) by hostility towards persons who are of a particular sexual orientation, or

(ii) by hostility towards persons who have a disability or a particular disability.

Eurasian Countries with no Hate Crime Laws

Albania, Cyprus, Estonia, San Marino, and Slovenia have no hate crime laws.

North America

Canada

The hate crime provision of the Canadian Criminal Code is Section 718.2. The section states (with regard to the hate crime):

A court that imposes a sentence shall also take into consideration the following principles:

(a) a sentence should be increased or reduced to account for any relevant aggravating or mitigating circumstances relating to the offence or the offender, and, without limiting the generality of the foregoing,

(i) evidence that the offence was motivated by bias, prejudice or hate based on race, national or ethnic origin, language, colour, religion, sex, age, mental or physical disability, sexual orientation, or any other similar factor,... shall be deemed to be aggravating circumstances.

Section 430(4.1) of the Canadian Criminal Code provides an increased penalty for "mischief" when the mischief affects a place of religious worship or religious property or a cemetery and is motivated by "bias, prejudice or hate based on religion, race, colour or national or ethnic origin."

United States

Defined in the 1999 National Crime Victim Survey, "A hate crime is a criminal offense. In the United States federal prosecution is possible for hate crimes committed on the basis of a person's race, religion, or nation origin when engaging in a federally protected activity." In 2009, the Matthew Shepard Act added perceived gender, gender identity, sexual orientation, and disability to the federal definition, and dropped the prerequisite that the victim be engaging in a federally-protected activity.

Forty-five states and the District of Columbia have statutes criminalizing various types of hate crimes. Thirty-one states and the District of Columbia have statutes creating a civil cause of action in addition to the criminal penalty for similar acts. Twenty-seven states and the District of Columbia have statutes requiring the state to collect hate crime statistics

According to the FBI Hate Crime Statistics report for 2006, hate crimes increased nearly 8% nationwide, with a total of 7,722 incidents and 9,080 offences reported by participating law enforcement agencies. Of the 5,449 crimes against persons, 46% were classified as intimidation and 31.9% as simple assaults. 81% of the 3,593 crimes against property were acts of vandalism or destruction.

However, according to the FBI Hate Crime Statistics for 2007, the number of hate crimes decreased to 7,624 incidents reported by participating law enforcement agencies. These incidents included 9 murders and 2 rapes(out of the almost 17,000 murders and 90,000 forcible rapes committed in the U.S. in 2007).

Attorney General Eric Holder said in June 2009 that recent killings show the need for a tougher U.S. hate crimes law to stop "violence masquerading as political activism".

South America

Brazil

In Brazil, hate crime laws focus on racism, racial injury, and other special bias-motivated crimes such as, for example, murder by death squads and genocide on the grounds of nationality, ethnicity, race or religion. Murder by death squads and genocide are legally classified as "hideous crimes" (*crimes hediondos* in Portuguese).

The crimes of racism and racial injury, although similar, are enforced slightly differently. Article 140, 3rd paragraph, of the Penal Code establishes a harsher penalty, from a minimum of 1 year to a maximum of 3 years, for injuries motivated by "elements referring to race, color, ethnicity, religion, origin, or the condition of being an aged or disabled person". On the other side, Law 7716/1989 covers "crimes resulting from discrimination or prejudice on the grounds of race, color, ethnicity, religion, or national origin".

In addition, the Brazilian Constitution defines as a "fundamental goal of the Republic" (Article 3rd, clause IV) "to promote the wealth of all, with no prejudice as to origin, race, sex, color, age, and any other forms of discrimination".

Support and Opposition

Support for Hate Crime Laws

Justifications for harsher punishments for hate crimes focus on the notion that hate crimes cause greater individual and societal harm. It is said that, when the core of a person's identity is attacked, the degradation and dehumanization is especially severe, and additional emotional and physiological problems are likely to result. Society then, in turn, can suffer from the disempowerment of a group of people. Furthermore, it is asserted that the chances for retaliatory crimes are greater when a hate crime has been committed. The riots in Los Angeles, California that followed the beating of Rodney King, a Black motorist, by a group of White police officers are cited as support for this argument. The beating of white truck driver Reginald Denny by black rioters during the same riot is also an example that would support this argument.

The U.S. Supreme Court unanimously found that *penalty-enhancement* hate crime statutes do not conflict with free speech rights because they do not punish an individual for exercising freedom of expression; rather, they allow courts to consider motive when sentencing a criminal for conduct which is not protected by the First Amendment.

When it enacted the Hate Crimes Act of 2000, the New York State Legislature found that:

Hate crimes do more than threaten the safety and welfare of all citizens. They inflict on victims incalculable physical and emotional damage and tear at the very fabric of free society. Crimes motivated by invidious hatred toward particular groups not only harm individual victims but send a powerful message of intolerance and discrimination to all members of the group to which the victim belongs. Hate crimes can and do intimidate and disrupt entire communities and vitiate the civility that is essential to healthy democratic processes. In a democratic society, citizens cannot be required to approve of the beliefs and practices of others, but must never commit criminal acts on account of them. Current law does not adequately recognize the harm to public order and individual safety that hate crimes cause. Therefore, our laws must be strengthened to provide clear recognition of the gravity of hate crimes and the compelling importance of preventing their recurrence. Accordingly, the legislature finds and declares that hate crimes should be prosecuted and punished with appropriate severity."

Opposition to Hate Crime Laws

The U.S. Supreme Court unanimously found the St. Paul Bias-Motivated Crime Ordinance amounted to viewpoint based discrimination in conflict with rights of free speech because it selectively criminalized bias-motivated speech or symbolic speech for disfavored topics while permitting such speech for other topics. Many critics further assert that it conflicts with an even more fundamental right: free thought. The claim is that hate-crime legislation effectively makes certain ideas or beliefs, including religious ones, illegal, in other words, thought crimes. In their book *Hate Crimes: Criminal Law and Identity Politics*, James B. Jacobs and Kimberly Potter criticize hate crime legislation for exacerbating conflicts between groups. They assert that by defining crimes as being committed by one group against another, rather than as being committed by individuals against their society, the labelling of crimes as "hate crimes" causes groups to feel persecuted by one another, and that this impression of persecution can incite a backlash and thus lead to an actual increase in crime. Some have argued hate crime laws bring the law into disrepute and further divide society, as groups apply to have their critics silenced. Some have argued that if it is true that all violent crimes are the result of the perpetrator's contempt for the victim, then all crimes are hate crimes. Thus, if there is no alternate rationale for prosecuting some people more harshly for the same crime based on who the victim is, then different defendants are treated unequally under the law, which violates the United States Constitution.

Critiquing Reliance on the Prison Industrial Complex

There are also those who oppose hate crimes laws because of the power such legislation gives to the prison industrial complex. The critiques from such a point of view are extensive and include, "Hate crime law sets up the State as protector, intending to deflect our attention from the violence it perpetrates, deploys, and sanctions. The government, its agents, and their institutions perpetuate systemic violence and set themselves up as the only avenue in which justice can be allocated; they will never be charged with hate crimes."

12

Rape and other Sexual Crimes

Rape is the most underreported crime in America as well the World over. Significant changes to improve the treatment of sexual assault victims have occurred in the last two decades. The impact of reforms, led by the women's movement, can be seen in the legal, mental health, medical, and victim services arenas. During the 1970s, the first rape crisis centre was established. The treatment of victims in the criminal justice system was questioned, and hundreds of laws were passed to protect rape victims in the courts. Medical protocols have been developed and widely accepted. The mental health impact of rape is well documented in the literature, and the practices of mental health professionals have improved.

Although the treatment of rape victims today is vastly different from three decades ago, many victims still do not receive the assistance and treatment they need.

Statistical Overview

Obtaining an accurate measurement of rape and other types of sexual assault is a challenge. Determining the scope and nature of rape and other types of sexual assault depends on how these crimes are defined and measured. It is important to note that statistics are derived from different sources employing different practices to gather information.

In 1997, there were 96,122 reported forcible rapes. (*Federal Bureau of Investigation. (released November 22, 1998). Crime in the United States, Uniform Crime Reports, 1997. Washington, DC: U.S. Department of Justice.)*

An estimated 70 of every 100,000 females in the country were reported rape victims in 1997, a decrease 1% from 1996 13% from 1993. *(Ibid.)*

1997 National Crime Victimization Survey, which includes both reported and unreported crimes, found that despite a decline of 7% in the nation's crime rate in 1997, rates of rape and sexual assault did not decline. *(Bureau of Justice Statistics. (1998, December). National Crime Victimization Survey. Washington, DC: U.S. Department of Justice.)*

The National Violence Against Women Survey, the first national study on stalking, found that in the 12 months preceding the study, 0.3 percent of all women surveyed experienced a completed or attempted rape, and 1.9 percent experienced a physical assault. *(Violence Against Women Grants Office. (1998, July). Stalking and Domestic Violence: Third Annual Report to Congress Under the Violence Against Women Act. Washington, DC: U.S. Department of Justice.)*

The National Women's Study (NWS), found that approximately 13% of adult women had been victims of completed rape during their lifetime (Kilpatrick, Edmunds, & Seymour, 1992; Resnick, Kilpatrick, Dansky, Saunders, & Best, 1993). During the year between interviews, 0.6% of adult women, or an estimated 683,000 women were victims of rape (Kilpatrick et al., 1992). In the two years between the first and third interviews, 1.2% of the adult participants in the NWS were raped. The results: an estimated 1.1 million women were raped in the United States during this two-year period (Kilpatrick, Resnick, Saunders, Best, 1997).

Using a definition of rape that includes forced vaginal, oral, and anal sex, the National Violence Against Women Survey found that 1 of 6 U.S. Women and 1 of 33 U.S. men has experienced an attempted or completed rape as a child and/or adult. According to estimates, approximately 1.5 million women and 834,700 men are raped and/or physically assaulted annually by an intimate partner in the United States. *(Tjaden, P. & Thoennes, N. (1998, November). A Prevalence, Incidence, and Consequences of Violence Against Women: Findings From the National Violence Against Women Survey, @ p. 2 & 5. Research in Brief. Washington, DC: National Institute of Justice, U.S. Department of Justice.)*

In 1996, more than two-thirds of rape/sexual assaults committed in the nation remained unreported. *(Ringel, C. (1997, November). Criminal Victimization in 1996, Changes 1995-1996 with Trends 1993-1996, NCJ-165812. Washington, DC: Bureau of Justice Statistics, U.S. Department of Justice.)*

The National Survey of Adolescents (NSA), a National Institute of Justice funded study of national household probability sample of 4,023 adolescents age 12-17, found that 8.1% of U.S. adolescents had been victims of at least one sexual assault (Kilpatrick & Saunders, 1997; Kilpatrick, Acierno, Saunders, Resnick, Best, & Schnurr, 2000). This indicates that an estimated 1.8 million 12 to 17 year olds have been sexually assaulted. More than 52 percent of all rape/sexual assault victims were females younger than 25. *(Perkins, C. (1997, September). Age Patterns of Victims of Serious Crimes, NCJ-162031. Washington, DC: Bureau of Justice Statistics, U.S. Department of Justice.)*

Women who suffered physical injury in addition to the injury suffered from the rape or sexual assault reported 37% of those crimes, while only 22% of rapes and sexual assaults without an additional physical injury were reported. *(Craven, D. (1994.) A Sex Differences in Violent Victimization, @ NCJ-164508. Bureau of Justice Statistics, Special Report. Washington, DC: U.S. Department of Justice).*

Although rape has occurred throughout history, the birth of the anti-rape movement in the US occurred only in the early 1970s. In 1972, the first rape crisis centers were established in San Francisco, CA (Bay Area Women Against Rape) and Washington, D.C. These grass roots centers grew out of the women's movement. They recognized that rape was an all-too-common part of women's lives and that it had a devastating impact on health and freedom. The goals of centers were to educate society about rape and rape-prevention and to improve the treatment of victims. In the nearly three decades since its birth, the anti-rape movement has accomplished many of its goals. Major accomplishments include:

Widespread reform of rape statutes and other legislation.

Improvements in the way criminal justice officials treat victims.

A better understanding of the scope and impact of rape.

Improved medical and mental health services.

Better funding for rape crisis centers and others who assist victims.

Despite this progress, there is much to be done. The fact that well over a million Americans of all ages are raped each year suggests that efforts to prevent rape have not been entirely successful.

Most rape cases go unreported. In turn, those cases are never investigated or prosecuted. Despite vast improvements in the investigation and prosecution of rape, more are needed. Too few victims who sustain rape-related mental or physical health problems obtain effective treatment.

This page will address the following issues:

- Defining rape and other types of sexual assault
- The scope and mental health effects of rape
- Victims' concerns
- Improving cooperation from victims
- Improving the way criminal justice officials and victim assistance providers
- Improving the investigation and prosecution of rape cases

Evolution of the Definition of Sexual Assault and Rape

Several authors have observed that many people still believe that rape occurs only when a stranger attacks an adult woman using overwhelming force. Using this definition, boys or men cannot be raped; girls and adolescents cannot be raped; no one can be raped by someone they know; and forced oral or anal sex does not constitute rape. Thus, attempts to discuss the topic are often frustrating because many people define rape differently. Before the 1960s, the legal definition of rape was generally a common law definition used throughout the United States that defined rape as "A carnal knowledge of a women not one's wife by force or against her will."

In 1962, the United States Model Penal Code (MPC) was established and updated the definition of rape. The MPC defined rape as " A man who has sexual intercourse with a female not his wife is guilty of rape if... he compels her to submit by force or threat of force or threat of imminent death, serious bodily injury, extreme pain, or Kidnapping" (Epstein & Langenbahn, 1994). In addition to *limiting* the definition of rape to a crime against a *woman*, this code was also very narrow because:

- It did not acknowledge rape within marriage or co-habiting couples.
- It focused on the victim's consent rather than the perpetrator's forcible conduct.
- Moreover, the MPC established a grading system for the rape and similar offences.

For example, it stated that rape by a voluntary social companion was a less serious offense than rape by a stranger. In addition, it treated the rape of men as a lesser felony than the rape of women.

In the 1970s and 1980s, extensive rape reform legislation was enacted throughout the country. And the legal definition of rape dramatically changed. Michigan's 1975 Criminal Sexual Conduct Statute, became the national model for an expanded definition of rape. Today, Illinois' Criminal Sexual Assault Statute is considered the national model. Both statutes broadly define rape to include:

- Gender neutrality, broadening earlier definitions of rape to include men.
- Acts of sexual penetration other than vaginal penetration by a penis.

Distinguishing sexual abuse by the degree of force or threat of force used. That issimilar to the "aggravated vs. simple" distinction applied to physical assaults.

Threats, as well as overt force, are recognized as means of overpowering victims.

Taking advantage of an incapacitated victim. This includes mental illness, victims under the influence of drugs and alcohol. Some states require that perpetrators give victims intoxicants to obtain sexual access.)

The Federal Definition of Rape

Despite these legislative changes, much of the debate that exists today about what constitutes sexual assault and rape stems from how rape should be defined. For purposes of this chapter, rape and other forms of sexual assault are defined using the Federal Criminal Code. Although criminal statutes regarding rape differ somewhat state-to-state, the Federal Code is national. For example, in addition to incorporating the reform provisions discussed above — gender neutrality and a broad definition of sexual abuse acts — the Federal Criminal Code: Distinguishes between types of sexual abuse on the basis of the degree of force or threat of force used.

Does not use the term "rape," and does not require the victim to label the act as rape to meet the elements of the crime.

The 1986 federal statute defines two types sexual assault:

- Sexual abuse
- Aggravated sexual abuse
- *Aggravated Sexual Abuse.*

Aggravated Sexual Abuse by Force or Threat of Force: When a person knowingly causes another person to engage in a sexual act... or attempts to do so by using force against that person, or by threatening or placing that person in fear that that person will be subjected to death, serious bodily injury, or kidnapping.

Aggravated Sexual Abuse by Other Means: When a person knowingly renders another person unconscious and thereby engages in a sexual act with that other person; or administers to another person by force or threat of force, or without the knowledge or permission of that person, a drug, intoxicant, or other similar substance and thereby:

a) Substantially impairs the ability of that person to appraise or control conduct
b) Engages in a sexual act with that person.

Aggravated Sexual Abuse with a Child: When a person knowingly engages in a sexual act with another person who has not attained the age of twelve years, or attempts to do so.

The definition for aggravated sexual abuse by force or threat of force is analogous to what is usually called *forcible rape*. Aggravated sexual abuse with children is a serious form of what is generally called *statutory rape*. However, aggravated sexual abuse by other means is a type of non forcible rape for which the perpetrator "shall be fined... imprisoned for any term of years or life, or both."

Sexual Abuse

The Federal Criminal Code definition of sexual abuse includes:

Causing another person to engage in a sexual activity by threatening or placing that person in fear.

Engaging in a sexual act if that person is incapable of declining participation in, or communicating unwillingness to engage in that sexual act.

Abusive Sexual Contact is defined as "when no sexual penetration actually occurred but when the intentional touching...of the genitalia, anus, groin, breast, inner thigh, or buttocks of any person with an intent to abuse, humiliate, harass, degrade, or arouse or gratify the sexual desire of any person occurs."

Sexual Abuse of a Minor or Ward is defined as "knowingly engaging in a sexual act with a person between the ages of 12 and 15 years.

Implications of Definitions

While great reforms have been made, the statute-based definitions for sex crimes fall short. They are lacking in the following areas:

- The victim's state of mind at the time of the crime, such as fear of death or serious bodily harm; and the victim's crime-related physical and psychological injuries.
- The types of unwanted sexual acts involved, the types of force or the coercion used, and the ages of victims and perpetrators.

Measuring Rape and other Types of Sexual Assault

Estimates of the number of rapes and/or the number of women who have been raped differ because the sources of these estimates use different samples, different definitions of rape, different time frames of measurement, different ways of measuring whether a rape has happened, and different units of analysis in reporting statistics.

The difference between *rape cases* and *rape victims* is that women can be raped more than once.

There is a difference between the *incidence* of rape and the *prevalence* of rape. *Incidence* generally refers to the *number of cases* that occur in a given time period (usually a year), and incidence statistics are often reported as rates (e.g., the number of rape cases occurring per 100,000 women in the population).

Prevalence generally refers to the *percentage of women* who have been raped in a specified time period (e.g., within the past year or throughout their lifetime).

There is clearly a difference between estimates based on reported vs. nonreported cases. Fourth, estimates of rape come from two basic types of sources: 1) government sources 2) studies conducted by private researchers funded by federal grants. With respect to government sources, the FBI Uniform Crime Reports (UCR) provides data on an annual basis only on the number of rapes and attempted rapes that were reported to US law enforcement that year. As noted by Crowell and Burgess (1996), another limitation of the UCR is that it uses the narrow common-law definition of rape (i.e., a carnal knowledge [penile-vaginal penetration only] of a female forcibly and against her will), meaning that other types of rape defined by federal law are not reported.

The Bureau of Justice Statistics conducts the National Crime Victimization Survey (NCVS) each year to measure reported and unreported crime, including rape and other sexual assaults. Every six months, the NCVS interviews residents 12 years or older in approximately 50,000 randomly-selected households about crimes that happened since the last interview.

In addition to data about the number of rape *cases* each year and rape *rates* (i.e., number of cases per 10,000 women), the NCVS provides information about the percentage of cases reported to police and characteristics of cases.

Because the NCVS is primarily measures the number of rapes per year among those 12 and older, it cannot measure rapes that occurred prior to the six-month reference period. Nor does it address children under age 12. Understandably, the NCVS and most other studies don't measure rapes of homeless women.

There are three major nongovernmental studies that provide additional information about rape.

- The National Women's Study (NWS), funded by the National Institute of Drug Abuse: longitudinal survey of a national probability household sample of 4008 adult women who were assessed at baseline and at one and two year follow-ups. The NWS generated the influential *Rape in America: A report to the nation* as well as a number of other peer reviewed scientific publications. The NWS measured rapes and other sexual assaults occurring throughout victims' lifetime as well as new cases occurring to adult women during the follow-up period.
- The National Violence Against Women Survey (NVAW), funded by the National Institute of Justice and the CDC: used similar methodology to that pioneered by the NWS and interviewed 8,000 adult women and 8005 adult men. Rape and sexual assault were measured using screening questions virtually identical to those used in the NWS. Like the NWS, the NVAW measured the lifetime prevalence of rape as well as rapes that occurred during the year prior to the interview.
- The National Survey of Adolescents (NSA), funded by the National Institute of Justice: conducted interviews with a national household probability sample of adolescents age 12-17. These adolescents were interviewed about sexual assaults and other crimes that occurred throughout their lifetimes. Also, information was gathered about important characteristics of these sexual assault cases and about the mental health effect of such experiences.

National Information About the Scope and Key Characteristics of Rape Cases

Accurate information about rape cases and victims is necessary to ensure victims receive effective treatment and cases are thoroughly investigated and prosecuted. The best information comes from the surveys described above. These surveys are ideal because they include information about reported and unreported cases.

Only a small percentage of rape cases are reported to police, and it is critically important that we learn more about these cases and the victims. Prior to describing the scope and case characteristics data, it is important to consider the following:

Encouraging victims to report attacks to police is critically important because most rapists are recidivists who will continue to rape they are apprehended, prosecuted, and incarcerated.

It is extremely important to understand the extent of America's sexual assault problem to properly address it.

Different types of sexual assault cases require different investigative and prosecutorial strategies to enhance the prospects of successful prosecution.

The size, funding, and staffing of law enforcement agencies in the US varies widely. A one-size-fits-all sexual assault protocol applicable across all jurisdictions does not exist.

Unreported Sexual Assault Cases

National research indicates that most sexual assaults are never reported to police. The best data on unreported crime comes from victimization surveys. The surveys interview representative samples of adults and/or adolescents asking if they have been victims and if they reported the crimes. Some surveys also ask why victims did not report these crimes.

- At the national level, major victimization surveys suggest that most sexual assaults go unreported. The National Crime Victimization Survey, conducted each year by the U.S. Department of Justice, found that only 32% of sexual assault cases were reported to police in 1994. The *Rape in America* survey conducted as a part of the National Women's Study found that only 16% of rape cases were reported to police or other authorities. Data from the National Survey of Adolescents indicated that only 14.3% of sexual assault cases had been reported. Thus, these national studies indicate that somewhere between 14% and 32% of all sexual assaults or rapes are ever reported to police.
- A study of nonincarcerated sex offenders conducted by Dr. Gene Abel and his colleagues found that 126 men

admitted that they had raped. *These 126 rapists had committed a total of 907 rapes involving 882 different victims. The average number of different victims per rapist was seven (Abel et al., 1987).*

These findings suggest that unreported rape constitutes a serious public safety problem. *The Scope of the Rape and Sexual Assault Problem*

As was previously described in the Statistical Overview section, the NVAW produced an estimate that 14.8% of adult women in the U.S. had been raped sometime during their lives and that another 2.8% had been victims of an attempted rape. For adult men, comparable lifetime prevalence estimates for rape and attempted rape were 2.1% and 0.9% respectively. The NWS found that 12.7% of adult women had been victims of completed rape and 14.3% had been victims of other types of sexual assault. The National Survey of Adolescents estimated that 13.0% of female adolescents and 3.4% of male adolescents had been victims of a sexual assault at some point during their lives. Data from the NWS and NSA indicate that revictimization is a problem for women and adolescents. Thirty-nine percent of rape victims in the NWS had been raped more than once, and 41.7% of the adolescent victims said that they had been sexually assaulted more than once.

National Research on Rape

Due to myths, misconceptions and social attitudes about sex crimes, the National Victim Centre, in partnership with the National Crime Victims Research and Treatment Centre of the Medical University of South Carolina, published *Rape in America: A Report to the Nation* in 1992.

The report was based on *The National Women's Study* — funded by the National Institute of Drug Abuse — a three-year longitudinal study of a national probability sample of 4,008 adult women, (age 18 or older), 2,008 of whom represent a cross section of all adult women and 2,000 of whom are an over sample of younger women between the ages of 18 and 34.

The study provided the first national empirical data about forcible rape of women in America: Seven-tenths of one percent of all women surveyed had experienced a completed forcible rape in the past year. This means an estimated 683,000 adult American women who were raped during a twelve-month period.

Thirteen percent of women have been victims of at least one completed rape in their lifetimes.

Based on U.S. Census estimates of the number of adult women in America, one out of every eight adult women, or at least, 12.1 million American women, has been the victim of forcible rape sometime in her lifetime.

While 56%, or an estimated 6.8 million women experienced only one rape, 39%, or an estimated 4.7 million, were raped more than once; and five percent were unsure as to how many times they were raped. Prior to this study, national information about rape was limited to data on reported rapes from the *FBI Uniform Crime Reports* or data from the Bureau of Justice Statistics, National Crime Survey (NCS) on reported and unreported rapes in the past year. The number of rapes per year in *Rape in America* was approximately five times higher than the Uniform Crime Reports or the NCS. Recently, the NCS has been redesigned amid concerns that it failed to detect a substantial proportion of rape cases.

Age of Rape Victims

The NWS found that "rape in America is a tragedy of youth," with the majority of cases occurring during childhood and adolescence:

Twenty-nine percent of all forcible rapes occurred when the victim was less than 11 years old.

Another 32% occurred when the victim was between ages of 11-17.

Slightly more than one in five rapes (22%) occurred between the ages of 18-24.

Seven percent of rapes occurred between the ages of 25-29.

Only six percent of rapes occurred when the victim was older than 29 years old.

The NVAW Survey found:

21.6% of first or only rape cases experienced by women happened before age 12.

32.4% of such cases happened between the ages of 12 and 17.

29.4% happened between the ages of 18 and 24.

16.6% happened at age 25 or greater.

Note: The NWS data represent a breakdown of victim's ages at the time of *all* rape cases; and the NVAW data are a breakdown of age at the time of first rape only.

The NSA also provides information about the age at time of 462 cases of sexual assault experienced by 12-17-year-old adolescents (Kilpatrick, 1996, from the *Mouths of Victims* paper).

29.9% had been assaulted before age 11.

16.3% between the ages of 11 and 12.

20.8% between the ages of 13 and 14.

20.8% between the ages of 15 and 16.

1.7% at age 17.

Note: In the remaining 8.7% of cases, victims were not sure or refused to provide age data.

Relationship of the Victim to the Offender

The NWS dispelled the common myth that most women are raped by strangers. For example:

Only 22% of rape victims were assaulted by someone they had never seen before or did not know well.

Nine percent of victims were raped by husbands or ex-husbands.

Eleven percent by fathers or stepfathers.

Ten percent by boyfriends or ex-boyfriends.

Sixteen percent by other relatives.

Twenty-nine percent by other non-relatives, such as friends and neighbours.

In addition to the data just presented, the NWS gathered information about new cases that happened to adult women during the two-year follow up period.

This information on the 41 such cases provides excellent information about the breakdown for new rapes experienced by adult women.

24.4% of offenders were strangers.

21.9% were husbands.

19.5% were boyfriends.

9.8% were other relatives.

9.8% were friends.

14.6% were other nonrelatives.

The NVAW survey used different categories for victim-perpetrator relationships but reported similar findings with respect to the types of perpetrators most prevalent in rape cases occurring after age of 18.

76% of perpetrators were intimate partners (i.e., current and former spouses, cohabiting partners, dates, and boyfriends/girlfriends).

16.8% were acquaintances.

14.1% were strangers.

8.6% were relatives other than spouses.

The NSA provides a different perspective because it provides data on cases during childhood and adolescence (Kilpatrick, 1996).

32.5% of perpetrators were identified as friends.

23.2% were strangers.

22.1% were relatives (fathers, stepfathers, brothers, sisters, grandparents, others).

18.1% were other nonrelatives known well by the victim.

Degree of Physical Injury

Another common misconception about rape is that most victims sustain serious physical injuries. Using lifetime cases from the NWS:

Over two-thirds (70%) of victims reported no physical injuries.

Only four percent sustained serious physical injuries.

Twenty-four percent received minor physical injuries.

Of considerable importance is that almost half of all rape victims (49%) described being fearful of serious injury or death during the rape.

Not surprisingly, the percentage of new rape cases (n=41) experienced by adult women in the NWS resulting in physical injuries was somewhat higher than cases that included childhood and adolescent rapes.

9.8% of victims reported serious physical injuries.

46.3% sustained minor injuries.

43.9% sustained no physical injuries.

58.5% said that they were fearful of serious injury of death.

The NVAW survey provides a detailed breakdown of physical injuries sustained and medical treatment of the recent cases of rapes women experienced since age 18.

31.5% of women sustained some physical injuries.

Only 35.6% of victims with injuries received medical treatment. In the NSA, 85.5% of child and adolescent cases resulted in *no* physical injuries. Only 1.3% of victims reported serious injuries, and 11% reported minor injuries.

Implications of these Findings about the Scope and Characteristics of Rape for the Investigation and Prosecution of Rape Cases

Information from all of these sources provides compelling evidence that most rapes are committed by perpetrators who are known well by their victims. This has profound implications for how rape cases should be investigated and prosecuted. If most victims know the identity of their perpetrators, then the key investigative issue is not collecting evidence to identify the perpetrator. Instead, most cases will likely require evidence refuting claims by the alleged perpetrator that the sexual activity was consensual. Known perpetrators are unlikely to claim they were mistakenly identified as a defence because forensic examinations can conclusively link the perpetrator to the assault

Second, Susan Estrich (1987) notes that successful prosecution of rape cases often requires victims to produce evidence of physical injuries to prove that they did not consent.

The fact that the vast majority of rape victims do not sustain major physical injuries also has clear implications for investigation and prosecution. The first implication is that most victims will not exhibit overt physical injuries, causing many people to conclude the victim consented. The second implication is that forensic examinations must focus on detecting evidence of physical injuries that are not consistent with consensual sexual activity. Law enforcement, prosecutors, and jurors need to be informed about these physical injury data.

This information indicates that most rapes and other sexual assaults involve relatively young victims - not adult women, as most people believe. This suggests that separate investigative protocols should be established for adult and child victims.

Implications for Sexual Assault Forensic Medical Examinations

In sexual assault cases, the victim's body is the primary "crime scene." The forensic medical examination is a critical part of evidence collection. Based on the victim's report of what sexual acts occurred, the forensic exam collects evidence from the victim's body that can establish: 1) sexual activity occurred 2) that a given person committed the acts 3) the sexual act produces physical injuries consistent with forced sex. The exam needs to collect evidence documenting that a sex act occurred to counter the defence that a suspect never had sex with the victim. The exam also needs to collect DNA or other evidence proving the named suspect committed the sexual act(s) in question. This evidence can be used to prove that the sexual act occurred and that the defendant was responsible for it.

The only remaining defence a suspect can use is a consent-defence. One of the few ways to counter a claim of consent is to collect evidence of physical injuries (to the vulva, vagina or anus) that are inconsistent with consensual sex.

Most sexual assault protocols for adult victims do not include state-of-the-art procedures for detecting physical injuries to the victim's vulva, vagina, or anus. Fortunately, new technology exists that may greatly increase detection of physical injuries.

The colposcope is a standard tool used by gynecologists for the evaluation of microscopic cervical, vaginal, or vulvar disease. Using a colposcope, the vulva, vagina, cervix, and/or anus can be examined at magnifications over 30 times the actual size. This permits detection of tears, bruises, or abrasions invisible to the naked eye. Colposcopic examination provides a much more objective and sensitive way of seeing and documenting genital, anal, and other injuries in sexual assault victims.

Conventional rape exams without colposcopes typically report evidence of genital injuries in only 19%-28% of cases. However, examiners using colposcopes find evidence of genital trauma in up to 87% of cases.

Another important finding is that colposcopic examinations of women who have had recent consensual sexual intercourse do not find evidence of physical injury. Thus, the colposcope is not only capable of detecting physical injuries invisible to the naked eye, but a trained expert examiner can also testify that such injuries do not occur during consensual sex.

The ideal acute sexual assault exam protocol would have two parts:

The first part would be similar to the existing protocol, which is conducted within 72 hours of the assault. However, the protocol would be changed to include a colposcopic exam.

The second part of the protocol would include a second colposcopic exam conducted 4-6 weeks after the assault. The purpose is to collect evidence of a victim's recovery from physical injuries detected during the first exam. That would provide evidence for an expert examiner to testify about recovery from injuries inconsistent with consensual sex.

A final advantage of the colposcope is that technology exists to take color photographs or make videotapes of the injuries detected. This documentation of injuries has been described as having a powerful impact on jurors. And defendants, who entered guilty pleas when confronted with this evidence.

The Need for a Comprehensive Approach

Improving the investigation and prosecution of rape cases cannot be accomplished by any single agency. At least two recent major reports strongly advocate interagency cooperation. The National Victim Centre Report, *A Looking Back, Moving Forward: A Guidebook* for *Communities Responding to Sexual Assault*, identified a number of agencies that should play a key role after an assault occurs.

These agencies and their roles are depicted in a figure contained in the above mentioned report. This figure identifies roles for five types of agencies/disciplines in responding to sexual assaults:

- o Medical
- o Law Enforcement
- o Prosecution
- o Corrections
- o Victim Services.

As the figure indicates, victims who report rapes to law enforcement will likely have contact with medical and victim service professionals as well as law enforcement. If an arrest is made, prosecution professionals become involved. If there is a conviction, then corrections becomes involved. The NVC report strongly advocates establishing community sexual assault interagency councils with representatives from these areas. The report also suggests these interagency councils should negotiate a multiagency protocol specifying how sexual assault cases should be handled.

Even though establishing an interagency council is difficult and may be impractical in some communities, the importance of cooperation cannot be overemphasized. Law enforcement is critically important, but law enforcement cannot succeed without the assistance and support of other agencies.

The US has numerous police and prosecutorial jurisdictions. No single policy will fit the needs of all jurisdictions. In large metropolitan areas or large departments, it might be feasible to develop sex crimes investigation units. This is not feasible in small jurisdictions. Likewise, large metropolitan areas have many law enforcement agencies as well as major medical centers, rape crisis centers, and other victim service agencies. Small law enforcement agencies are often in small towns or rural areas that lack ready access to medical centers and victim services. Large agencies often have victim advocates, but small agencies rarely do.

Even though victims' needs and the elements of effective investigation and prosecution are the same regardless of jurisdiction, protocol should reflect the circumstances within different jurisdictions.

Bibliography

Akers, Ronald L.: *Deviant Behavior: A Social Learning Approach*. Belmont, Calif.: Wadsworth, 1985.

Ashraf, A.: *Political Sociology : A New Grammar of Politics*, Universities Press, Delhi, 1983.

Becker, Howard S.: *Outsiders: Studies in the Sociology of Deviance*. New York: Free Press, 1963.

Bennett, James: *Oral History and Delinquency, The Rhetoric of Criminology*, Chicago, University of Chicago Press, 1981.

Bonger, William Adrian: *Criminality and Economic Conditions*. Boston: Little, Brown, and Company, 1916.

Braithwaite, John: *Crime, Shame, and Reintegration*. New York: Cambridge University Press, 1989.

Cohen, Albert K.: *Deviance and Control*. Englewood Cliffs, N.J.: Prentice-Hall, 1966.

Felson, Marcus: *Crime and Everyday Life, Insights and Implications for Society*, Thousand Oaks, California, Pine Forge Press, 1994.

Gottfredson, Michael R.: *A General Theory of Crime*. Stanford, Calif.: Stanford University, 1990.

Gove, Walter R.: *The Labelling of Deviance: Evaluating a Perspective*. Beverly Hills, Calif.: Sage, 1980.

Grupp, S. E. : *The Positive School of Criminology; Three Lectures by Enrico Ferri*, Pittsburgh, PA: University of Pittsburgh Press, 1968.

Hirschi, Travis : *A General Theory of Crime*, Berkeley, California, Stanford University Press, 1990.

Hoebel. E. Adamson: *The Law of Primitive Man*. New York: Atheneum, 1968.

Kramer, Laura : *The Sociology of Gender : A Brief Introduction*, Rawat, Delhi, 2004.

Lander, Bernard : *Towards an Understanding of Juvenile Delinquency*, New York, Columbia University Press, 1954.

Langbein, John H.: *Torture and the Law of Proof, Europe and England in the Ancien Regime*, Chicago, University of Chicago Press, 1977.

Malinowski, Bronislaw: *Crime and Custom in Savage Society.* London: Routledge and Kegan Paul, 1926.

Marvin, E.: *Patterns in Criminal Homicide,* Montclair, New Jersey, Patterson Smith, 1958.

Mccaghy, Charles H.: *Deviant Behavior: Crime, Conflict, and Interest Groups.* New York: Macmillan, 1976.

Peltason, Jack : *Federal Courts in the Political Process,* New York, Random House, 1955.

Quinney, Richard: *The Social Reality of Crime.* Boston: Little, Brown, 1970.

Rathod, P B : *Fundamentals of Political Sociology*, ABD, Delhi, 2005.

Schur, Edwin M.: *Labeling Deviant Behavior: Its Sociological Implications.* New York: Harper and Row, 1971.

Scott, J. R. : *Russian Political Institutions,* New York, Frederick A. Praeger, 1961.

Stewart, Michael : *Modern Forms of Government: A Comparative Study,* New York, Frederick A. Praeger, 1961.

Sumner, Colin: *The Sociology of Deviance: An Obituary.* New York: Continuum, 1994.

Susan, J.: *Crime, Space and Society*, Cambridge, England, Cambridge University Press, 1986.

Tannenbaum, Frank: *Crime and the Community.* Boston: Ginn, 1938.

Thakur, A.P. : *Webers Political Sociology*, Global Vision Pub, Delhi, 2006.

Tittle, Charles R.: *Sanctions and Social Deviance: The Question of Deterrence.* New York: Praeger, 1980.

Walter, B: *Lower Class Culture as a Generating Milieu of Gang Delinquency, Journal of Social Issues* 14, 1958.

William Ebenstein : *Communism, Fascism, Capitalism, Socialism,* Englewood Cliffs, N.J., Prentice-Hall, 1958.

Index

□□□